BEYOND NUCLEAR DETERRENCE

New Aims   New Arms

edited by

JOHAN J. HOLST

UWE NERLICH

Crane, Russak & Company, Inc.

NEW YORK

Published in the United States by
Crane, Russak & Company, Inc.
347 Madison Avenue
New York, New York 10017

Published in Great Britain by
Macdonald and Jane's (Macdonald and Company (Publishers) Ltd.)
Poulton House, Shepherdess Walk
London N17 LW, England

Library of Congress Catalog Number 76-20283

Crane, Russak ISBN 0-8448-0974-8
Macdonald and Jane's ISBN 0354 01093 X

Printed in the United States of America

This book is the first in a series from the European-American Workshop. It was written under the joint auspices of Pan Heuristics, Los Angeles; the Norwegian Institute of International Affairs (NIIA), in whose book series it can be identified as No. 22; and the Foundation of Science and Politics (SWP), Ebenhausen/Munich.

European-American Workshop Organizing Committee

Johan Jørgen Holst*
Uwe Nerlich
Laurence W. Martin
Albert Wohlstetter
Henry S. Rowen
James F. Digby
Thomas Brown

*Mr Holst resigned in January 1976 upon his appointment as Undersecretary of State for Defense in Norway.

TABLE OF CONTENTS

Editors' Preface   vii
Foreswords
    James R. Schlesinger   ix
    John J. McCloy   xiii
Editors' Introduction   1

I. Political Developments and Military Power in Europe: The Political Setting   7
  1. Continuity and Change: The Political Context of Western Europe's Defense   9
    Uwe Nerlich
  2. Détente and the Politics of Instability in Southern Europe   41
    Pierre Hassner

II. Limited Military Responses: The Doctrinal Framework   61
  3. Limited Options in European Strategic Thought   63
    Laurence Martin
  4. Selective Nuclear Operations and Soviet Strategy   79
    Benjamin S. Lambeth

III. Promises of Technology   105
  5. New Technologies: The Prospects   107
    Cecil I. Hudson, Jr. and Peter H. Haas
  6. New Technologies: Some Requirements   149
    Erik Klippenberg

7. Precision Weapons: Lowering the Risks with Aimed Shots
   and Aimed Tactics   155
       James Digby

IV.   **Changing the Alliance Posture: Some Constraints**   177
    8. Technological Change and Arms Control: The Cruise
   Missile Case   179
       Richard Burt
    9. Limits of Budgetary Flexibility   193
       David Greenwood
    10. Precision Guidance for NATO: Justification and
   Constraints   207
       Graham T. Allison and Frederic A. Morris

V.   **Developing the Ability to Respond Selectively**   223
    11. Varying Response with Circumstance   225
       Henry S. Rowen and Albert Wohlstetter
    12. Limited Options, Escalation, and the Central Region
   Region   239
       239
       Peter Stratmann and René Hermann
    13. Flexibility in Tactical Nuclear Response   255
       Laurence Martin
    14. Flexible Options in Alliance Strategy   267
       Johan Jørgen Holst

Glossary   291
Bibliography   299
Contributors   303
Index   309

EDITORS' PREFACE

This book is the result of a broadly based effort to examine emerging security issues which now confront the Atlantic Alliance. The book was planned when the original collaborators, the members of the Organizing Committee of the European-American Workshop, saw that no projected publication seemed to provide a cross-cutting discussion of these issues which are affected by new technology, new economic pressures, shifting political factors, and a changed power balance.

The chapters in the book have been discussed in two workshops devoted to a reexamination of Western security problems: The first was held in Ebenhausen near Munich in March, 1975, and organized by the Foundation for Science and Politics. The second took place in Copenhagen in September, 1975, and was organized by the Norwegian Institute of International Affairs. Pan Heuristics of Los Angeles, California has provided the framework for a continuous examination of the issues involved. The workshops are part of a systematic and continuous effort at joint assessment of emerging issues before governmental positions are crystallized and hardened. They provide an unprecedented opportunity to build on ongoing research on both sides of the Atlantic in ways which hopefully will prove to be conducive to both more scholarly effort and future policy formation.

These workshops have become possible through various financial contributions. We wish to acknowledge in particular the role the Thyssen Foundation has played in these endeavors. We are also grateful to the Annenberg Foundation which helped to set up the Ebenhausen Workshop and to the Council on Germany (the John J. McCloy Fund) for its generous assistance in the preparation of this book for publication. The Fund of the Council is the result of a gift of the Federal Republic of Germany to the United States on the occasion of the Bicentennial. The Council decided to assist in the presentation of this volume to a concerned public because they believe the essays are worthy of attention and thought in a rapidly changing world. Their assistance does not, of course, imply that either the Fund or Mr. McCloy necessarily share the views expressed herein.

European-American bridge-building in the preparation of this book was also facilitated by the fact that Uwe Nerlich was a Fellow of the Center for Advanced Study in the Behavioral Sciences at Stanford in 1974-75. This unique place provided both a detached reappraisal and a most stimulating environment. The kind assistance of the Center's staff and the contribution from the National Science Foundation are much appreciated.

The editors want to thank their fellow contributors for the patience and competence they have shown in preparing their contributions to the present volume. We want to thank also all those who participated in the workshops and gave us all the chance to benefit from their wisdom and insight. Above all we are indebted to our fellow members of the Organizing Committee for the European-American Workshop. Our special thanks go to Dr. Thomas Brown for his valuable assistance in the preparation of this book.

January 20, 1976

Johan Jørgen Holst   Uwe Nerlich

FOREWORD

The strength of the Atlantic Alliance remains, as it must, the touchstone of the security of democratic societies around the world. Periods of political vigor and of compelling military doctrine and force structure are associated with self-confidence among the Western allies. By contrast, low morale and diminished confidence within the alliance both reflect and reinforce political weakness among the democracies. It is to be hoped that the recognition of difficulties will elicit the vision, the energy, and the dedication that will restore political and military self-confidence.

Adaptation to changing opportunities and threats is indispensable for the maintenance of adequate deterrence. The twin impediments to successful adaptation are complacency and hopelessness. Complacency reflects the belief that somehow retention of a military balance is of secondary importance and, therefore, that *any* military posture is adequate for the alliance. Hopelessness reflects the conviction that Warsaw Pact forces are so preponderant that no action by the alliance can alter its position of conventional military inferiority—or the doubt that the alliance, consisting of free and independent states, can successfully coordinate actions with sufficient rapidity to stay abreast of the Warsaw Pact buildup.

In a world of continuing tension, complacency is hardly justified, but neither is hopelessness. Free societies by their nature do have their ups and downs, but they possess a dynamic and a potential responsiveness not available to totalitarian states. The challenge remains—the response must be forthcoming.

For the Western Alliance, the chief point of potential military pressure remains Europe, not North America. In changing circumstances the preservation of European security requires serious and continuing thought. Yet the alliance has been afflicted by the drag of obsolescence, reflected in General Steinhoff's observation that NATO is in danger of becoming a "military museum." Historically there has been a fear of change that stems, in part, from insufficient trust among the several nations that constitute the alliance—and notably on oscillating concern in Western Europe regarding the steadfastness of American purpose. The fear of change reflects the concern that in the process of change each of the allies will attempt to lessen its obligations. Consequently, change is likely to be for the worse.

Nevertheless, it is necessary to face the necessity for change—that imperative for adaptation—with confidence and imagination. The collection of essays produced in the European-American Workshop on the Defense of Europe makes a signal contribution in that direction.

An adequate deterrent is a necessary, if not sufficient, condition for political self-confidence in Western Europe. The requirements of deterrence have changed over the years, and inevitably have become more complex with the decline of the preponderance of American strategic nuclear forces. Increasingly, the alliance has recognized that mutual reinforcement among the three elements of the NATO Triad —conventional, tactical nuclear, and strategic forces—provide the ingredients for continuing, effective deterrence. No longer do we indulge in the profitless debate of the early 1960s which treated conventional forces as a substitute for nuclear forces. There is general recognition that there is synergy among the three elements of the Triad, that conventional capabilities ease the demands on nuclear forces, and that nuclear forces necessarily reinforce the deterrent effect of the conventional forces.

It should also be recognized that deterrence must be based upon a credible response. Deterrence is not based upon an accumulation of weapons, even nuclear weapons. There must exist both the strategy and the force structure to respond credibly and effectively under widely varying conditions. Deterrence is not free-floating; it must be carefully thought through. A credible response has frequently, though somewhat misleadingly, been referred to as a war-fighting strategy. Preferably it should be referred to as a peace-maintaining strategy. The ability to respond effectively is what underlies the ability to deter effectively.

The rudiments of successful deterrence in these changing circumstances are reasonably clear. An existing deficiency lies in adequate conventional forces that permit the raising of the nuclear threshold. A higher nuclear threshold does not weaken deterrence; it reinforces it. All that it does is to assure a potential foe that medium-level provocations will fail. If the determination to employ nuclear weapons remains firm, one's opponent recognizes that it would be his own decision to initiate major aggression, which, even if successful at the conventional level, would inevitably lead to a nuclear response. Thus, the greater the effort on his part, the greater would be the corresponding burden for creating the risks that would bring about nuclear engagement.

With respect to the nuclear components, the unquestioned ability to implement an all-out response must be maintained. Yet, for certain aspects of deterrence, the number of weapons is less critical than the existence of a doctrine, the will to abide by that doctrine, and weapons systems consistent with that doctrine which permit the deliberate use of weapons in those circumstances that may require a nuclear response. Such changes in doctrine have been forthcoming, but still more work is required. Deliberate use, based upon selectivity and flexibility, maintains the coupling between the main strategic forces of the alliance, provided by the United States, and the security of Western Europe.

Our Western world today faces a threat, less blatant than but just as perilous as that of the 1930s. The steady accretion of Soviet military power continues its momentum. Negotiations have not significantly altered that reality. In particular, the Mutual Balanced Force Reduction (MBFR) negotiations in Vienna show little promise of providing any panacea permitting reduced Western military efforts. Soviet objectives at Vienna have been clear. The first goal has been to obtain control over the Bundeswehr; the second, to prevent any movement toward a common European defense effort. Acquiescence in such Soviet objectives would seem far too high a price to pay, just for an alleviation of short-term budgetary or diplomatic pressures. The fundamental goal for MBFR must remain increased stability, thus *enhancing* the security of Western Europe.

The essays in this volume deal with the newly emerging conditions, both the risks and the opportunities. They provide new and stimulating ideas bearing on the future of European security. The belief that European security is either static or hopeless is explicitly rejected. Adaptation in the face of change is an unavoidable, if painful, necessity. Eternal vigilance remains the price of freedom. In making a contribution to that continuing vigil, these essays deserve careful attention.

—James R. Schlesinger

FOREWORD

Although Americans may be inclined to think they are immune from the intellectual and bureaucratic inertia that historically has often affected participants in the last wars, they are not. Generals Eisenhower and MacArthur experienced such a period of inertia in this country after the victories of World War I. In the era between the two World Wars, as young officers, they agitated, largely in vain, for greater recognition of armor and aircraft in our defense posture. General Doolittle felt he had to sacrifice a brilliant career to get an adequate hearing for the importance of aircraft to our security. He took his case to the public in defiance of orders, but he had to wait a long time before his views were generally accepted. The argument in the United States over whether battleships were dated was largely settled when two of the finest units of the British fleet were quickly dispatched by Japanese airmen in the South China Sea.

It is important to insure that new ideas and new developments in defense as well as in other fields are given their proper hearing. We may not have the time to recover from our lethargy and our mistakes when the next challenge presents itself. It is hoped that this collection of essays may contribute to a debate which sifts out the truth. It is the product of qualified observers and, in a number of cases, of real operators on the security scene. What they have to say should be weighed carefully.

The collection contains an interesting review of current political changes, past strategic doctrines, and the military technology which influenced such changes and doctrine in the past. It reviews the coming of the nuclear age in military affairs, the evolution of current doctrines, and present current political and strategic problems, many of which have yet to be solved. It also discusses in detail new technological development, the new emphasis on precision techniques which are provoking advanced military thinking and could affect new strategic and force positions.

Not all technical innovations are significant. Most of them, indeed, fall short of their promise. But there are certain inventions in military history which can fairly be said to have changed the course of history. One of the essays discusses these landmarks of military history. The Battle of Adrianople is remembered for the introduction of new cavalry weapons and tactics. The longbow ended the reign of the mounted and armored knight, who had been the centerpiece of military prowess for centuries. The musket in turn doomed the longbow and the crossbow. In our own time, the tank and the airplane caused abrupt shifts of military power, and certainly altered the course of modern Western history.

If the promise of technology holds true for the next five or ten years, perhaps the emphasis on precision described in these essays will cause some alteration in our defense thinking and structures. It could amount to a change in orders of magnitude in the cost, effort and speed of waging war. Even leaving aside some of the caveats, and the over-dramatization of some of the technological possibilities described in these essays, they are somewhat staggering in their concepts.

The debate over these concepts is commencing in informed military and government circles. There is evidence also that the Soviets have engaged in at least a part of this debate in their strategic journals. The concepts might well be of real significance for us and for our relations with our principal allies. The essays relate to matters not generally discussed in the usual international interchange of economic and political ideas and it seems appropriate that the Fund help make them available to interested thinkers and readers.

—John J. McCloy

Beyond Nuclear Deterrence:
New Aims, New Arms

EDITORS' INTRODUCTION

THE CHANGING SETTING OF WESTERN SECURITY

We are currently witnessing profound changes in the environment of Western industrialized nations, the political framework of the Western Alliance, the nature of the Soviet threat, and military technology. Obviously, the first three kinds of changes strongly reinforce each other. The Yom Kippur War and its consequences for Western economies and, indeed, for political stability in the industrial world, the potential American-West European cleavage over growing political heterogeneity inside the alliance in view of potential communist government participation in Italy or other Southern European countries, the Soviet intervention in Angola and the evidence of Soviet interests in Portugal prior to the accession to power of the democratically elected Soares government which was interpreted by many as a possible Soviet disposition to exploit domestic conflicts in European countries—all point in the same direction.

Western nations have barely begun to reorganize their relations with the "Southern" countries, even though this task now appears more manageable than under the impact of the oil crisis. The alliance has managed to create more favorable conditions in Portugal, not because of multilateral efforts inside the alliance context, but due to a combination of political cooperation on the party level (with active roles on the part of some neutrals) and economic incentives provided by the EEC. But no consensus has emerged yet between the United States and

1

Western Europe, or indeed between Northern and Southern European governments, as to how to reconcile the continuing need for protection and the potential heterogeneity of governments inside the alliance. There is thus a growing range of political contingencies which the Soviet Union could try to exploit. Soviet military power might be applied in a variety of ways short of major aggression, which could affect outcomes. The alliance has hardly begun to prepare itself for these more indirect or remote threats.

While there may not be a need to restructure the alliance posture with regard to classical contingencies, it certainly has to be reviewed in regard to such "novel" contingencies as indicated above. At the same time, the conditions have to be established for using the potential of new weapons technology. This does not require new doctrines. The doctrinal consensus which is enshrined in NATO's basic document, the *MC 14/3*, allows for sufficient flexibility. What is needed, however, is to generate additional response options, to unfreeze core beliefs and philosophical distinctions like the one between war-fighting and deterrence capabilities, and to refine strategic thinking about the controlled use of force, which hitherto was based on thresholds, escalation, and similar concepts that originated from a situation of Western strategic superiority and excessive dependence on nuclear weapons.

While no new doctrine seems to be required, new conceptual approaches that will result in new ways to implement existing doctrinal consensus are in fact vitally important. New instabilities combine with a growing awareness of bureaucratic inertia and propensities to maintain endowments rather than buy usable options, with the inflexibilities of multilateral institutions, important though these will remain, and with the conceptual freezes which more often than not reflect parochial outlooks.

Whether these unpleasant insights will be translated into viable defense policies remains to be seen. Intellectual endeavor and conceptual innovation surely will make a difference. Fortunately, intellectual energies are once more increasingly being allocated to issues that are vitally important in any framework of Western security. To some extent, new strategic thinking began to develop along the emerging new technologies. As in the fifties, when the acquisition of high-yield nuclear weapons together with the perception of a monolithic Soviet threat profoundly changed Western security concepts, new technologies that allow for extreme discriminateness are now combining with specific contingencies and a perception of Soviet military power that can be applied in a wide variety of ways, so as to provide a strong challenge to analytical professionalism as well as political leadership. Some of the new thinking is reflected in this book.

SOME OF THE MAIN ISSUES

The political map of Europe has undergone a series of major changes since the NATO Alliance came into being. The East-West conflict no longer maintains the dominant saliency of the forties and sixties. Détente and the arrival of strategic parity has created a more complex and ambiguous environment than that which generated the feared contingencies of a major Soviet drive to the Channel. Recognition of the territorial status quo in the Center of Europe has contributed to shifting the focus of attention to Southern Europe. The social volatility of Mediterranean Europe and the increasing tension between state and society in that area has created a kind of Third World instability problem, which interacts with a series of actual and potential succession crises. The Soviet imperial position in Eastern Europe remains dependent on Soviet armed might and vulnerable to the social dialectics of industrial societies of the Marxist variety. Extra-European conflicts may pose differentiated challenges to the security interests of the NATO states. Uwe Nerlich and Pierre Hassner analyze the novel sources of instability and the potential dynamics of crisis eruption and spillover in Europe. The fluidity of the situation poses requirements for flexibility of response.

NATO has experienced a series of great and not-so-great doctrinal debates, instigated primarily by unilateral American decisions in favor of a change in emphasis with respect to conventional options. New weapons technologies will pose novel requirements for doctrinal adjustments. However, current concepts seem inadequate as currencies of reform. There is a long-term European interest in flexible options, as we are reminded by Laurence Martin. Johan J. Holst points to the need for providing more operational substance to the concept of flexible response. The new weapon technologies will provide hitherto unavailable options.

There is a broad panoply of novel technologies permitting a discriminate and effective application of military power. These technologies include those of information sensing, precision guidance, very effective nonnuclear munitions, data processing, and communications. No sudden breakthrough has taken place, but the cumulative effect of improvements in these technologies promises to have a considerable overall impact. If political authorities make the right decisions, they will have available a wide array of less than suicidal responses. Hence deterrence should be susceptible of improvements. Peter Haas and Cecil Hudson describe the broad base of technological options that are becoming available. Erik Klippenberg points to the need to look at costs and operational efficiencies.

New weapons technologies promise to blur some of the accepted distinctions and break down some established concepts. Thus the tactical-strategic dichotomy will be subject to cruise missiles. Smaller countries may consider options of shallow cross-border responses. Long-range cruise missile attacks may involve the employment of conventional rather than nuclear munitions. Accuracy will render great explosive power unnecessary. There is always a dual criterion, as Albert Wohlstetter and Henry Rowen point out in their chapter, of target destruction and avoidance of collateral damage. Thus the technologies may, as James Digby asserts, permit of new ways for dealing with old dangers.

However, there is no way of denuclearizing conflict in Europe in the sense of leaving nuclear weapons out of the calculus. Any conflict will take place in the nuclear shadows. The capacity to dominate escalation on the central front will remain essential to the efficiency of the Western security order in Europe, as Peter Stratmann and René Hermann point out.

But how will the distribution of roles and missions within the Western Alliance be affected by the new technologies? Will the alliance be able to transcend the propensities for incrementalism? Will incrementalism provide adequate responses?

CONSTRAINTS ON INNOVATION

The ability of the alliance to implement change and adapt to altered circumstances and opportunities is not only a function of intellectual awareness of the choices ahead; it is to a large extent a function of the economic constraints that apply to decision-making in the defense sector. Most of the European governments are already committed to major procurement programs. The margin for innovative change is extremely narrow, as David Greenwood illustrates in his contribution. Procurement programs constitute inflexible trajectories because of industrial and institutional vested interests and compromises. There is a strong propensity to extend existing priorities and mission assignments into the future, rather than engaging in systemic reassessment. Some big procurement decisions, such as those associated with lightweight fighters (F-16), a new medium tank, or airborne warning and control systems (AWACS), tend to eat up the available funds at the margin.

As always in complex organizations, we are up against bureaucratic and political inertia, a natural tendency to protect existing structures and processes against the onslaught of the forces for change. Some of those reflect an understandable fear of the unfamiliar. In Europe there is an automatic fear of American "gadget" solutions and technological panaceas. There are fears of "industrial imperialism" and of Trojan horses concealing American interests in disengagement and in taking the American cities off the Soviet nuclear hook in Europe.

In such circumstances, it is necesary to inject the process of reassessment into the existing institutional machinery in an imaginative and unorthodox fashion. Informal bilateral studies could gradually produce the framework for a novel consensus. A confrontation between nuclear and conventional advocacy should be avoided. It is useful therefore that an assessment of the broad family of new weapon technologies has been undertaken by the Nuclear Planning Group (NPG) in NATO. There is a need to emphasize continuities in the face of an altered environment and novel means of response.

MANAGING INNOVATION

At the present juncture the alliance is not in need of another "great debate" with the misunderstandings and vicarious argumentation that normally attend such encounters. The conceptual categories are available, but what is needed is a political awareness of the choices ahead. Incrementalism will be the natural response. But incrementalism is inadequate as a framework for reconstruction. There is a need to make the defense posture and options socially acceptable so as to retain plausibility in the eyes of domestic audiences. A heavy nuclear emphasis posture will not be able to pass the test of public credibility. Suicidal options should not define the available responses in a crisis. A range of flexible options will enhance credibility in the eyes of adversaries and domestic audiences alike.

The challenges of tomorrow are likely to be less clear-cut and unambiguous than the design contingencies of yesterday. NATO faces the need to develop postures and responses which are relevant to the challenges that may emerge. There is a need for agreement in the alliance with respect to the adaptations required and the options for defense that may become available in the years ahead. This book constitutes an attempt to promote such agreement.

I

POLITICAL DEVELOPMENTS AND MILITARY POWER IN EUROPE:

The Political Setting

CHAPTER 1

Continuity and Change: The Political Context of Western Europe's Defense

Uwe Nerlich

IN SEARCH OF A FRAMEWORK

The political agenda of Western governments today is much more complex and diffuse than in the early sixties. Strategic policy issues thus may not regain the central role they once had. Nevertheless, the elements of another controversy seem to be in the making. The focus is on new technologies. Like earlier strategic debates, the emerging controversy displays characteristic paradoxes. Some Western governments are about to expend considerable portions of available investment budgets on major weapons systems whose usefulness has barely received parliamentary consideration.

Modernization: Some Approaches

Generally, the acquisition of new weapons systems leaves room for major choices only in the more distant future—in today's context, 1985 and beyond. Any judgment in this area is associated with considerable uncertainties. Hence, a priori judgments are in the market. For some, new technologies are a panacea; for others, they are a threat to perceived vital security interests. Neither position deserves much credit. Yet political assessments usually are made in terms of today's priorities, preoccupations, parochialisms, modes of thought, and perceived interests. It is the combination of technological choice for the late eighties

9

and beyond with today's pressures that tends to determine any framework for analysis and decision-making.

Two approaches prevail. One stresses unresolved issues in the present security structure, many of which result from permanent conditions like the differences in perceived vital security interests among various members of the Alliance. The other approach tends to emphasize the potential inherent in new technologies for taking fresh looks and for unfreezing doctrinal frameworks that have a propensity to foreclose options. There is some truth in both approaches. Naturally, West Europeans are more inclined toward the first position while Americans tend more easily to adhere to the second.

An assessment of inherent and unresolved issues in the present defense context would have to be a major element in any analysis of such issues as what type of war is a conceivable contingency, what kinds of objectives ought to govern Western defense operations, what are the requirements for a nonsuicidal strategy in Western Europe, what are the prospects of any nuclear escalation both in terms of a Western denial strategy and in terms of likely outcomes, what is the importance of the Central Region with regard to the stability and military flexibility elsewhere in Europe, and what new options the Soviet Union may acquire in Europe through new technology and force modernization.

It seems hard to escape some unpleasant truths: First, major conventional Soviet campaigns are plausible only if Moscow can reasonably expect to win without going nuclear. Second, if there is anything NATO has never been able to agree on, it is on objectives of NATO defense and conditions for terminating a conflict; demonstrating resolve, identifying enemy intention when the aggression has started, and buying time for unidentified purposes are the usual kinds of substitutes. Third, most arguments on conventional defense and escalation are based upon the premise that the Soviet Union would draw back if the level of violence threatened to reach an unexpectedly high level: This premise requires agonizing reappraisal. For while Soviet military behavior in crisis situations tends to be cautious, once they start a major military campaign they will probably carry it through with utmost determination. This premise does not rule out Soviet perceptiveness toward emerging risks, but it renders irrelevant the kinds of sequences of a probing nature that usually dominate Western thinking. Finally, it may turn out to be true that future threats will be more indirect in kind and will result from political instabilities in Southern European or continguous areas in the Middle East and Africa. But any Western capacity to cope with such contingencies is based on a sufficient degree of military stability in the Central Region. By the same token, it raises the requirements in the Central Region for increased flexibility.

It is against this background that a framework for analysis of new technologies and their military implications should be designed. In fact, for the first time since the late fifties, genuine efforts to design new strategic concepts are unfolding. Some are reflected in this book. However, in the fifties the focus was on strategic forces, their composition, their protection, and their possible uses, and, notwithstanding the Sputnik shock, strategic rationales were conceived under conditions of Western escalation control and superiority. Under foreseeable circumstances the emphasis will henceforth be on theater forces. The task of constructing a coherent framework may be tantalizingly difficult, but given current vigorous research, it may not be lack of ideas that prevents desirable changes. The odds are that organization of policy formation as well as political circumstance will militate against major innovative change.

Bureaucratic Inertia

There is every reason to believe that bureaucratic acceptance of a coherent framework or simply bureaucratic commitment to reach new doctrinal consensus will not be strong enough. The causes would be structural and intentional; the results, piecemeal and incremental. Hard-core beliefs and maintaining suborganizational endowments would be prime factors. The delay of various types of precision-guided munition over the last thirty-odd years underscores this fact. Change has to be implemented by organizations, and organizations naturally tend to perpetuate themselves and to keep their budgetary shares.

But if technology is the driving engine of potential innovation, the difficulties are more complex. The following are some of the reasons. First, organizations charged with research and development (R&D) responsibilities tend to focus on performance on a system-by-system basis rather than on theater-oriented operational requirements, and since they naturally try to avoid early service interference, broader conceptualizing efforts are the exception rather than the rule. Second, if service endowments appear to be threatened, only strong evidence will generate the political will to overcome bureaucratic resistance, but the change of roles and allocation patterns has to be planned at early stages in a long-term perspective. Given the inherent uncertainties of technological promises, inertia tends to be strong. Third, there exist obvious economic disincentives for the early dissemination of technological data. Potential large-scale sales are at stake. This factor is particularly important in intra-alliance communications, and the inherent difficultes are reinforced by the fact that in order to become eligible for technological information, countries start R&D programs of their own, which in turn delay conceptualizing efforts even further. Finally, given these bureaucratic and economic incentives for high secrecy, consultations between governments suffer from two restraints: In more visible consultative multilateral bodies, the technological base simply remains too vague to be conducive to doctrinal and structural change. On the other hand, richer data exchanges are confined to more encapsulated suborganizational units, for example, to certain air force organizations of two countries where the receiving organization can claim not to be entitled to disseminate information within its own defense establishment because of restrictive data exchange agreements. The result of all these mechanisms is a widespread propensity to disregard functional interdependencies and to follow piecemeal approaches, rather than coherent efforts toward a generally acceptable framework, despite the existence of the need and the promises of current research.

In order to generate an alliance capacity to match future challenges in Europe, a much more comprehensive conceptual framework is needed than that within which NATO's options were considered in the past. Yet reform-minded communities within the alliance still display a propensity to believe that "science and technology are responsible for our present predicament but offer the only means of escaping the misfortunes for which they are responsible."[1]

Current defense policy should recognize the promises of the new technologies, as indeed it does. But unlike twenty years ago, when NATO agreed to nuclearize its forces, technology does not itself prescribe political solutions. The different nature of the new technologies is one reason. More importantly, however, the political framework is different. NATO reforms in the past were essentially confined to means or institutions. Policy formation in the years ahead will have to establish new priorities, and it will have to redefine the very ends of the alliance. At the same time, the political viability of the alliance will ultimately depend on more urgent and pressing issues, on levels not altogether within the framework of alliance politics.

The Imperative of Political Leadership

Given the inertia of bureaucratic policy-making, only strong political leadership could create the conditions for utilizing the technological potential to the extent possible. However, political will has become a scarce commodity within the Western Alliance. In fact, most Western societies suffer from political stalemate and bureaucratic inefficiency, if not fading governability. The quality of political elites is one fact of life; the immensely complex structure within which today's multilateral problems ought to be defined is another. While the two obviously interact, intellectual efforts to establish a framework within which definitions, if not solutions, of future Western security issues could be achieved and agreed upon, could make an enormous difference.

CHANGING PATTERNS OF ALLIANCE POLITICS

Bureaucratic inertia and the lack of political will notwithstanding, both future threats to Western Europe and the generation of appropriate Western responses will have to be considered in the broadest political terms. Compartmentalization of policy formation is a sure recipe for incrementalism and, indeed, political erosion. Some lessons will have to be remembered from earlier NATO experiences. More importantly, however, the political conditions have to be identified that will be conducive to both a sufficient Western military posture in the eighties and beyond and to the political purposes which such a posture could be expected to serve.

American Initiatives: Some Lessons of the Past

Past "great debates" within the alliance were essentially over redistributions of political influence in peacetime situations rather than over resolving NATO's strategic deficiencies in view of potential military crises. Moreover, the sequence of structural changes within NATO and public debates over how to reform the alliance were somehow implausible. Rather than preceding and shaping structural changes, debates usually occurred in the aftermath of changes which by and large resulted from unilateral action. Suez with its structural implications or de Gaulle's decision to leave NATO were exceptions to the rule that changes within the alliance resulted from American domestic developments or technological promise or both. "Great debates" then were usually over the implications of previous changes or over the implementation of policies that were touched off by those changes.

But whenever consensus seemed to emerge in Western Europe after painful processes of adaptation and reappraisal,[2] the conditions that had determined American unilateralism in the first place ceased to exist. Thus when the alliance finally agreed, under considerable American pressure, to accept a major West German conventional contribution, the United States pushed through the decision to nuclearize NATO forces, thus changing dramatically the rationale for the German defense contribution. When West European governments, including Bonn, came around to supporting this new NATO posture, a new administration in Washington again turned things upside down by forcefully favoring stronger conventional defense. But when the alliance (under the impact of France's decision to leave NATO) eventually agreed on a flexible response doctrine (*MC 14/3*), congressional pressure was mounting to reduce American forces in Western Europe, a process that was strongly reinforced by the drains of the Vietnam War. Similarily, when, in addition to Turkey, Italy, and Great Britain, other West European governments gave up their resistance to the deployment of IRBMs on their territory, Washington had already changed its deployment policies (primarily due to the deployment of ICBMs and SLBMs), thus reinforcing the very concerns they had made West Europeans aware of a few years earlier. Again, as at least some West European governments became committed to the American MLF substitute formula, that project became the victim of President Johnson's rising interest in offsetting the impact of the Vietnam War with the conclusion of a non-proliferation agreement with the Soviet Union.

Each case can, of course, be stated in more complex terms, and in each case there are plausible reasons why the United States acted the way it did. But these cases nevertheless display a characteristic pattern of major efforts within the alliance to reach consensus on issues of strategic policy.

Like American unilateralism, paralysis in Washington is also bound to affect the whole alliance. Thus the agony of the Johnson Administration marked a turning point in NATO's development. Until 1967-68, multilateral policy controversies within the alliance were over alternate innovations and/or redistributions. Ever since, they have been over how to maintain the major elements of NATO's posture.

The currently unfolding US-West European controversy is evolving around conservative choices—technological substitution versus mere preservation. In the United States the vigorous defense research establishment exhibits both technocratic optimism and unusual organizational tolerance for early publicizing and politicizing of R&D policies. These characteristics tend to be perceived as merging with tendencies to replace or dismantle major elements of NATO's current posture in order to reduce burdens or risks or both.

Moreover, given its size, the American defense establishment is capable of lending weight and considerable political priority to projects. By the same token, however, there usually are competing forces and concepts which make it difficult for West Europeans to pick the likely winner before policy formation in Washington is finalized. This substantially reduces the chances for West European influences.

In Western Europe, on the other hand, there is a propensity not only to stress uncertainties, but to emphasize alleged motives rather than feasibility. Suspicion—not always unfounded—has a large constituency whenever substitutive American offers come up. There is also little political flexibility in terms of existing budgetary commitments, bureaucratic inertia, suborganizational interest in maintaining endowments, and requirements for policy coordination among West Europeans. Nor are standard fears implausible that, given uncertainties over feasibility and motives as well as diverse signals from Washington, West Europeans may engage in self-fulfilling prophecies.

Most importantly, however, the dynamism of the huge American defense establishment is capable of setting priorities which are likely to survive the varying strains on budgets and political will within reasonable limits. That means above all that the administration has considerable control of political outcomes. West Europeans are not only perennially a possible victim of American unilateralism, but priorities are much more likely to shift under pressure. The multitude of constraints which are operating in West European policy formation thus substantiate a more general political feeling of not rocking the boat. For West European leaders the best and most important way to save the viability of the alliance is to solve current problems of trade and the monetary order, and in order to achieve this goal, NATO itself should become as much of a political untouchable as possible.

The Fallacy of Shifting Priorities

The conservative framework within which currently dominant choices have emerged thus in a sense reflects the state of Western societies. Political and economic conditions justify giving first priority to maintaining stability as the principal ingredient of security. But there exists a potential for crises, in that American pressures to change the military posture of the alliance conflict with West European resistance to change what they consider a modestly pivotal stance in a process of seemingly increasing destabilization. Similarly, West European pressures to change trade relations as a prerequisite for economic and thus political stability conflict with what may be a narrowly conceived American interest not to jeopardize prospects for a recovery of the US economy by making concessions to Western Europe. This unfolding conflict is likely to set the stage for whatever specific proposals for modernizing the alliance posture may be tabled in the near future.

Governments could well be overloaded if too many things in the Atlantic framework were changed at the same time. But while meeting West European economic demands halfway is likely to serve vital US long-term interests, even though it may not pay off domestically in the short run, West Europeans for their part should realize that their legitimate concern over the risks of instability cannot be confined to the economic level, crucially important though that may be. They have to face the fact that instability in Western societies is also a decisively important stage for Soviet political strategy, in ways that require an "agonizing reappraisal" of political uses of Soviet military power in European contingencies. And the present posture of the alliance is not likely to provide appropriate responses. Therefore, while West Europeans accord first priority to economic recovery, which is highly dependent on American cooperation, they should be aware that in the longer run, US-West European efforts to change the alliance posture are also vitally important, in the event that stabilizing efforts fail and this failure invites more massive Soviet pressures.

In the immediate postwar period, economic reconstruction was pursued as the most promising as well as the most feasible security policy for Western Europe. In the early fifties, military security began to dominate West European and Atlantic affairs and, in fact, provided the framework for basic economic decisions as well. In the early sixties, efforts to harmonize security and economic policies within the Western world more or less failed, and when some misconceived specific security policies—above all, Vietnam—worsened the economic situation dramatically, the result was a perceived primacy of economic stability instead of what used to be a primacy of military security. In the early seventies, economic crisis and the erosion of NATO coincided. Again an effort to harmonize the two policy areas—Kissinger's Atlantic Declaration framework—failed. It was the economic threat resulting from the Yim Kippur War which began to make political elites aware of crucial interdependencies. And yet no major effort to design a coherent framework has been undertaken since. However, both economic stability and military security appear somewhat stronger in 1976. Whether this will be conducive to a growing awareness of the fact that economic stability in the long run will require military security, and that security in turn is a matter of political and economic stability as well as military protection, remains to be seen.

The Fallacy of Negotiating Requirements

In the mid-fifties, strategic policy became a currency of both alliance diplomacy and domestic politics in the West. While the earlier nuclear debate at least reinforced the political framework that could be expected to be conducive to an agreed-upon Western strategic policy, East-West negotiations provided instrumentalities of a different nature. Bilateral as well as multilateral frameworks emerged. From a NATO point of view, MBFR was naturally most closely related to European defense.

This shift was one of the major ironies in recent European history. In the fifties and beyond, the West had tried hard to link Soviet demands for force reductions in Europe to Western demands for Soviet concessions on the German issue. When the German issue changed its character and ceased to be the core of Western diplomacy in Europe, this coincided with a shift from redistributive alliance reform to efforts for mere preservation. The seemingly reluctant Soviet side was now urged to enter into negotiations over force reductions that were expected to stabilize the Western defense posture in a number of ways.

West Europeans were increasingly facing not only abrupt domestic changes as normal outcomes of US presidential elections, but also perennial domestic pressures to reduce US forces and commitment in Western Europe. To some extent, however, the secular importance of the American military engagement had also escaped West Europeans. While in the past they normally resisted any change before "falling in with the preferences of the United States," they now hoped to preserve the alliance's military status quo by changing the pattern of East-West relations. MBFR was expected to serve the same purpose that clinging to massive retaliation doctrines had served only a few years earlier: the latter was meant to prevent unilateral change, whereas the former was somewhat perversely intended to secure US force levels. Not surprisingly, this approach looked promising to West Europeans only as long as it was not capitalized upon by Washington. As soon as the United States became committed to MBFR—gradually after May 1971—West Europeans became more and more opposed to it.

In terms of multilateral policy coordination, MBFR became—at least during the prenegotiating phase—the single most important alliance issue since the late sixties; indeed, in its absence, diffusion of political interests within the alliance might have been worse. By the same token, however, strategic criteria became even more confounded with various political interests than in earlier years. NATO's nuclear debates were essentially over redistributions of political influence, but strategic issues were at least the vehicles of those controversies. MBFR served above all to neutralize domestic pressures, but as consultations went on, priorities shifted from strategic to negotiating requirements.[3] Not only was MBFR designed so as not to provide for constraints on Soviet military behavior as the one desirable negotiating outcome, but for a number of years NATO's posture was essentially considered in terms of what was compatible with negotiating policies, if not negotiable on the conference table.

The structure of Western threat perceptions was equally affected. The prospects of negotiations reinforced perceptions of a declining Soviet threat in spite of increasing Soviet capabilities in Eastern Europe. Furthermore, the emergence of a European geographical framework for East-West agreements combined with a shrinking readiness on the part of all alliance members to enter into new commitments to reinforce preoccupations with Central Europe by imposing an artificially narrow geographical definition of negotiable force relationships. At the same time, Soviet political strategy was scoring major successes outside Europe, with a more or less direct impact on European security. While MBFR was thus focusing political attention on the least unstable region, Central Europe, in a way which might well have affected military rules of engagement, Soviet political strategy should have made the alliance more aware of the crucial importance for Western Europe of who was pushing liberation wars—in Angola and Mozambique, for example—or, more importantly, who was gaining control over Middle East oil supplies for Western Europe.

After actual negotiations with the Soviet Union got under way, MBFR steadily lost momentum, even though some structural by-products may well turn out to be of a more durable nature (Central

European preoccupation or issues of compatibility with negotiating requirements in view of continued domestic pressures). Only American unilateralism could reinvigorate MBFR in the near future. On the other hand, only American foreign policy is vigorously addressing itself to some of the crucial extra-NATO regions of instability, notably in the Middle East.

MBFR thus was invented as a conservative alliance policy, which, not surprisingly, more or less ruled out meaningful long-term negotiating objectives. Not the reduction of forces in a given, artificially delineated area, but rather agreed constraints which would reduce the political usability of Soviet forces in European prewar situations, was a prudent aim of Western diplomacy. By the same token, however, MBFR tended to reinforce the traditional framework of strategic policy. Its basically conservative nature, while giving priority to "gimmicky" negotiating objectives, helped to delay reappraisals of NATO's strategy, force structure, and arsenal. During the earlier nuclear debate, failures of strategic policy efforts simply meant the end of a "game." MBFR may turn out to be different: given the lack of meaningful objectives, the criteria for failure may not even exist, but potential Soviet reactions at future negotiations may well remain a basic factor in any major effort to create new defense options within the Western Alliance. Obviously Soviet advice is not easily reconcilable with the imperatives of Western prudence.

The Fallacy of West European Institutionalism

MBFR negotiations may be expected to continue, with somewhat uncertain prospects, but emphasis undoubtedly has shifted back to defense. However, while in the United States the focus has been on new threats as well as technologies, renewed West European emphasis on defense has focused on preventing the loss of the European Defense Community (EDC) type of option in MBFR or of designing the architecture of a political union in order to boost political cooperation among the Nine.

This renewed interest in defense had relatively little in common either with the EDC of the early fifties, which was meant to utilize West Germany's potential under maximum political control, or with subsequent trans-Atlantic controversies over nuclear control which "Europeanists" hoped would result in a redistribution of peacetime influences. European history of the past twenty-five years has shown that except for political instrumentalities, a West European defense community belongs to the realm of gimmickry rather than strategic policy.[4] But while some may argue that options of the EDC type are at least necessary fictions for regulatory purposes in West European integration processes, such policies have lost options time after time. The sequence from West German power integration to diminishing American power to the more recent blend of mere institutionalism does not seem to reflect progress.

Combined West European defense efforts today may seem more desirable than ever, but they can only be modest in scope. There is no way to generate a meaningful spectrum of defense options outside the framework of US-West European defense cooperation. Any such effort is bound either to revive the insoluable issue of West European nuclear sharing or else to end up in vague institutionalism. Most importantly, however, not only is West European community-building unlikely to allow for more than mere consultations on defense matters in the foreseeable future, but, unlike integrationist concepts in the past, adding a defense community level would most probably disrupt the process of community-building itself. And since community-building is the most promising way to generate the kind of political stability in Western Europe that is the most important ingredient of its security, there is every reason not to confine future revivalist efforts to an EDC framework.

Like MBFR, the EDC drive has lost momentum again, but like MBFR it may once more be revived as a result of domestic changes. The absence of a persuasive defense concept is likely to favor zigzagging shifts of emphasis which are inconsequential in terms of postural outcomes, yet can make a big difference by absorbing or neutralizing political factions capable of supporting or generating usable options.

Scope and Limits of a Conservative Alliance Framework

In the past, changes in alliance politics occurred in terms of American initiatives to reform NATO, shifts of priority between different action levels, a temporary primacy of East-West negotiations, or efforts to create an institutional framework for a West European defense entity. While these various types of processes could have resulted in major changes in the alliance, they nevertheless were all consistent with what appeared to be a basically conservative alliance framework which rested on a prestabilized harmony of domestic forces in the member states.[5]

Until the early sixties, multilateral strategic policy formation was driven more or less within a relatively homogeneous political environment, and within a framework that was accepted together with its insoluable built-in conflicts. The system thus provided for a limited number of structural options which could be capitalized upon by competing political forces in domestic or interallied competitions. It was in the nature of this redistribution that competing strategic concepts came close to being considered in a political vacuum. All major competing political forces appeared to be identifiable on the strategic policy level.

Obviously, the conditions for this kind of game no longer exist. For all practical purposes, the classical options have gone: security is becoming weaker, so as to be a scarce commodity rather than an abundantly available currency. Moreover, there no longer is an accepted framework, and diversification of domestic forces with a chance to determine outcomes is still increasing.[6] As Henry Kissinger put it: "The domestic structure is taken as a given; foreign policy begins where domestic policy ends. But this approach is appropriate only to stable periods because then the various components of the international system generally have similar conceptions of the 'rule of the game.' "[7]

Conservative parties ceased to dominate the system in the early sixties when moderate social-democratic opposition parties like the SPD in West Germany had come around to supporting the Atlantic Alliance.[8] While the earlier opposition of these parties had provided domestic leverage for the conservatives, this major policy shift in turn helped to make nonconservative parties more eligible for government responsibility. In a sense, this broadened the political base of the Atlantic Alliance; in fact, it made the alliance politically less vulnerable both in the international arena and with regard to the needs for societal modernization. At the same time, supporting NATO no longer was a decisive means to maintain political power, and alliance politics began to lose some of its domestic functions. This was bound to reduce the domestic political status of the alliance, and while the alliance ceased to be the major framework for policy harmonization, the growing diversification of political parties which shared government responsibilities within the alliance made itself increasingly felt.

In the seventies, the political landscape of the alliance changed drastically. Except for France, where ruling conservatism never had an Atlantic orientation, and Italy, where governability simply is in jeopardy, conservative parties have by and large ceased to govern in Western Europe. They may regain power in one country or another, but for some time to come political conservatism has run out of structural options in Europe. But while social-democratism has become the dominant political force in Western Europe, the alliance has maintained its conservative framework. Given the strong American role, this condition could change only if Washington took the initiative. But in terms of respective domestic policies, there is a growing disparity between the United States and Western Europe. In the United States, the conservative swing back is likely to continue for some years. The "making of the president" in 1976 underscores this fact: in both parties, conservative candidates dominated the scene. In Western Europe, social-democratism is likely to remain the dominant force (even though "reformism" obviously has slowed down), but the very party elites which produced the policy shift in favor of supporting NATO will increasingly be replaced by the next political generation.

As long as the need to change the conservative alliance framework is not overwhelming, this disparity may not be very different from the relationship between Washington and today's SPD in Bonn, which still allows for dominant cooperation. But American governments may continue not to realize that social-democratism in Western Europe has a crucial integrative function, that of absorbing or moderating more radical leftist forces. This not only is a basic requirement for political stability and thus for Western Europe's security; it also explains why Moscow is most hostile to social-democratism. Indeed, if in Soviet perspective there is a genuine West European threat, it is the menace of a European Community which is increasingly dominated by social-democratism, which still maintains military protection within an Atlantic framework, and which generates increasing political attraction in Eastern Europe. For the first time, increasing political stability in Western Europe may also increase the need for its military protection.

On the other hand, if Washington fails to harmonize its Atlantic policies with the domestic realities in most West European countries, genuine American efforts to modernize NATO's military posture will be widely perceived in Western Europe as yet another effort to stabilize a conservative framework for maintaining American influence in Western Europe. Obviously, such perceptions would not be apt in terms of means, but they would be plausible in terms of the common purposes modernization is supposed to serve.

Without a strong commitment of West European political leaderships, bureaucratic inertia would probably suffice to prevent innovative change within the alliance. And without changes in the political orientation of US alliance politics, this commitment is not going to develop. However, in the United States the strongest support for NATO comes from conservative groups which are least likely to intend, let alone achieve, a major change of the existing conservative framework of the alliance. Those factions most strongly committed to NATO have an understandable propensity to prefer West European conservatism, and they are unlikely to recognize that a Western Europe moving somewhat more to the left than the United States may pose a much more serious threat to the Soviet Union than to the United States.

This situation results not only from the conservative frame of mind, but from the West European situation as well. In the present West European universe of political discourse, most nonconservative forces have a disposition not only to assume a declining Soviet threat, but also to reduce NATO's means, if not functions. Conservative forces are more likely to overrate the importance of Soviet military power in Europe. They also have a greater propensity to support revivalist efforts within the alliance, but their basic status-quo-mindedness tends to rule out the kinds of changes without which the alliance may well turn out to become dysfunctional politically and incapable militarily of meeting future challenges.

Thus strategic concepts can no longer be separated from the conditions of their political implementation. American policy statements to the effect that a continued American military presence is inconceivable if communist parties participate in West European governments, simply demonstrate that the conservative alliance framework tends to divorce strategic policy from the realities of Western Europe's domestic scene. While communist participation remains undesirable, it may be unavoidable. The American threat to withdraw will hardly prevent such outcomes; in fact, it has been rather counterproductive. More importantly, however, political integration of the less than moderate left is the basic requirement for political stability, a crucial fact that is hardly recognizable within the conservative framework of American alliance policies. Nor do those West European political forces which are most involved in this process of political integration always realize that the need for military protection may increase. The scope of a new trans-Atlantic alliance consensus is uncertain. But a redefinition of the Soviet threat to Western Europe is likely to be a sine qua non for any new consensus.

THE CHANGING NATURE OF THE SOVIET THREAT

Unlike Western military capabilities, Soviet military power in Europe has not ceased to be a determining factor on the Continent since 1945. Yet in the years following Hitler's defeat the Soviet threat was not primarily perceived in military terms. Vast expansion of Soviet political control over Eastern Europe and the destruction of the political fabric in most, and of the economies in all, West European countries combined to create profound uncertainties. Participation of communist parties in two West European governments with the prospect of more was widely regarded as a further step in Moscow's effort to penetrate Western Europe. Soviet performance in Iran, Greece, and Turkey suggested that while the threat was political, involvement of Soviet military power could make a crucial difference. Exploitation of Western political weaknesses was the name of the game—military power would be employed if it were appropriate.

The Doctrine of Generalized Threats

Since the late forties, Western threat perceptions have changed profoundly. Three events in particular shaped concepts and perceptions for the decades to come. First, while the Soviet role in Greece and Turkey was essentially defined by local conditions, President Truman had but one chance to present his case domestically—by generalizing the Soviet threat.[9] Second, although West Germany was most exposed to the threat of Soviet penetration and, indeed, was the highest stake in the emerging East-West confrontation, threat perceptions in Western Europe related to the German menace as well as to the Soviet threat and thus created the profound ambivalence of the emerging Western security system. Third, the nuclearization of NATO, the required centralized command structure, and the unavoidable American dominance were conducive to a defense system which reinforced both the mechanics of generalizing threat perceptions and its depolitization.

If the essence of the massive retaliation policy was the threat to generalize any conflict in terms of means, regions, and participants, any Soviet consideration to apply military power in a given situation would have to reckon with the prospects of generalization. In other words, as long as nuclear deterrence is dependable in any major conceivable contingency, the potential use of Soviet military power can indeed be perceived in terms of a generalized threat. The origins and dynamics of potential crises and military conflicts could, in a sense, be neglected as long as the assumption of instant multilateral response made all uses of Soviet military power more or less alike; nor did war termination draw much attention within a doctrine that was supposed to prevent conflict by deterrence. Within this framework, all that mattered was Soviet capabilities, that is, military power usable in major European conflicts under unspecified circumstances. Given this doctrine of generalized threats, the definition of threats was, in fact, a nonissue.

A vast Soviet military potential on the Eurasian continent simply has to be understood as a permanent factor which can strongly affect outcomes of political processes in Europe. In Soviet doctrine this means creating favorable conditions for political change. In Western perspective this is the Soviet threat. But while the Soviet threat is genuine, the structure of its perception in the West certainly is not. Accidental as the origins of the doctrine of generalized threats may be, it obviously is a function of profound political interests in the West.

Generalized Threat Perceptions: Their Political Functions

The most obvious pattern of interactions between genuine threats and Western interests is that perceived threats provide a favorable pretext for integrationist efforts. The political will to unify Western Europe certainly had a more complex basis, but growing readiness to accept West Germany as a key member of the Western community was directly related to the rise of Soviet power in Europe. This interest shaped or reinforced the structure of threat perceptions in the West. On the other hand, this political function of threat perceptions also shaped integrationist concepts in the West. The result was a primacy of military integration. Western integration policies in the fifties obviously were driven successfully by unifying threats, while the decline of the perceived threats in the sixties and beyond tended to slow down integration.

The international pattern may be more obvious, yet the domestic pattern may be more important. The doctrine of generalized threats tends to ignore the political nature of the Soviet threat in Europe: potential interactions of domestic or regional situations in the West and Soviet power. At the same time, however, this doctrine helped to make such contingencies less likely. Dominant threat perceptions and the resulting high priority for multilateral integration in Western domestic politics tended to neutralize political forces that originally were opposed to the prevailing blend of integrationist policies, and they tended to ostracize those political forces in Western countries that could have interacted with Soviet interests so as to provide incentives for Soviet support.

While conservative dictatorial regimes were reluctantly tolerated in terms of the primacy of common security interests, radical leftist regimes were not, because of their potential coalition with the Soviet Union. Similarly, radical leftist opposition parties for many years were denied any chance to participate in government simply because they could not reconcile their objectives with the reality of NATO, and this in turn was bound to reduce their potential constituencies. The doctrine of generalized threats thus was instrumental in the process of chanelizing domestic developments. Diminishing Soviet political leverage in Western Europe was the major outcome.

This concept of Western Europe's security obviously did not express adequately the factors that determined the political viability of postwar Europe. In fact, it has often misled political actors as well as observers to ignore the fundamental conditions of Western Europe's security: political stability and economic growth. However, the founding fathers of the alliance understood the instrumental nature of that concept, nor was this original insight ever completely lost in the years that followed. Threat simplification has helped to suppress or even eliminate internal conflicts, thereby minimizing the leverage for Soviet interference in West European politics. And focusing on joint responses produced a degree of political cohesion that was a prerequisite for political, social, and economic reconstruction of Western Europe after World War II. The alliance framework provided a projective mechanism that produced a dominant outward orientation in allied countries.[10]

There was no obvious alternative to achieving political stability by military integration. Neutralism would have encouraged domestic polarization. Priority for economic integration would have institutionalized traditional conflict patterns among West European countries. And there never was a serious possibility of a West European defense system; moreover, even if there were, this too would have institutionalized traditional conflicts. While neutralism would have induced only fragmentation, the two integrationist concepts would have favored opposite distributions of influence, one favoring Germany, the other France. In addition, each of the three alternatives would have raised a disturbing issue of Soviet political and military restraint. None would have generated a capacity to respond militarily, had Soviet military power been used against Europe.

These instrumentalities of the Atlantic Alliance have indeed proved to be of fundamental importance, but they have not lent themselves easily to public understanding. Military action refers to extreme situations and thus fails to convey a sense of common purpose in times of political stability. This is a fault of the system rather than a failure in judgment.

In the final analysis, the causes are common to all modern Western societies. They are essentially twofold. First, there is a decline of political responsiveness in Western democracies as experienced, for example, in the United States by Wilson, Roosevelt, Truman, Johnson, and beyond. Second, generalized and multinational defensive threats display a characteristic abstractness which stems from inherent presentational difficulties in view of low responsiveness as well as from the nature of means. Collective security concepts of the thirties[11] and NATO's nuclear deterrence share most of the characteristics and, in fact, instrumentalities of this abstractness.[12]

In the early sixties, to be sure, nuclear-sharing formulas appealed to some Western foreign policy elites as a conceivable surrogate for international order. By and large, however, the abstract nature of nuclear deterrence instead reinforced what Stanley Hoffman has called the "spontaneous depolitization towards force" in Western societies.[13] It is a Soviet contention that this indeterminateness "favors [Western] imperialism,"[14] but while this was true for the stalemate phase of the fifties and possibly a few years beyond, it now displays a profound weakness of the Western Alliance, especially in view of countervailing tendencies in the Soviet Union, where the "armed forces are being given a role and kept at a size that goes far above and beyond their functionality in the present international system."[15]

In a way it was the privilege of the radical New Left to point out these political functions of the alliance, but while they had no qualms about its stabilizing functions, they caricatured the state of Western society either by identifying it with rightist fringe countries or else by claiming the militarization of Western societies at the same time as the depolitization toward force almost self-defeatingly "exceeds the actual decline of the functionality of military force."[16] In attacking the alliance, the New Left tried to hit not defense per se (which it considers somewhat useless anyway), but the state of societies which tend to be preserved by the alliance. Not international security, but domestic change is their imperative. But while they obviously understood the political nature of the alliance and the threat perceptions on which it was based, they could make themselves heard only when the alliance was failing anyway as a political framework. The publicity the New Left received was thus essentially a windfall from the Vietnam War.

Some of the founding fathers of the Atlantic Alliance were probably aware of its transitory nature as a framework for political and social reconstruction. Certainly Adenauer was. The European Community was then conceived as a second layer—which it may well become in the future. But the divorce of international security functions from domestic purposes has gone very far. The Portuguese experience displayed the magnitude of change. While Washington tended to ignore strategic interests in order to expel Portugal because of its domestic situation, both Cunhal and the leftist military leadership assumed that domestic change could best be protected against outside interference by staying in NATO.[17]

What appeared to be a paradox—a decline of the perceived Soviet threat in Europe in spite of steadily increasing Soviet power—thus turns out to be a simple fact of life. Given the structure of Western threat perception and its domestic function, it was in fact a decline of political instrumentality within the West. This decline is not a result of détente, although it has the same endemic causes. The politics of détente in the West thus simply had to run its course. Whatever the need for genuine détente in East-West relations, the current politics of détente is certain to decline as well: it too is running out of domestic options.[18]

While the doctrine of generalized threats was a function of internal needs, and in this respect tended to lose its political relevancy, it nevertheless served a security purpose as well. Paradoxically it did so only as long as it maintained its domestic functions. The traditional deterrence posture of the West was expected to guard against overt Soviet aggression under unspecified circumstances which constitute a NATO case and thus generalize the conflict with no significant Soviet clients in Western Europe and no compelling restraints on Soviet destructive capabilities. This assumption helped to create a posture which was ill-conceived with regard to potential failure of deterrence, yet proved to be a sufficient deterrent. Moreover, it was politically viable because the political framework still did not deny generating responses to European worst-case contingencies. Generalizing the threat helped to create domestic situations in Western Europe which denied any prospects for

Soviet interventionism; under the circumstances, the conditions for expanding Soviet political control there simply did not exist. It helped to create a deterrence posture. Probably the security of Western Europe rested more on the former than on the latter. In any case, as long as domestic homogeneity and stability prevailed, the Soviet doctrine of using military power suggested that the deterrent would work.

However, this situation is likely to change. Increasingly there appear to be specific situations where the Soviets could use their military power more indirectly, without constituting a NATO case and thus without the risk of generalized responses. Many of these situations might involve political clients in Western Europe, which would make escalatory responses even more unlikely. The same domestic developments which rendered generalized threat perceptions and the alliance framework for generalized responses dysfunctional domestically, may in fact create in some West European countries the very political situations the Alliance was meant to prevent. Recent American testimony has it that in such circumstances "the Alliance as it now is could not survive. . . . The Western Alliance has always had an importance beyond military security. There would be a shocking change in the established patterns of American policy."[19] Obviously this would be conducive to Soviet interventionism. But even with the alliance functioning militarily, its present posture would not be wholly apt to match potential Soviet pressures.

Western Crisis Contingencies and Types of Soviet Military Involvement

In one sense this situation is anything but new. The political nature of what in Western perspective is the Soviet threat becomes apparent again in ways not too dissimilar from the years following World War II. Indeed, it was observed more than a century ago:

> The significance of Russia for Europe. A threat? Yes. Unavoidably so, because Russia's backwardness, the uneven rhythm of her own development and her inability to come to terms with herself forbade it to be otherwise. A nation that was not at peace with itself could not be at peace with its neighbors. But the menace Russia presented was something that could be measured only in terms of Europe's own weakness.
>
> Russia was aggressive—yes—out of a desire to be something it was not. Europe, however, was threatened primarily by its failure to be all that it really was.
>
> Russia was aggressive—yes—for lack of quality it recognized and envied in others but did not itself possess. Europe was threatened pri-

marily by its failure to respect and to preserve a quality that was already its own.

Russia was a menace to itself and to others—yes—by virtue of the fact that it had no past to believe in. Europe was threatened primarily by its failure to respect the past that it had.[20]

Today, however, Russian power no longer is checked within a European balance of power. During World War II, the Soviet Union emerged as the one dominant power on the Continent. It continues to unfold, and is checked only by American influence, which is based not on geographical reality but on political commitment. Whatever its intentions, Soviet power cannot be perceived in Western Europe except as a potential source for political expansionism. The mere fact of huge power and seemingly opaque processes of political decision-making in Moscow is bound to have an impact on Western Europe, whatever outcomes its adaptive behavior may produce. Moreover, Western Europe as a stake in Soviet-American competition and the complex nature of their relationship in Europe add to unavoidable rivalry. Most importantly, however, internal legitimacy and, indeed, stability will continue to require active Soviet hostility toward the social order in Western industrialized countries.[21]

These are structural causes for what in many Western perspectives appears as Soviet aggressiveness. It may or may not be a matter of Soviet intentions, desirable as Soviet cooperation may be. It is a secular problem, whatever the outcomes of East-West negotiations or adaptive changes resulting from the politics of détente may be. And it explains why military power continues to have political utility for the Soviet Union, whatever the chances of its actual exploitation for military aggression may be. The objective of developing a mutually accepted system of constraints is also a perennial one. But except for Soviet hegemony on the Continent, Soviet power maintains its political utility under any circumstances. There thus remains a challenge for Western democracies for the rest of the century.

Possible use of Soviet military power can be seen in four categories. First, there is the classical assumption of overt Soviet aggression for purposes of conquest without any legitimizing cause or any major coalescing political forces in the invaded territory. This is what NATO planning has tried to cope with over the years. Second, there is the impact of the mere existence of Soviet military power. In the broadest sense, military superiority may shape perceptions of the political environment so as to induce adaptive behavior.[22] But this utility can take on a number of more dynamic forms also. Developing a naval threat to Western maritime lines of communication is one. Demonstrating interventionist capabilities through maneuvers or troop movements is another. Remote threats are yet another type. While classical alliance policy obviously was a sufficient answer to potential overt aggression, arms control, however unsuccessful, was meant to cope with the political effects of Soviet power or at least with its demonstrative usability. A third and intermediate category which received much less attention during the classical period of alliance politics, from the early fifties into the early seventies, for reasons which relate to what has been labeled the doctrine of generalized threats is the opportunist use of military power outside the Soviet orbit. One could add a fourth category which in a different context may even be considered the most important one. It relates to what has recently been called the "unorganic relation" between the Soviet Union and the socialist states within its orbit.

These categories of political utility of Soviet military power ought to be distinguished more explicitly in Western strategic policy than has been the case in the past. For practical purposes they can be referred to as categories A (overt aggression), B (political influence without actual use), C (exploitive use interacting with political developments in the countries concerned), and D (suppression in order to maintain political control inside the Soviet orbit).

Category C pertains to expanding political control and/or improving the strategic environment in the Western sphere of influence by Soviet action. In either case, Soviet policy would interact politically with some developments outside the Soviet orbit.

Moves to improve Soviet strategic conditions (in addition to diplomatic efforts to weaken the fabric of the Western Alliance) might take the shape, for instance, of the acquisition of infrastructural facilities that could be used for military purposes. Thus before the moderates took over in Portugal on November 15, 1975, a Polish-Portuguese agreement was about to be signed that would have opened up broad possibilities to the Soviet Union. Given Western traffic around the Cape of Good Hope, Angola should also be mentioned here. Spitzbergen may be a possible future contingency, and Egypt might have become one except for the impact of Soviet-American bilateralism. In each case, the strategic conditions are being improved, from a Soviet point of view, with a straightforward expansionist zeal; none can be explained in terms of a defensive posture.

The more important kind of Soviet military involvement outside its orbit is the application of Soviet power in order to change the outcome of political developments within the West or vitally important to the West. Political support or simply expansion of political control are the objectives. This kind of Soviet military involvement can be described in terms of the four types of contingencies from which they could originate. First, the Soviet Union could try to maintain or change a domestic power distribution in a Western country under conditions of turmoil or civil war, by projecting military power in order to support a political client or simply establish a responsive regime. For example, an assassination of Soares might have produced a situation in Portugal where, in the aftermath of the Chilean disaster and in view of conceivable American hostility to any of the major competing forces in Portugal, the Soviet Union might have felt a need to shape the outcome. It may be relevant that Secretary Brezhnev is reported to have pointed out to President Gomes during the Helsinki summit that while the Soviet Union is bound by the Helsinki principle of nonintervention, the CPSU is not.

Second, the Soviet Union could try to project power in order to take sides in a violent conflict between Western nations. For example, in the absence of a charismatic figure such as Karamanlis, Greece might have become the recipient of Soviet military support, had the conflict over Cyprus in 1974 escalated so as to put Greece in a desperate situation.

Third, contingencies may arise in European "gray area" countries. Yugoslavia after Tito is widely regarded as a possibility, the likelihood of which could be affected by whether or not a "historical compromise" has been achieved in Italy. Austria and Finland are less likely, but conceivable. The ominous "Polarka Plan" at least suggests how Austria could be affected in conjunction with a Yugoslav contingency.

Fourth, there is a possibility of Soviet intervention in areas or countries vitally important to Western Europe, above all Iran or Saudi Arabia, or even South Africa. The application of Soviet military force is conceivable in at least four different ways. There could be a Soviet takeover, say, in Iran, in the context of a succession crisis or of a subregional military conflict where the Soviet Union chooses to assist "the other side"; there could be a request for Soviet military help in a domestic or subregional conflict, or simply a Soviet assumption that help is being requested, with subsequent Soviet military action; there could be a perceived threat of Western or specifically American intervention in the area which could trigger Soviet decisions to assist the Arabs, for example, by taking action at Berlin or other vulnerable spots in Europe; and there could be situations where the Soviet Union simply takes advantage of the consequences of Arab oil embargoes in Europe.

These types of contingencies are meant as paradigms rather than predictions. However, while none of these possible contingencies is new, interactions between exploitable crises and Soviet power have become more likely. They are certainly more likely than the kinds of worst cases NATO tries to guard itself against. Such contingencies deserve close study in terms of indigenous situations, levels of Soviet commitment, status and nationality of forces involved, military means applied in the conflict, and the like.

Since the early fifties the Soviet threat has been described in terms of the Type A threat described above. It will increasingly have to be described in terms of A and C. While D does not pose a direct threat to the West, recent discussions of the so-called "Sonnenfeld Doctrine" have reminded the West that Soviet suppressive action in Eastern Europe could in fact escalate into a more general conflict. Paradoxically, the impact of détente on Eastern Europe may increase the likelihood that this may happen. But while category D does not determine requirements for the Western military posture, category C does.

NATO planning has almost exclusively focused on A. While political elites were aware of category B as well, the considerable political stability and homogeneity in Western Europe allowed the doctrine of generalized threats and the system of multilateral responses built on it to minimize political influences of Soviet military power. In fact, as has been pointed out, this doctrine turned out to be counterproductive because it was conducive to perceptions of a declining threat in spite of a worsening military situation. Category C with its various ramifications poses the most serious analytical and political deficit in Western strategic policy. While the Western military posture will have to continue to meet the requirements of A, it has to be changed in order to meet the new requirements of B and C as well. Notwithstanding the obvious utility of doctrinal and institutional coherence and unity, these more complex challenges require that Western strategic policy provide for several distinctly different types of action.

SOME REQUIREMENTS FOR FUTURE WESTERN STRATEGIC POLICY

Given the changing political framework of Western strategic policy and the changing nature of the Soviet threat, some basic requirements for future Western strategic policy emerge with regard to the military posture, the political homogeneity of the alliance and its institutional flexibility. Three additional requirements also have become obvious. First, whatever the needs for shifting emphasis of governmental action from one level to another, denying the use of Soviet military power remains a precondition for political stability and economic growth. Second, whatever the desirability and in fact the need for mutual constraint, negotiating objectives must not be perceived as a measure for defense planning. Third, whatever the impact of Western institution-building on political stability, defense efforts ought not to be oriented toward institutional spillover at the expense of an improved military posture.

Requirements for a Western Military Posture

A Western military posture for the eighties and beyond has to be designed with regard to what have been labeled categories A, B, and C. While the existing deterrence-only posture will turn out not to be politically viable in the face of the changing political framework of the alliance, or militarily sufficient in the face of the growing complexity of the Soviet threat, a deterrence posture remains the answer to Type A threats. However, the deterrence posture must be designed to allow for escalation control, that is, for politically usable escalatory potential should deterrence fail. Moreover, the requirements for such a posture will have to be based on the assumption that should a Soviet Type A threat materialize, it will most likely be a determined effort. At the same time, a future deterrence posture will have to be compatible with requirements that emerge with regard to categories B and C.

In order to neutralize the political influence of Soviet military power, there must be stability of political expectations in Western Europe. This is primarily a political matter, but various military postures may have different impacts on perceptions and political expectations. In the past a vague notion of credibility and a straightforward fear of budgetary restraints accompanied Western strategic policy considerations. In the future, political requirements will be more complex. First, the military posture of the West must be designed so as not to become the domain of particular factions of the spectrum of democratic political forces. Second, it must be politically viable in a long-range perspective in terms of diminishing domestic pressure on particular deployments or commitments. Third, it must be presentable as a nonsuicidal security arrangement for plausible contingencies. Finally, it must be perceived by political constituencies as a posture that credibly denies specific Soviet options. Different postures will have different degrees of political acceptability in any of these dimensions.[23]

In order to make Type C threats less likely, appropriate domestic policies as well as preventive diplomacy are most important. If the Greek domestic change in 1974 had gone to more bizarre extremes, it would have had to be blamed on those who tolerated the preceding regime. On the other hand, the Angolan cause was lost not because of a lack of military support, but because diplomacy failed to recognize that the competing factions were separated by tribal rivalry rather than ideological differences. It thus avoidably drove Netto to seek Soviet support, which he readily received. Kissinger's African tour in April 1976 may suggest that a lesson has been learned. It also underlines the fact that preventive diplomacy did not come into play during the formation phase of the Angolan crisis.

In addition to political and diplomatic requirements, the military posture, too, is crucially important for dealing with Type C threats. The likelihood of their materializing will depend to some extent on how acceptable a future posture will have become in Western political processes in the four dimensions described above. Given the possibility that any Type C conflict could escalate into a general conflict between the two alliances, deterrence as designed against Type A threats will be a decisive constraint on Soviet escalatory potential.

But since Soviet military power can be used in ways that will not be perceived as constituting a NATO case, the posture will have to meet additional military requirements. Nonnuclear options will have to be expanded. Mobility will have to be improved. Command and control will have to allow for more political flexibility. To meet such requirements, new technologies are most promising. On the other hand, Soviet constraints as well as nonmilitary coercive potentials also have to be considered for any type of contingency.

As for Type D contingencies, it may seem paradoxical that while continued détente policies may in the long run increase the likelihood of Soviet suppressive military action in Eastern Europe, which may in turn spill over into more general conflicts, modest but perennial efforts to constrain growing Soviet power through détente remain essential. Moreover, in order for the alliance to have a viable and sufficient military posture, a degree of superpower détente also is needed before the defense efforts can be politically acceptable to broader political constituencies. Thus there is in fact a need for complementarity of defense and détente policies, even though in recent developments the opposite seems to have been the case.

Defense and Political Homogeneity

For some twenty-five years the Atlantic Alliance operated on the assumption of political homogeneity: it embraced countries governed by political forces that would not coalesce with the Soviet Union. Defense against a Soviet threat and denying communist government participation were then two sides of the same coin. Except for brief interludes in Iceland and Portugal, political homogeneity has by and large prevailed. It may not last. But while the shadows of Soviet power become longer and communist government participation becomes more likely, at least in some Southern European countries, the interests of the Soviet Union and West European communist parties are now less easily identifiable than they used to be.

Whatever the diplomatic utility or domestic necessity of Kissinger's warnings that should communist parties join governments in Italy or France, the alliance would begin to lose its viability, his contention is based on three assumptions which require a closer look. The first is that NATO will cease to function if communist parties participate in one or several NATO governments. The second is that if elections in Italy and/or France should bring communist parties into governmental responsibility, a chain reaction is bound to start all over Western Europe so as to turn it communist or radically socialist within the next ten years. And the third assumption holds that if this should happen in some or most or all West European countries, these nations could then become the objects of American manipulative power diplomacy, but not the recipients of American protection.

It is one thing to approach this issue from the point of view of reducing the likelihood of such election outcomes, and another to consider how to live with communist government participation should it occur.

In spite of counterproductive Western blunders in Portugal in 1975,[24] developments there suggest that communist rule may not be irreversible under military protection, let alone in electorial trials. But while communist government participation may occur, the alliance may be capable of developing pragmatic ways to maintain arrangements for military cooperation. Kissinger's second assumption seems highly unlikely. The danger is rather the political fragmentation of Western Europe—which may be just as bad from a security point of view.

Kissinger's third assumption touches fundamental issues. While the implied automaticity is untenable, two major security considerations arise with regard to such a process should it happen. On the one hand, communist parties will not be able to maintain power forcefully without direct Soviet support. This could in fact lead to a Type C threat. Such a situation must not be tolerated, and would require a combination of measures that would have to include the threat of Western military countermoves. On the other hand, it is widely assumed that Yugloslav leaders hope to enjoy some degree of Western protection. Recent public controversies in the United States over the "Sonnenfeld Doctrine" go even further. In spite of the record since 1953, they display a political will to support efforts to achieve greater independence from Moscow. If this is so, it seems reasonable to assume that should some West European countries go communist, they would be eager to maintain protection against Soviet interventionism, and there would be a potential in the West to provide it. Thus the fundamentals of Western Europe's security may have to be redefined.

What is really at stake, however, is whether Soares in Portugal or Mitterand in France would be able to square the circle of not disrupting relations with respective communist parties and maintaining protection within an Atlantic framework. In the final analysis, political integration of the more radical Left and some degree of multilateral military cooperation are two sides of one coin—West European security. Given the Kissinger approach, this requirement tends to be ignored in some Western governments. Without redefining the basic security purposes of the alliance, the modernization of its military posture may well turn out to be of marginal political importance.

Multilateralism and Institutional Flexibility

The doctrinal and institutional uniformity and coherence of military cooperation in NATO was never met by political realities within the alliance. Thus to some extent NATO's multilateralism is little more than an ideologized defensive political posture of its bureaucracies. But whatever its virtues, future developments may require increasing institutional flexibility in two important ways: a growing diversification of membership and a growing diversification of threats the alliance is expected to cope with.

While NATO's multilateralism ought to be maintained with regard to Type A threats, it could even be an obstacle with regard to most Type C's. The alliance's military posture would have to be designed to meet both kinds of threats. This has implications for existing rules of engagement, conditions for stationing forces, geographical limits as required by the Treaty of Washington, and so on. This dual capability cannot be reproduced institutionally. While the NATO system ought to be maintained and modernized to the extent possible in order to provide a multilateral deterrent, it will have to be complemented to a much larger extent than hitherto by intergovernmental arrangements, both for crisis management of Type C contingencies and for joint action should such contingencies emerge.

The unfolding debate on Western security has developed in a compartmentalized manner. Efforts are under way to reconsider all issues—the posture, the political framework, and the institutional requirements. Unfortunately, some of these debates are unfolding in terms of domestic infighting rather than through deliberate reform efforts. But while this situation may change, the fundamental challenge for Western political leaders will be to redefine the political requirements for Western Europe's security in ways which recognize both the need for political stability and the growing utility of Soviet military power.

NOTES

1. Sir Peter Medawar, "Technology and Evolution," in Saul Bellow, Daniel Bell, Edmondo O'Goman, Sir Peter Medawar, and Arthur C. Clarke, *Technology and the Frontiers of Knowledge* (Garden City, N.Y., 1973), p. 108.
2. As Laurence Martin puts it: "In the last resort most Europeans . . . have perceived the better part of wisdom in falling in with the preferences of the United States. . . ." (see Chapter 3 of this book).
3. For a discussion of a specific example of shifting criteria, see Uwe Nerlich, *The Alliance and Europe: Part V: Nuclear Weapons and East-West Negotiation, Adelphi Paper 120* (London: The International Institute for Strategic Studies, Winter 1975/6).
4. For a fuller discussion of recent efforts to revive EDC-type options, see Uwe Nerlich, "West European Defence Identity: The French Paradox," in *The World Today*, vol. 30 (May 1974). See also Uwe Nerlich, "NATO, EEC and the Politics of Détente: Regulative Frameworks of Western Foreign Policy Making," in Nils Andrén and Karl Birnbaum,

eds., *Beyond Détente: Prospects for East-West Cooperation and Security in Europe* (Leyden, 1976), pp. 51-64.

5. The concept of conservatism is used here loosely to describe a political disposition which would give priority to national security over societal modernization if hard choices were to arise, which would tend to identify vigilance toward the Soviet Union with domestic anticommunism, and which is primarily status-quo oriented with respect to the external environment. This kind of conservatism, like other political tendencies, attaches great importance to preserving Western cooperative structures, above all NATO. As a corollary, the emphasis on security was usually justified so as to require that shared values be reflected by stated objectives of the Atlantic Alliance. Obviously conservatism in this sense cannot always be equated with conservative political parties.

6. The Portuguese case illustrates some of the more paradoxical processes. While Cunhal and the radicals in the MAF assume that staying in NATO is the safest way to protect the revolution from outside intervention, most political forces in Western Europe are opposed to ousting Portugal from NATO—the leftists in order not to cut off remaining ties, the conservatives in order to preserve at least the institutional facade of NATO.

7. Henry A. Kissinger, *American Foreign Policy* (New York, 1969), p. 11.

8. Norway is the major exception to this rule. With one brief interlude, its Labor Party has ruled in Oslo ever since the alliance was founded, and Norway has indeed played an important role in the formation of NATO.

9. See Ernest May, *"Lessons" of the Past: The Use and Misuse of History in American Foreign Policy* (New York, 1973), pp. 46 ff.

10. See Morton A. Kaplan's discussion of projection as a mechanism of regulation, in *System and Process in International Politics* (New York, 1951), pp. 262 ff.

11. See Arnold Wolfers, *Britain and France Between the Two Wars* (New York, 1966), pp. 337-43.

12. See Henry A. Kissinger, "Coalition Diplomacy in a Nuclear Age," *Foreign Affairs*, July 1964, p. 531. See also Uwe Nerlich, "Nuclear Weapons and European Politics: Some Structural Interdependencies," in Johan Holst, ed., *Security, Order, and the Bomb* (Oslo: *Universitets-forlaget*, 1972), pp. 78 ff.

13. *Force in Modern Societies: Its Place in International Politics*, Adelphi Paper 102, Papers from the Travemünde Conference (London: The International Institute for Strategic Studies, Winter 1973), p. 7.

14. In Wassili Kulisch, *"Militaerische Potenz und Aussenpolitik des Imperialismus," IWP-Berichte*, September 1972, p. 10.

15. *Force in Modern Societies*, ibid.

16. Idem.

17. See Oriana Fallaci's interview with Alvaro Cunhal in *The New York Times Magazine*, July 13, 1975, p. 47.

18. Uwe Nerlich, "NATO, EEC, and the Politics of Détente," op cit.; also *"Détente und Westpolitik: Zum Verhältnis von aussenpolitischem Pluralismus und innerer Stabilitat in Westeuropa," Europa-Archiv* 1976/4, pp. 105-12.

19. See summary of Secretary of State Kissinger's remarks to the London meeting of twenty-eight US ambassadors, *New York Times,* April 7, 1976, p. 16.

20. For George F. Kennan's résumé of what "Russia's Toqueville," the Marquis de Custine, observed more than 130 years ago, see George F. Kennan, *The Marquis de Custine and his Russia in 1839* (Princeton, N.J., 1971), pp. 90 ff.

21. See Richard Loewenthal, *"Die Sowjetunion—eine Weltordnungsmacht,"* in *Die Sowjetunion als Weltmacht* (Berlin, 1975), pp. 16 ff. Also see Fritz Ermarth, *Internationalism, Security, and Legitimacy: The Challenge to Soviet Interests in East Europe 1964-68,* The Rand Corporation, RAND-RM-5909-PR (Santa Monica, Calif., 1969), and Uwe Nerlich, "Soviet-American Bilateralism: A Constraint on Soviet Policy?" in Lawrence Whetten, ed., *Political Impact of Soviet Military Power* (New York, forthcoming).

22. For a useful discussion of these "shadows of power," see R. J. Vincent, *Military Power and Political Influence: The Soviet Union and Western Europe,* Adelphi Paper 119, (London: The International Institute for Strategic Studies, Autumn 1975), pp. 19-29.

23. Given current trends within the alliance, recent polls may not be surprising. E.g., in West Germany, 37% assumed that by the end of the century the Soviet Union will be more powerful than the United States; only 11% were expecting the United States to be stronger. What is of particular significance is that considerably more supporters of conservative parties were assuming the Soviet Union to be stronger than supporters of the SPD (42% versus 36%). See *Allensbacher Berichte* 1975/ No. 29.

24. See Tad Szulc, "Lisbon and Washington: Behind Portugal's Revolution," *Foreign Policy,* Winter 1975, pp. 3-62.

CHAPTER 2

Détente and
the Politics of Instability
in Southern Europe

Pierre Hassner

"The owl of Minerva," Hegel said, "rises only at dusk." Similarly, great debates tend to develop when their subject matters are losing their relevance. This may be the case with the polemic waged, especially in the United States, about détente. The debate seems to reach its peak precisely as détente itself is, if not disappearing, at least losing its claim to constitute the central characteristic phenomenon of present international relations.

This probably inevitable gap between reality and discussion is, however, profoundly ambiguous. It may be linked to a new realism, but also to a new misunderstanding. If the debate on détente is so lively in 1974-76, it may be because the optimistic expectations of 1971-73 about the consequences of détente have been proven false, or because other more depressing events of the last two years, unexpected or predicted by pessimists and skeptics, are being attributed to détente.

It may well be that the first perception is true but that the second is misleading.

After having been oversold, détente may be overattacked. In both cases, its effects upon what happens in the world may be exaggerated, because of too hasty and dogmatic answers to a real question, namely, the mutual influence of the state of relations between superpowers and of the political evolution of the world. This general question itself raises two distinct issues concerning the relative importance and mutual effect of global versus regional and local, and of military and diplomatic versus domestic, social, and economic factors.

The trouble with the concept of détente is probably that it is either too broad or too narrow. The philosophical disagreements about détente usually are really about the size of the defense budget, the value of arms control or trade agreements, or the analysis of Soviet policy and its role in given countries or crises. All of these are topics which would be more usefully discussed on their own terms. On the other hand, the real general problem of international relations today concerns the mutual influence (or the dialectical relationship) between the evolution of the strategic balance of the interstate system and the evolution of domestic and transnational society. Many issues usually connected with the notion of détente, such as the effect of economic interdependence or of communication upon domestic regimes, the effect of domestic crises upon foreign policy behavior, or the effect of superpower intervention upon regional conflicts, obviously enter into this broader framework. The problem, if one is to have a meaningful discussion of détente, is to isolate its specific nature and role, if any, within these more diffuse interactions. But this can only be a means toward returning to the global structure and dynamics of a given political situation, such as that of Southern Europe which, in Europe, is the area where the contradictions of security and change are the most acute.

DETENTE AS A CONDITION OR AS A POLICY

In Southern Europe, perhaps even more than elsewhere, the central problem obviously lies in the relation between the policies of governments and the evolution of societies. Applied to the notion of détente, this consideration suggests that insufficient attention may have been devoted to the distinction between détente as a situation or a condition of public opinion and of social attitudes, and détente as a policy aimed at promoting, exploiting, or adapting to the former.

It may be more useful to start from détente as a situation, if only in order to take a clue from the word itself: before being a positive policy, détente is a psychological notion and a negative one. It represents neither cooperation nor settlement, neither a change in long-range objectives nor a change in objective structures, but rather a decrease in tension between adversaries or in attention between allies. Détente represents a decrease in subjective feelings of fear or hostility as distinct from objective insecurity or opposition.

On this subjective and negative level, détente certainly represents an objective reality. Perhaps the case where this reality can be observed in its purest form is that of Chinese-American relations: not very much has changed in actual military or economic policies since the start of Ping-Pong diplomacy and President Nixon's visit to Peking, but the subjective feelings of mutual hostility and threat have been radically altered. These subjective changes have, of course, objective causes and consequences. Again, from the US-Chinese case, one factor appears as particularly important in both categories: it is, rather than the disappearance of conflicts, their relativization or their decrease in psychological salience, because of the appearance of other conflicts, within states, within alliances, or with other groupings.

The Cold War has not disappeared but it has tended no longer to appear as *the* Cold War because of the appearance of other cold wars: Sino-Soviet, North-South, between the executive and legislative branches within the United States, or between Greece and Turkey within NATO. This says nothing about the relative importance of these various conflicts; but a loss in visibility may mean a loss in subjective priority and a modification in the way one issue affects all the others. Even in this first and basic meaning, détente may turn out to be more fragile than was assumed for the past few years: clear Soviet strategic superiority, direct use by the Soviet Union of its new conventional power (whether against Norway or in Angola), or attribution to the Soviet Union of communist successes in Western Europe may revive feelings on the Western side of direct threat and hostility. Already a certain intermediate stage of suspicion and skepticism, distrust and unease, seems to gain in the Western perception of the Soviet Union over the more optimistic feelings associated with détente.

Conversely, Soviet internal difficulties and ideological hardening may revive the need for Western scapegoats, especially if a normalization of relations with China made the latter less useful as a unifying enemy. But for the time being, domestic, intra-alliance, and North-South factors maintain their priority in public attention and frustration, as well as in the dynamics of political evolution.

What is, however, increasingly under challenge, both politically and intellectually, is the second aspect of détente. This second aspect is a policy built upon the first, in the sense in which Ceral Bell has defined détente as "an artifice of statecraft by which a reduction of tension is induced into a diplomatic relationship."[1] The question is the nature of this diplomatic relationship, and the relation of détente in both the psychological and the diplomatic aspects to the third and decisive level of reality, which the Soviet literature calls the "total correlation of forces" and which includes both the military balance and, even more important, the evolution of social and political regimes.

Here it becomes increasingly obvious that the expectations built upon the reduction of tensions, and the strategies built upon these expectations, show a great measure of divergence and varying degrees of frustration corresponding to the uncontrolled or unexpected developments of specific areas or countries.

For Henry Kissinger, détente as a policy meant using the reduction of tension for establishing a basically conservative concert of which the Soviet-American relationship would constitute one important element among others. Between these two countries, nuclear cooperation on the basis of parity to limit the arms race would be supported by economic interdependence. Toward their allies, restraint in the support of each other's rebels, or their outright discouragement, amounted to a de facto sphere-of-influence policy. In disputed areas, détente would make possible a mutual restraint in superpower competition. This would mean, under the cover of the meaningless "no unilateral advantage" formula, a greater freedom of action for the United States to withdraw gracefully where it had to and to use its leverage for exercising a central role, consisting of various combinations of hegemony and mediation, in the rest of the world.

For the Soviet Union, the uses of détente were seen in an even more asymmetrical and a much more dynamic light. Détente would be one element among several (such as favorable changes in the military balance, the inner divisions of the West, and Western difficulties with the Third World) in the shifting of the "world correlation of forces" in its favor. It would permit an opening to the West in terms of economic and technological cooperation, which would create risks for the domestic stability of the empire and contribute to an increased centralization and control in Eastern Europe. In the West and in the Third World, it would encourage a weakening of cohesion and of American domination and an increase in Soviet influence. The process had to proceed in a slow and controlled fashion, however, to avoid the twin dangers of, on the one hand, a strong American reaction, such as a victory of right-wing forces leading to a return to the Cold War and to denying the Soviet Union the benefits of détente, and, on the other hand, a spreading of instability to the Soviet empire through the influence of "social-democratism" or of "pluralistic communism."

The Kissinger concept and the Soviet concept were, ultimately, deeply at odds with each other but perhaps even more at odds with the concepts of smaller European powers, West or East, which were looking to détente as an opportunity for change in their domestic regime, their external alignment, or their general role. For a Gaullo-Rumanian conception, détente was to mean the dissolution of blocs, a partial disengagement of the superpowers, and an increased scope for the diplomacy of small and middle powers. These hopes were quickly shattered after 1968, when it appeared that détente, in Europe, would be based upon the acceptance of existing realities, first and foremost among which was the Soviet domination of Eastern Europe and, as a consequence, the general acceptance of American presence in Western Europe. Therefore, an opposite conception seemed to be more in tune with the character of a détente based on "Big Twoism." For countries like Kadar's Hungary in the East and Brandt's Federal Republic in the West, the acceptance of détente between the superpowers was the basis upon which an inner transformation and a mutual opening of societies, East and West, could take place: détente would act as a legitimizer of social change and East-West cooperation.

A similar conception was, and still is, entertained by the Italian communist party. Its assumption, which is shared to some extent by most of the Left in Southern Europe, was that détente would help blur the opposition between capitalist and communist regimes or parties, would legitimize the latter in the West, would deemphasize both ideological and military confrontations, and would allow domestic compromises, as between Christian democrats and communists, under the legitimizing umbrella of the international compromise between the United States and the Soviet Union.

Of course, these expectations and strategies clash directly with both the nature of the superpower détente and its present crisis. There is one thing in common between the phases of predominant cooperation and predominant confrontation between the two superpowers: in both cases each wants to maintain or increase its control over its respective sphere, applying the principle *cuius regio, eius religio*. The difference, if any, lies in their attitude toward the other superpower's control over its own allies: the degree of "Holy Alliance" versus "International Civil War" varies according to degrees of cooperation, but also according to opportunities: here the difference between the two sides is as important as between different phases.

This is why the most interesting and at the same time the most controversial position is a fifth one, which was formulated by the leader of the Spanish communist party, Santiago Carrillo, in an interview given to the Italian leftist journal *Il Manifesto* on November 1, 1975. According to Carrillo, the Left can come to power in Southern Europe only against the opposition of both superpowers, for both have an interest in the status quo: the United States to maintain its control, the Soviet Union because a West European model of pluralistic communism and/or socialism would create difficulties for its own control in Eastern Europe. However, prospects of success do exist because of the pressure of societies for change, because the ability of the United States to intervene militarily is severely hampered, and because if Western communist parties severed their links with the "party states" of the East, this might help remove Western objections.

This synthesis of Gaullist and Italian strategies seems based on the clearest recognition of the contradictory variables present in the situation, in particular the conflicting directions of the desires of the superpowers and of the dynamics of local situations, and the limits on the power of the former to block the latter. But the assumption of symmetry or of the diffusion of diversity from West to East is more debatable, so that the dilemma between autonomous sociopolitical trends within the West and the maintenance of the political-military balance with the East is all the more acute, and the relationship between both and détente all the more ambiguous.

The character of détente itself—bilateral or multilateral, one-dimensional or multidimensional, symmetric or asymmetric—is affected just as much by the character of the various instabilities, crises, and conflicts within societies as by the reactions and policies of the different states.

Neither détente nor, more generally, the action of the Soviet Union or of the United States has created the new crises and conflicts which seem to characterize the present period; rather, it is these new crises and conflicts which have made détente inevitable. But, in turn, détente, by removing or attenuating the inhibitions coming from the perception of a common enemy, has contributed to bringing these crises and conflicts into the open. The result has sometimes been revolution (particularly in the South), sometimes erosion or absorption, sometimes paralysis or adaptation (particularly in the West), and sometimes preventive repression (particularly in the East). The various outcomes of the crisis in turn affect the East-West balance, and the various reactions to modifications of the East-West balance affect both détente (or attitudes toward the opposite alliance) and the domestic or intra-alliance situations.

In these dialectical processes, the importance of perceptions can hardly be exaggerated. In particular, gaps or lags between the conscious and the unconscious, the specific and the diffuse, between changes in external reality and in collective consciousness, severely limit the ability of governments to practice the desired selectivity in détente, or more generally, to practice discrimination and flexibility in political strategies aimed at reaching the right combination of conflict and cooperation, of identity and interpenetration.

Two examples are particularly relevant to the present situation. The first concerns the paradoxes of self-denying security and self-deluding reassurance. Détente, in its psychological and negative meaning, involves a coincidence between a well-founded lessening of the fear of both nuclear attack and conventional invasion on the one hand, and, on the other hand, Cold War fatigue everywhere, ideological erosion within the East, and disaffection with military values and organization in the West. When these two aspects—the decrease in military insecurity and the decrease in political hostility—become separated, a dangerous gap may open. Their coincidence leads to taking for granted the impossibility of war and to the lowering of defense budgets. This in turn may endanger the stability of the balance and increase the likelihood of war. But the phenomenon known as "cognitive dissonance," based on the self-perpetuating force of obsolete perceptions and on the continuing force of the other priorities, leads to either ignoring the objective change or to finding in it, consciously or unconsciously, yet another reason for détente and hence for the blurring of ideological opposition. This is what "Finlandization" really means: adopting the most reassuring interpretation of Soviet behavior precisely because one is not reassured.

The other example concerns the difficulties of centralization and discrimination in détente. While there is a rational case for trying to separate détente into that between the leaders of the two alliances, that between all their states, and that between and within all their societies, this position is untenable because of psychological and moral dynamics. What is good for de Gaulle or Kissinger inevitably looks also good for Brandt, no matter how much the first two would have liked to keep a monopoly on relations with the East. Similarly, East-West détente legitimizes the communist parties within Western countries and makes it very difficult for socialist parties to renounce the prospects of change through alliance with communists because of their links with Moscow, or because of the consequences for NATO. The alternation between the rhetoric of reconciliation and that of resistance to the totalitarian danger inevitably endangers the credibility of both.

The first case is more characteristic of the situation in the North of Europe, the second in the South.

In general, while the Cold War tended to produce a partly artificial unity both between actors within alliances and within societies and between dimensions (territorial, military, diplomatic, and ideological), détente, or what I have called elsewhere "hot peace,"[2] tends to produce discrepancies and asymmetries. It encourages centrifugal trends between and within units and differentiation between and within dimensions. This happens both East and West, North and South, but to different degrees and, above all, with different consequences and counterreactions, due to the different nature of relations between leader and allies, or between state and society. While the US-Soviet military balance remains the ultimate foundation, there is a trend toward the emancipation of nonstate, national, regional, and nonmilitary relations from its direct control. This trend is particularly visible, although its consequences are particularly ambiguous, in Southern Europe.

SOUTHERN EUROPE: MORE SOUTH THAN EUROPE?

Both the advent of détente and a number of developments, ranging from biological accidents to historical trends, conspire toward what might be called, in more than one sense, the "Third-Worldization" of Western Europe. In the sense which is relevant here, the discrepancies and unpredictabilities of social change, political regimes, and international alignments raise, for the superpowers as well as for multilateral organizations, problems of choice or priorities between ideological and strategic considerations and between direct and indirect methods which it was possible to ignore in the stability of earlier years.

This is particularly true of the southern part of the Continent, for more than other regions it is involved in a crisis of legitimacy which in various respects touches both Western and Eastern systems.

Nationally and internationally, there is a tension between the persistence of old structures and the push of economic, social, cultural, psychological, and, ultimately, political forces which they contain or repress, channel or absorb, or which erode them, overwhelm them, or break them up. In the south of the Continent, this tension is particularly spectacular and explosive. First, the structures of authority are more fragile, because of the legacy of archaic dictatorships, as in Spain and Portugal, or because of the lack of renewal of political elites, as in Italy. Second, social tensions are increased by the fact that these societies and economies are struggling with the problems of transition between agriculture and industry, between traditional models and those of a modernity which is itself in crisis.

While the strategic and, to a large extent, the diplomatic and ideological structures of the Continent remain dominated by the East-West relationship, social and economic tensions in Western and, above all, in Southern Europe are dominated by the East-West and North-South dimensions, which go between countries and through each of them. Unequal wealth and development, unequal vulnerabiilty and dependence, as between the United States and Western Europe, between the North and the South of the Continent, or between the North and the South of Italy, Spain, or Portugal themselves, are the more relevant conflict structures in this respect.

To some extent this has always been the case; but for about twenty years the East-West conflict has pushed all the others into the background. The coincidence between the geographic situation of a country, its diplomatic and military alignment, and its social and economic regime has been taken for granted. The great shock of 1968 was the demonstration that revolution is not inconceivable in Western Europe, and that, in Eastern Europe, a country could slide away from the Soviet model. In both cases, the system succeeded in reasserting itself, but by very different methods and with very different degrees of solidity.

The Soviet Union has succeeded remarkably well in stabilizing its own camp, but by doing violence to the spontaneous tendencies and aspirations of its nations and societies; and it still lives in constant fear lest communication with the West or economic crisis bring them back with a vengeance. In the West, destabilizing trends have been much more free to unfold, helped by détente which diminishes the preoccupation with military security toward the East and legitimizes communist parties, and by the social and economic crisis which increases economic tensions and blemishes the model of Western democracy. In any case, it is clear that the danger to stability and hence, ultimately, to security comes from these trends much more than from Soviet action itself.

In the three types of crises which have been distinguished by Uwe Nerlich in Chapter 1 of this volume—crises linked to the economic vulnerability of Western Europe, to the domestic instability of some of its countries, or to conflicts between two of them—the situation offers opportunities to Soviet power but is not created by it. Nor is it subjectively felt by the actors involved that opposing the Soviet threat is the main key to the evolution of their problem. For instance, the security preoccupations of Greece and Turkey are defined much more in terms of their mutual threat and of their respective domestic tensions than in terms of the Soviet Union. This was already the case to a great extent in the sixties, but the residual fear of the Soviet threat and the credibility both of American protection and of American sanctions gave the United States a crisis-management capacity which has been dramatically reduced by détente for all three types of crisis—while the American role in Greek domestic politics has made the United States, at least in Greece, more unpopular than the Soviet Union. Of course, both in Greece and in Turkey, leading social and political circles are aware of their need for American support and of the longer-run risks of Soviet dominance, but beyond the difficulties of a solution on Cyprus or on Aegean oil, their diplomatic and strategic stance must take into account the passions of public opinion today, and is exposed to the risks of revolutionary or counterrevolutionary change for tomorrow.

This is even more true for Portugal, Spain, and Italy. There the risk is of civil war or of revolution, of a takeover by a minority or of anarchy, or of communist participation in power which, even if it resulted from a democratic process, might lead to the isolation of the respective countries and to the paralysis of Western institutions. But in these crises—except in Yugoslavia—the military role of the Soviet Union occupies only an indirect and subordinate role.

Yugoslavia, indeed, has the unhappy privilege of being at the crossroads of every possible crisis, both domestic and international, both economic and political, both ideological and national, both through the risk of political exploitation by the Soviet Union of an internal legitimacy crisis after Tito and through the risk of direct or implicit Soviet military pressure. Hence the schizophrenic attitude of many Yugoslavs, both toward détente and, for instance, toward developments in Italy or in the Arab world, where their ideological sympathies and their desire for stability and security often go in different directions.

One thing is in common for all these countries: each has its own structure and dynamics, where the army, the communist party, and nationalism play a different role and often have a different nature. Of course, it is no less true that none of them can escape from the economic or strategic interdependence which links it to Europe, or from the psychological and ideological contagion of its neighbors. It is even extremely likely that in all or almost all of them, a substantial majority of the popuation share the same aspirations toward a Western type of regime and, above all, toward stability and prosperity. But these aspirations and influences are but one component in a national and social consciousness which, as a whole, is different in every case, for each of these countries is in the throes of its own identity crisis. This entails (as in the opposition to Russia of Westernizers and Slavophiles, repeated since in every developing country) a countervailing set of aspirations and influences which are no less strong and, in many cases, run deeper and with greater violence, toward a return to national or regional origins —whether Balkanic, in the case of Greece, or Islamic, in the case of Turkey, or Mediterranean or Third-Worldist in the case of almost all. The fact that these origins or ties are often rather mythical and almost never lead to viable political or economic choices does not detract, at least in the short run, from their mobilizing power.

Hence Southern Europe today, corresponds to a Third World torn by divergent social forces more than to the fifties image of a Western Europe united in its refusal of communism and its fear of the Soviet Union.

The problem of containing the latter and its expansionist ambitions, therefore, must be seen in a different light. Already in the early fifties, authors like Raymond Aron and Hans Morgenthau were indicating that in this respect the situation was profoundly different in Europe and in Asia. In Europe, the problem was essentially to balance the power of the Red Army and to inspire confidence in populations which, west of the Iron Curtain (and, incidentally, east also) were favorable to the West. In Asia, the problem was less military and more political, the direct presence of the Soviet Union and of China were much less considerable, and the communist problem was inextricably linked with those of nationalism and development.

This opposition was always less clear for Southern than for Central and Northern Europe: there, from the beginnings of the Cold War, the Western connection was one of the main factors for maintaining, encouraging, or tolerating a certain type of domestic regime, whether democratic, conservative, or reactionary. But the element of direct Soviet threat was either clearly present, as in Turkey, or thought to be clearly present, as in Greece, or undistinguished conceptually from the domestic communist challenge, as in Italy. Today, the emergence of

"Third-World" situations is both much more definite (for the reasons, domestic and international, which have already been mentioned) and more diffuse, since in some respects France and Britain, the first through the possibility of the Left gaining power with communist participation and the second through the role of social unrest, of terrorism, and of ethnic rebellions, are partial (or "candidate") members of this new Third World, characterized by domestic, leading to international, unpredictability.

DETENTE AND RESISTANCE: WHO WITH WHOM, AGAINST WHOM?

Yet at the same time this new Third World is in Europe, that is, in a continent which strategically has the same crucial importance, the same bipolar structure, and the same vulnerability to the direct presence of a massive Soviet power that it had in 1949. Hence the necessity for any Western policy to be geared to the basic dilemma inherent in the situation. On the one hand there is, in Mediterranean Europe as in the Third World, a primacy of internal politics as compared to the Soviet military threat, and a diversity of national situations leading to various degrees of neutralism and nonalignment. But on the other hand there is a massive geostrategic presence of the Soviet Union and, in front, there is the Atlantic Alliance which has no equivalent in the Third World and which fulfills an indispensable stabilizing function, above all by keeping the military balance but also by providing a reassuring political framework.

How can one reconcile the political dimension and the military one, the need for stability and the need for change, the acceptance of diversity and the maintenance of unity?

The answer—to the extent there can be one—would seem to lie only in controlled diversification, corresponding to the diversity of national situations and to the diversity of actors and dimensions involved in each of them. In turn, this diversification must involve not only the actors and the instruments of Western policy, but, in a certain sense, its aims and the very structures of Western organizations.

In all these respects, the lessons of 1974 and 1975 would seem to be reasonably clear, and to contradict the apparent assumptions of Secretary of State Kissinger. These assumptions themselves are hard to reconcile with each other except insofar as they spring from a general distrust of small and middle powers and of popular forces, and from a more surprising intolerance of ambiguity. They can be grouped into three: (1) Europe is seized by a catastrophic trend toward the left and "will be Marxist within ten years." (2) In spite of the seemingly irresistible character of this fatal trend, the United States can and should oppose it by every means at its disposal, by manipulating domestic situations or excluding the guilty or the suspect, and by favoring conservative forces in every country. (3) The worst outcome is ambiguity, whether within a given country or within a given Western organization. It is better to have a "people's democracy" in Portugal than a Third World military regime, for it would serve as a deterrent against communist progress in Italy or France. By the same token, reform communists or left-wing socialists are more dangerous than Stalinist communists, for they entertain ambiguity and blur political and geographical differences.[3]

In contrast to these assumptions, the trend of events seems to have underscored at the same time (1) the diversity of situations, the absence of any single unifying trend, and the limits of the domino effect; (2) the limits of external, particularly American, ability to analyze, predict, and manipulate foreign domestic situations, but at the same time the existence of built-in restraints or counterreactions which have so far limited the range of catastrophic evolutions; and (3) the diversity, ambiguity, and complexity of the evolution of various communist parties and of their relations with various other political forces.

First, not only is the leftward trend not universal, but the problem lies precisely in the lack of congruence between the evolution of various members of Western organizations: for example, the future of Franco-German cooperation if, as seems to be the present trend, France moves to the left and Germany to the right, raises many questions. Even in Southern Europe, while there is a general trend toward each country getting into a special position in relation to NATO and to the United States, the nature of this special position and, even more, the nature of the respective domestic evolutions have varied considerably. The Portuguese model of dictatorship has not been duplicated so far either in Greece beforehand or in Spain afterward. Indeed, it is Portugal which seems, at this writing, to be following the two other countries into at least provisional and fragile moderation. Second, this is not due (to any substantial degree at least) either to a counter-domino effect or to American actions: neither the exploitation of the Portuguese events, which at the time were quite threatening, nor President Ford's visit prevented the defeat of the Democrazia Christiana and the success of the communist party in the Italian elections of June 1975. Rather, each country tends to respond much more to internal factors than to the example of its neighbors. On the other hand, among domestic forces there *are* analogous reactions to analogous crises. The constraints of economic interdependence, through their objective effects, through the perception of the country's actors, and through the manipulation of foreign and transnational forces, sharply limit the range of viable political alternatives: here the examples of Portugal and Italy, in spite of their differences, are quite eloquent. But rather than a sharp and final choice between a conservative formula excluding the communists and a revolutionary one dominated by them, the political responses to these constraints are likely to involve a choice between polarization (itself involving an unpredictable alternation between the extremes of left-wing and right-wing authoritarianism) and ambiguous compromises which are equally unpredictable but more manageable and hence hold the promise of a more stable kind of instability.

If this description is more accurate than the alternative one, a number of consequences flow for Western, and particularly American, policy.

First, it is clear that the instruments or strategies of the late forties and early fifties will, for the most part, not do the job. If the main source of insecurity is the internal instability of countries and their main external targets of fear or hostility are their allies, in particular the United States, no ringing call to Atlantic unity against the Soviet threat is going to be very productive unless the Soviet Union itself resorts to direct and spectacular bullying tactics which would bring détente—even in its minimum negative sense—to an end. The collective framework of NATO may be accepted as insurance; it can no longer serve as a positive guide or inspiration, particularly for domestic politics. The same goes for unilateral American intervention. Both in words and in deeds, direct political and military action by the United States has been delegitimized at both ends and has been made unworkable or counterproductive both from an American and from a European point of view. Only indirect methods have a chance, if not of achieving their aim by themselves, at least of being one element in influencing the evolution in the desired direction.

But what indirect methods? Again, covert, CIA-type activities aimed at influencing the domestic political life of the respective countries are likely in most cases to be counterproductive. As shown by revelations about Italy, the consequences of Vietnam, Watergate, and détente make secret measures unlikely; once revealed, their decline in acceptability, both in the United States and in the target countries, is just as great as that of open intervention. Of course there are some distinctions between, on the one hand, helping right-wing plots or rich and corrupt political factions already in power, as in Italy, and, on the other hand, helping beleaguered democratic opposition parties, deprived of their normal activities and resources by an authoritarian regime. But the general principle seems to hold true that the use of economic power for secretly influencing the politics of European countries is illegitimate and counterproductive.

But what about the use of economic power to affect the situation of a country as a whole? Here, perhaps, lies the central question, for politically motivated economic pressures are hard to distinguish from the normal play of economic interdependence, and the latter is clearly the most important external influence or brake (short of military invasion) on a country's domestic orientation. Whether for Chile or for Italy, for Portugal today or for France tomorrow, the state of foreign reserves, the flight of capital, and the availability or refusal of loans clearly are more important for determining the fate of left-wing experiences than for any rhetorical exhortations or cloak-and-dagger operations.

Here again, however, some distinctions are in order. There is no reason for the United States or the European Community to go out of their way to prop up confidence in an unfriendly government if it is undermining confidence in itself by its own actions or incapacity; moreover, actual economic help is naturally more forthcoming to compatible countries—even though the denial of positive sanctions can be construed or perceived as hostile or negative. But there is an essential difference between, on the one hand, making the degree of help or the intimacy of cooperation dependent upon the degree of friendliness and, on the other hand, isolating, boycotting, or "destabilizing" a country. The latter raises problems both of ends and of means, of legitimacy and of efficacy. Again, the question is what the danger to avoid consists of. If it is not social change or independence from the United States but instability and dependence upon the Soviet Union, then it may well be that national or even left-wing coalitions including the respective communist parties are in the interest of the West, provided the Soviet Union is not allowed to exploit these domestic evolutions for its diplomatic and strategic goals.

The question, then, becomes that of diversity within conflict and détente. There are two attitudes which negate this diversity and the problems it raises, by making no distinction between attitudes toward the Soviet Union and toward the various communist revolutionary or simply left-wing forces of different countries. The first, that of unconditional confrontation, consists of being equally hostile to both, since they are supposed to be parts of a unique reality and to pose a unique threat. The second, that of unconditional détente, consists of being equally friendly toward the Soviet Union and the left-wing movements of various countries, since, with the demise of the Cold War, the East-West ideological conflict and the danger of Soviet military power are equally obsolete.

Two other attitudes are based, on the contrary, upon a fundamental distinction between the two realities they face. The attitude of the United States, in particular of Dr. Kissinger, seems to lie in being as conciliatory as possible toward the Soviet Union, in celebrating the era of negotiation, of détente, and of peace, and in being intransigent toward any form of evolution toward the left in Western countries which would involve a risk of communist participation. The logic of this attitude, inspired by realpolitik, consists in accepting communism where it is strong and fighting it where it is weak. It is inspired by the principle of *cuius regio, eius religio:* in other words, it means proposing a division into spheres of influence, the Soviet Union and the United States each remaining master in its own sphere.

There is a certain realism to this notion, but is it really tenable to consider the Soviet Union as a power among others, with which one can run a partial condominium and build a "structure of peace," while at the same time considering the Italian communist party as an incarnation of evil with which any contact should be avoided? Again one runs into a strong moral objection from those who take democracy seriously. This was well expressed by the young Soviet dissident Andrei Amalrik when he wrote, "The United States supports communism where it is unpopular and fights it where it is popular." But even on its own terms, the policy is ultimately unrealistic. It rests upon illusions about the Soviet Union's conservatism and about the ability of the United States to stop evolutions it dislikes in Western countries, where the situation is anarchic or revolutionary.

A fourth attitude, which would be the opposite of the third one, would seem more reasonable. It would consist in being more vigilant toward Soviet military power and more tolerant toward national evolutions which one is unable to prevent, which spring out of situations that one is unable to manipulate, and which lead to results that the Soviet Union itself is unable to control. The lessons of Western failures in the Third World when faced with complex situations where neither social and ethnic realities nor regional rivalries could be readily reduced to the East-West opposition should be learned, if NATO is not to become as oppressive as the Warsaw Pact or as artificial as SEATO or CENTO.

And yet the East-West opposition does exist; the risks of the Soviet Union's exploiting in strategic terms any Western tolerance of domestic evolutions or revolutions (as well as Western intolerance which, precisely, risks throwing them into Moscow's arms) are only too real; the necessity of the Atlantic Alliance as a multilateral framework which gives a tangible expression to the East-West balance and the American guarantee is all the more obvious. None of our remarks against ascribing military causes or cures to political evolutions is meant to minimize their military consequences. The fact is that with Turkey, Greece, and Portugal all getting into special situations of semiwithdrawal regarding NATO or American bases, the "Southern flank" of the organization is already in a shambles. If tomorrow Portuguese, Spanish, and Italian bases were all denied to the United States, the military balance in the Mediterranean and the South Atlantic would be seriously affected, with consequences for the Middle East as well. Finally, two countries, by virtue of their strategic position in relation to the Soviet Union and to the central front, would directly affect the European and global military balance if they should slide toward the Eastern camp: Turkey and France.

This evolution could be all the more serious since strictly military factors could, after an apparent decline, gain again in importance in the global and European "correlation of forces." While it remains true that, in situations of global parity and local stalemate, the emphasis is on the internal evolution of opposing systems, and the hopes of the Kremlin lie in the controlled disintegration of the West rather than its forcible conquest, this political evolution, coupled with growth in Soviet military strength and mobility, may lead to a more active projection of this military power. This is, after all, actually happening in such different ways and places as Soviet pressures against Norway and Soviet and Cuban presence in Angola. There is no reason to exclude it in Mediterranean crises.

But there is every reason to exclude the wrong Western response. This would seem to be typified by the Angolan example—first picking the wrong local allies between the Portuguese and the African liberation movements and between the African liberation movements themselves, then trying to achieve a covert local response which turned out to be precluded by domestic American conditions as well as by African ones (the alliance with South Africa), and finally trying only halfheartedly and belatedly to raise the problem with the Soviet Union while being unable or unwilling to use whatever leverage is left in the area of superpower détente and cooperation: grain, technology, arms control negotiations, attitudes to Soviet rule in Eastern Europe.

This spectacular failure—along with the specifics of Southern Europe as outlined—should provide some guidance as to more appropriate policies, on the lines of opposing controlled diversification to the Soviet-promoted controlled disintegration. The United States should concentrate on deterring Soviet intervention or military advances. This certainly involves restoring a capacity for answering Soviet actions locally and in kind. But above all it involves indicating as firmly as possible to the Soviet Union that détente, with its expected advantages, depends, in a zone like Europe where the two superpowers are directly present, upon the maintenance of the military status quo, a concept to which the Soviets themselves claim to be so attached in the Vienna negotiations on force reductions.

Toward particular countries, such as Turkey, the strategic considerations involved may dictate giving priority to the maintenance of American presence and a close bilateral relationship, whatever the political costs involved with other countries, such as Greece.

Toward all countries, however, there should be a cessation of the pursuit of the paradise lost of ideological, political, and military unity through pressures or statements, manipulations or excommunications, which can only provoke hostility, defiance, or, at the least, destabilizing polarization.

On the contrary, the European Community, its governments (particularly those of Germany through its financial power and of France and of Italy through their Mediterranean status), and its political forces (particularly the social-democratic and socialist parties) can, without replacing the primary role of local forces, play a useful role of mediation (in the conflict between Greece and Turkey), of solidarity (in Portugal), or of encouraging the accommodation of desirable or inevitable evolutions (in Italy or Spain). Their main leverage probably lies in the existence of the Community itself, in the legitimizing value attached to its membership, and in its economic role.

Militarily, the role of the Community can only be much more

modest. It is truer than ever that there is no substitute for NATO and for the American guarantee backed up by physical presence. But it is no less true that NATO, as a collective organization with no regional fragmentation and no partial membership, has become even more obviously and irreversibly a myth than ever. It is clear that the trend is toward the distinction between two or several tiers within the alliance, according to membership in the organization, and in more restricted caucuses, according to regional, political, or functional considerations. Whether to formalize this diversification or to keep it flexible and ad hoc cannot be answered in the abstract. The generally valid point, however, is that to negate diversity and change means ultimately to perish by them. While institutions and organizations exist precisely in order to limit diversity and change, they can function only if, to use or adapt the expressions of other contributors, "institutional flexibility" as a response to "contextual fluidity" is made an element of the precision-guided diplomacy and of the flexible political options required by a time of social crisis—instability and mutual but unequal ideological vulnerability.

NOTES

1. In her contribution to R. Rosecrance, *America as an Ordinary Country: U.S. Foreign Policy and the Future* (Ithaca, N.Y.: Cornell University Press, forthcoming).
2. See "The New Europe: From Cold War to Hot Peace," *International Journal*, Winter 1971-72.
3. Among many sources, see Tad Szulc, "Washington and Lisbon," *Foreign Policy*, Winter 1975.

II

LIMITED MILITARY RESPONSES:
The Doctrinal Framework

CHAPTER 3

Limited Options in European Strategic Thought

Laurence Martin

In the mid-seventies two related debates are proceeding within the Western Alliance. One concerns so-called "limited strategic options": an attempt to review the relevance of long-range nuclear weapons to political issues. The other is stimulated by technological advances in conventional and low-yield nuclear weapons, particularly with respect to accuracy of delivery. Taken together, the debates reopen many strategic questions, including that of the relationship between what have commonly been called the tactical and strategic levels of military balance and conflict.

The debate is a new one in its present form, but the underlying issues are familiar. In particular the issues affect the persistent problem of how to reconcile the divergent geostrategic perspectives of the United States and its allies so as to preserve and advance the community of interest which maintains the Western Alliance. Already in the early fifties, as the tide of rearmament stimulated by the Korean War receded, two facts were becoming apparent. On the one hand, the Western capability to fight a conventional war on World War II lines was likely neither to be provided nor to be welcomed, because of the costs involved and the implied levels of damage that those who live in the battle areas would suffer. On the other hand, the Soviet acquisition of nuclear and thermonuclear weapons revealed the limitations of reliance on the threat of nuclear retaliation. Admittedly governments

63

were not eager to acknowledge those limitations and, given the sobering effect of even questionable threats of catastrophe, their reluctance had some justification. Nevertheless, the divergence between strategic logic and official pretensions created an uneasy tension within Western strategy that has persisted to this day and from time to time opens up troublesome divergences of outlook between the United States and its allies.

In the later seventies, when nuclear "parity" is reaching a codified form, many of the issues of the fifties are reviving. It is possible, however, that technical and doctrinal innovations have now emerged to let us go further in reconciling strategic theory to political reality. Certainly it is highly desirable to bring such a reconciliation to pass, and it may help to recall something of the earlier debate. For not only are the fundamental questions less than novel, but many of the principles of an answer have also long been familiar. Thus it does not call for any amazing feats of imagination or will to come to terms with the new developments and employ them in our interest.

The variegated American strategic debate so often drowns out its sparser European equivalent, that there is some value in trying to retrace specifically European thinking about limited options. If by "limited options" we mean the limited strategic options that have recently won attention, there is only a little elaborated in earlier European thought or practice to illuminate our current deliberations. But if we look at European attitudes to limited responses in general, there is rather more to be said. Certainly the problems to which limited options respond have long weighed on European minds and their partial answers suggest some of the criteria that a solution must satisfy.

In Europe, as in the United States, it was the appearance of the H-bomb, the supposed implications of "massive retaliation," and, above all, the unexpectedly rapid Soviet acquisition of nuclear weapons, that stimulated the search for alternatives to all-out war. The speed of Soviet nuclear development created an impression of relative decline in American strategic power that was soon to be reinforced by the appearance of the Sputnik and the alleged missile gap. Europeans, or at least Englishmen, had played some part in evolving the strategic ideas espoused by the Eisenhower administration, particularly Sir John Slessor, whose succinct formula, "The dog we keep to take care of the cat, can also take care of the kittens," summed up the cheerful simplicity infusing the early years of the British nuclear program. When the advent of nuclear bipolarity cast some doubt on this aphorism, Europeans began their own reappraisal, heavily influenced by reports of the American debate. Their early formulations make a starting point for a review of early European thinking about more limited options.

The core of the debate was recognition that bipolar nuclear deterrence might mean stalemate or paralysis. Any threat of the actual use of nuclear weapons under such circumstances was, according to Liddell Hart in 1954, "perilous folly or bluff"; later he concluded, "the natural consequence of nuclear parity is nuclear nullity."[1] Bipolarity negated the use of nuclear weapons for less than "life or death issues": Helmut Schmidt approvingly cited von Weizacher's observation that nuclear deterrence might preserve your life but not your briefcase. Yet Europe was, as it were, America's briefcase.[2] The British scientist Patrick Blackett believed that "the doctrine of total war includes little or no provision for any threats less than the almost wished-for case of 'pure' aggression; it left the United States practically powerless to use its great military power in any less vital circumstances."[3] Clement Attlee's judgment was: "the more absolute the sanction, the greater the reluctance to use it."[4] American reluctance to use the nuclear weapon in Korea and Indochina was invoked as empirical evidence of this theoretical inhibition.

Europeans derived a dual fear from this state of affairs. On the one hand, the United State was inhibited from the positive use of its military power. On the other hand, the Soviet Union, which did possess a full range of military means, might be free to exploit them. Denis Healey warned that no "general threat" would be effective against "probes,"[5] and his Labour colleague John Strachey feared that, below the level at which nuclear action would be credible, there were "a hundred most unwelcome acts which our potential opponents can do to us with relative impunity."[6] Raymond Aron endorsed Helmut Schmidt's belief that "*à condition de ne pas employer immédiatement les grands moyens, l'aggresseur ne provoquerait pas la réplique totale, même si le détenteur de la force de dissuasion était lui-même attaqué.*" Even more would the Soviet Union be unleashed at the level of Cold War which it preferred.[7] Another British commentator suggested that by undertaking conventional aggression, the Soviet Union could "show an alternative—albeit one that involved limited defeat—to the vastly more unpalatable prospect of mass destruction by thermonuclear assaults."[8]

To many, the fact that the Soviet Union might have limited options while the West did not, suggested the danger that the United States would blow up the world for want of an alternative. Even some who saw that this could scarcely be in American interests, feared that it might nevertheless be the result of the situation. Aron cited the development of World War II from Britain's quixotic guarantee to Poland. But to many others, the consequence seemed more likely to be Western defeats. Richard Crossman did not fear "the ultimate horror of nuclear annihilation . . . the real danger is Western retreat and surrender."[9] This could break up the alliance. Liddell Hart thought that, offered defense only by massive nuclear action, many others would opt for neutrality.

The task for European strategists was, then, to design a defense posture that "includes the ability to use effective force."[10] In the search for expedients between annihilation and surrender, Europeans coined a variety of terms: "intermediate deterrence" (Buzzard); "intermediate courses" (Liddell Hart); "the middle game" (Strachey); "measured retaliation" (Healey); "*stratégic d'emploi progressif et raisonné*" (Aron). Of all the terms, the most evocative and typically European was Buzzard's "graduated deterrence."[11]

The speculation that produced these phrases was all aimed at discovering strategies which the United States could plausibly threaten to implement on behalf of its more exposed allies, and which the latter might actually be willing to have implemented if the occasion arose. Only such a strategy could deal with the problem that "NATO is an odd organization and almost unique in history in that the possessors of its decisive and most destructive weapon are not there in the front line."[12]

Such a policy would have to be one that did not threaten the mutual survival of the superpower cities. The peoples of both Europe and America needed to be offered some options that were less than suicidal: "If public opinion in the West believes, as it does at present, that the use of any atomic weapon means starting down the slippery slope that ends with the hydrogen bomb, then the democratic governments will have their hands tied behind their backs."[13] The point of a limited nuclear strategy, according to André Beaufre, was to set limits to the indirect strategies of the enemy but, insofar as such a "nuclear capacity with a certain offensive potential" could have any plausibility at all, it must indeed be a limited one.[14] Indeed, according to Aron, once the idea of limited strategy has been conceived, it is essential to work one out, for otherwise the enemy may prevail with limited strategies of his own. Once free of the idea of "*la guerre*," "*la continuité se rétablit d'elle-même entre la stratégie traditionelle et la stratégie de l'arme atomique.*"[15] The ultimate purpose of such a strategy is both to counter enemy probes and to give "more latitude to our diplomacy." This latitude would be enhanced by a strategy that also responded to "the moral principle of never using more force than necessary."[16]

In the initial debate over graduated deterrence in the mid-fifties, the strategy chiefly espoused was one employing tactical nuclear weapons, but, in contrast to the emerging official NATO strategy, as an alternative rather than a supplement to strategic strikes. Tactical weapons were to be used chiefly for local defense, under restrictions of yield, range, time, and type of target. Buzzard's original version called for city avoidance, for a return to the allegedly classic military objective of destroying the enemy's armed forces, and accepting, if the enemy would also, restraint in attacking military targets colocated with centers of population. Subject to that restriction, the use of nuclear weapons was not confined to the battlefield. Targets close to populations could still be attacked with conventional munitions, in the accurate delivery of which the West was said to excel.

Such a strategy was said to demand good command and control, and careful preplanning. There was no agreement as to whether the enemy's clear consent to such rules had to be assured beforehand. The dominant opinion seems to have been that Western strategic nuclear weapons could, as a monitor, enforce the rules. Buzzard argued that while NATO would enjoy a *relative* advantage from the restraints, both sides would gain *absolutely* from the absence of strategic warfare. Critics, however, suggested that the enemy might discover rules to suit him better and enforce them by his own strategic threat.

It was not made entirely clear whether the tactical nuclear strategy was intended as a deterrent signal of escalatory prospects or as a way to physically defeat the enemy attack. The latter seems to have been the preponderant view. The strategy was intended to meet aggression "on its own terms" and to "repel" the enemy. Nuclear weapons were to be used "against the forces engaged in aggression." Buzzard defined a tactical target as a military one; provided this criterion was met, targets within the Soviet Union were apparently as legitimate as any elsewhere. The deterrent element of "punishment" and of what now might be called a limited "strategic" option was therefore not wholly absent; John Strachey spoke of the enemy's knowledge that the victim of aggression might "go over to the counterattack." But the chief deterrent effect was anticipated from the plausibility of actually employing the strategy if the occasion arose. Liddell Hart claimed that the better a strategy as a defense, the better as a deterrent. Buzzard spoke of the "removal of the element of bluff." Blackett, who came to be very skeptical about tactical nuclear strategies, nevertheless gave his approval (as a former naval man) to the principle of having a precise plan for implementation in every contingency.[17]

We now know that most of the European members of NATO came, however skeptically, to accept tactical nuclear weapons as an element in flexible response. Many of the doubts that still persist were, however, raised at the outset. There was considerable skepticism about the practicability of singling out military targets with sufficient precision. The London *Times* was concerned that the targets most suited for nuclear action would be well behind the battle area. Many of them would be close to centers of population. Strachey believed that the "shorts and overs" of a would-be discriminatory policy would effectively kill a great many Europeans. This argument, that the technical capacity was lacking to be sufficiently discriminating, was later espoused by open enemies of limited strategy, such as General Ailleret. Aron feared that the intention to use nuclear weapons would create a great pressure to preempt them. Blackett thought the idea of limited use of nuclear weapons would call for an improbable complexity of rules. The burden of all these objections was that unintended escalation would take place beyond the limits that made the strategy tolerable.[18]

Some Europeans naturally feared that, while the superpowers might observe limits between themselves, their mutual understanding would permit attacks on a wide range of European targets. In the early fifties, when the vision of war still reflected much of the traditional image of the two world wars, there was particular anxiety about Atlantic ports as a preferred Soviet target. Much of the insistence on the foregoing of attacks on military targets in centers of population had this Western weak spot in mind. Schmidt had a similar anxiety that attempts to hit military targets of opportunity would break down the rules of engagement. One derivative line of thought went back to the all-conventional defense; another advocated confining the use of nuclear weapons to an increasingly narrowly defined battlefield. So far as the Soviet Union's temptation to escalate was concerned, however, very few Europeans saw the answer in denying the Soviet Union immunity even from limited nuclear action.

Such a course had not been excluded in the original presentation of graduated deterrence; at one early discussion, Richard Lowenthal stressed the importance of ensuring that the "graduated" element in the strategy did not negate the "deterrence."[19] The *Economist* had voiced the uneasy question: "Would a graduation of deterrence lead a would-be aggressor to believe the game might conceivably be worth the candle?" By the early sixties, a few European writers were toying with the idea of the limited strategic "countervalue" strikes espoused by some Americans. Well before that, however, Slessor had asserted the importance of denying the Soviet Union sanctuary. Drawing on the Royal Air Force's cherished memories of imperial "air policing," he suggested deterrence by the threat of attack on "nominated cities."[20]

Such bold ideas did not win much hearing. The preferred solution to the dangers of offering the enemy limited liability was to declare the principle of limitations but not to define them too clearly. Buzzard conceived of this strategy as not "committing ourselves unalterably in advance or showing our hand too clearly." The British Minister of Defense, Duncan Sandys, spoke of "an area in between about which I will not speculate and which I will not define."[21]

While many believed that uncertainty was an essential part of deterrent strategy, vagueness of this kind also struck critics as one of many reasons to believe limited nuclear strategies would prove uncontrollable in practice. Raymond Aron saw no reason to believe the leaders would be any wiser than those who created World Wars I and II. An enemy might well base his policies on despair rather than rational calculation. Helmut Schmidt also feared one could not assume a rational foe. Sir Solly Zuckerman, chief British defense scientist, argued that, as always in the past, the "fog of war" would thwart oversophisticated strategic doctrines.[22]

The many suggested ways in which calculated military, particularly nuclear, defensive and deterrent measures might lead to unintentional escalation contributed to the anxiety that graduated deterrence might do more to undermine than to reinforce political will. Helmut Schmidt argued that the prospect of nuclear action would do as much if not more to demoralize the defender than the aggressor. *The Observer* suggested that "Western public opinion, increasingly alarmed at the implications of any form of nuclear warfare, may lose patience with the attempt to find a middle way between suicide and appeasement, and choose the latter."[23] Moreover, graduated strategies raised difficult questions of the relative impact on specific allies, while reliance on the deterrent effect of a threat of general war could be presented as a way to avoid any fighting at all, and insofar as implementation was concerned, left only a vague and equitably distributed sense of undifferentiated horror. The idea that anything less than "massive retaliation" was both divisive and ineffective was, of course, welcomed by many in authority, not on grounds of strategic doctrine, but because it could be used to justify economies in men and money.

All of the European allies had historic as well as contemporary economic and social reasons to shrink from strategies that demanded the intensive use of manpower. This made the strategies of "massive" deterrence attractive and, where these were rejected, enhanced the case for the use of new technology in graduated deterrence and local resistance. The idea of compensating for communist "hordes" had percolated from the Asian theater. It was therefore to be expected that one of the main lines of criticism of the "graduated" strategies was that they relied excessively on hollow assumptions of Western superiority. These assumptions were of several kinds. Simplest was the belief that a residual strategic superiority, whether based on quantity of nuclear weapons, on better methods of delivery, or, in the age of Soviet encirclement by American bases, on geographic advantage, was necessary to impose the rules of the limited engagement. There was fairly general agreement that at least parity was necessary for such enforcement.[24]

A second kind of superiority involved an advantage in the weapons for local, limited engagement. Buzzard's original thesis had been based on "Allied superiority in techniques and precision attack," "our great tactical atomic superiority, our atomic and chemical weapons used in defense, and our precision with high explosives." This faith that the West had a technical superiority to exploit was linked to a third assumption, familiar ever since, that tactical nuclear weapons had an inherent tendency to favor the defense.[25]

Given these themes, it was only to be expected that critics should insist that the assumption of superiority was unfounded or anachronistic. Such rebuttals were common; one of the more succinct was Richard Crossman's attack on "the presupposition . . . that the Russians would always be behind the West in technical development and therefore unable to retaliate in kind. . . . this delusion made (advocates of nuclear strategies) swallow the idea that the weapon of annihilation could render obsolete old-fashioned war and the need for fighting soldiers."[26]

This criticism clearly leads toward the alternative prescription of an all-conventional defense. It must be realized that many of the exponents of graduated deterrence with tactical nuclear weapons were primarily concerned to attack the ultranuclear school of deterrence and to advocate practical schemes of defense into which they built, faute de mieux and with some skepticism, the tactical nuclear weapon. An all-conventional defense is not usually thought of as a limited option, but, insofar as it tries to find a solution short of using the ultimate weapons, it does derive from similar sources, though it notably fails to offer an economical solution.

Probably the most thoroughgoing European exponent of the all-conventional defense was Helmut Schmidt. In expanding his view, he emphasized that conventional weapons were already a limited option for the Soviet Union to which the West had no adequate answer: "The risk of an outbreak of hostilities does not lie superficially in the Soviet Union's strategic missile armament but . . . in the very flexible nature of Soviet armament and strategy."[27] This approach was founded on the belief that escalation was likely to be uncontrollable once the conventional-nuclear firebreak had been crossed. In any case there was no reason to believe that nuclear weapons favored the defense. Aron also came to believe that the collateral damage from tactical nuclear weapons would be intolerable, that strategic nuclear weapons were becoming immune to counterforce, and consequently that conventional defense would be the only recourse. Strachey argued that it would be politically and psychologically easier for an aggressor to accept defeat after losing a reasonably drawn-out war on traditional lines than to forego the next move in an exchange of escalatory strikes.[28] The prime argument of the conventional school was, however, the deterrent value of having a strategy it would not be insane to implement. Hence Schmidt's demand for "continuity in the balance of military power." Only this could "make it possible for the political leadership to make graduated use of the armed forces."[29]

Insofar as the theory of conventional defense requires both sides to prefer the verdict of the battlefield without appeal to nuclear weapons, either tactical or strategic, it is something of a limited option, even though it accepts the possibility of a very substantial war if deterrence fails. Advocates of the theory would quickly point out that even such a war would be considerably less horrific than that which might follow the failure of massive nuclear deterrence.

The doctrine of conventional defense has further significance for the limited option debate, however, since its followers, while adamantly opposed to the naked "massive retaliation" approach, have been forced to recognize the failure of the alliance to provide the wherewithal for this strategy. Consequently their line of thought might yet be invoked in support of more convincing nuclear strategies, and could certainly be used to support any new conventional technology or strategy that offered the prospect of reaching its goal by new routes. Indeed, in his later writing, even Schmidt seems to waver slightly when he suggests that, below the all-out strategic level, but apparently above the purely conventional, "the defender needs the possibility of posing less extreme forms of defensive threat."[30]

Yet another prominent line in European strategic thought and practice has been that supporting independent national nuclear forces. Given the doctrine of those forces, they may seem far removed from and even antithetical to the idea of limited options. But while this is certainly the main significance of the national forces, there are elements in the underlying thought unmistakably relevant to the search for more moderate courses.

There has always been an element of national independence in the thought behind the British nuclear force. Carefully muffled behind the predominant ideology of Anglo-American solidarity and a loyal "contribution to the Western deterrent," has been the idea of insurance against American infirmity of purpose, or divergence of national policies. The supreme exponents of national nuclear independence and, indeed, of the belief that there is an inherent implication of independence in nuclear power, have been the French. President de Gaulle did not flinch from proclaiming the inadequacy of a foreign nuclear guarantee: a nation would only die for itself. According to General Gallois, a nuclear power "can only ensure its own protection, since it is hardly credible that it would expose its entire property to destruction merely to ensure the protection of another state."[31] Paradoxically, perhaps, this observation accords very well with the spirit of a search for limited options, which is also founded on skepticism about reliance on all-out deterrent strategies for the alliance.

But while, according to French thinking, a foreign nuclear guarantee is inadequate, especially given the stable deadlock overtaking the specific Soviet-American balance, a nuclear element in defense is essential given the inherent instability at the conventional level. This idea, diametrically opposed to Schmidt's thinking, is associated above all with André Beaufre. Stable deterrence could never be firmly based on conventional arms, given the difficulty of calculating the balance and the consequently endemic hope of success. The answer had to come from reintroducing a degree of instability into the higher, nuclear balance, thereby extending an element of deterrent risk down into the conventional level. A national nuclear force could do this both by relating a plausible nuclear response to lesser issues which might otherwise seem limited stakes to a superpower and by the uncertainty engendered simply by multiplying centers of decision.[32]

Fortunately the task of creating a national nuclear force from modest resources was not insurmountable, because it need only threaten a degree of damage proportionately greater than the value of enemy designs on the deterring state. Thus a minimal force would be adequate. According to de Gaulle, a nation can only die once. If, Gallois argued, Americans thought some twenty million deaths would deter all hostile Soviet enterprises against the United States, how much less would anything offered by the conquest of France be worth? Certainly deterrence came well below annihilation.[33]

From this brief and doubtless distorted summary of earlier French thought on deterrence there curiously emerge some ideas to support the search for limited options. The United States cannot be expected to implement threats endangering its ultimate survival for allies. Less than ultimate threats may, however, be expected to deter the Soviet Union if plausibly made. Even according to Gallois, the United States might plausibly pledge itself to run moderate risks; it was only sacrifice of its "entire" property he found incredible. One could therefore conclude that if the United States designed limited actions that exceeded what the Soviet Union would willingly endure, such a strategy would serve the purposes of national deterrence for US allies.

At once it must be conceded that this is only a partial and illustrative conclusion. It says nothing about the element of prestige in national nuclear policies or the sense of insurance against future political and technological uncertainties. Nor could one go very far without investigating the degree to which credibility is related to the idea of "self" in a nation state. Even the earlier Denis Healey argued that, were limited nuclear strategies adopted, national strategic forces would be required to ensure that limited action did not exceed the bounds tolerable to particular allies, and went on to regard the consequent incentive to proliferation as a major argument against limited strategies.[34] This and much more French thought also requires us to recall that the desire for nuclear independence has been partly inspired by fear that the leading ally might do too much rather than too little on one's behalf. Moreover, it would be useful and necessary to consider how a controlled, limited option compares qualitatively as a deterrent with a response which, even if limited by resources, would be the dying retort of a national force trying to do its worst. Whatever the objective consequences, the latter might well be thought to involve a quite different order of uncertainty.

Admitting all this, it still seems only prudent to recognize that the idea of limited options is intimately related to the question of proliferation and to the incentives toward national nuclear power within the alliance, not all of which tend toward the position of unqualified independence. This recognition implies that how limited options are orchestrated within the alliance may be at least as important as what the options are to be. The relationship between independence and credibility in the theory of national deterrence also suggests the need for a broadminded exploration of whether limited options should be related to greater devolution or greater centralization within the alliance.

The vein of theory exposed in this brief review of some earlier European strategic thought, much of it generally forgotten, is not elaborated in much detail as regards limited options. It does, however, contain certain recurrent themes that new proposals should take into account. It may be useful to conclude by summarizing some of them:

1. Ideas of limited or graduated response have been directly linked to perceptions of the strategic balance between the United States and the Soviet Union, particularly the appearance of parity as early as the beginning of the fifties. In these perceptions, degrees of relative strategic superiority and inferiority have played a considerable part.

2. Once the US loss of invulnerability was perceived, American strategies on behalf of peripheral allies were widely regarded as credible only if they were limited in consequences for the United States.

3. By the same token, limited strategies were closely scrutinized for their differential impact on allies, particularly for the degree to which their implications for Europe were worse than those, not so much for the United States, as for the Soviet Union, against which the balance of disadvantages determined deterrence.

4. The foregoing concern has repeatedly raised questions about the location of decision-making in the application of limited strategies, leading in extreme cases to the demand for national forces.

5. The emergence of particular limited strategies and the reception accorded them has commonly been related to the appearance of new technology.

6. Some early thinking about limited options envisaged the combined use of nuclear and conventional weapons.

7. Proposed strategies frequently implied the technological super-

iority of the West; this assumption was severely scrutinized by critics who suggested one could only safely base strategy on the inherent tendency of particular weapons or tactics to favor the defense, not on a relative advantage in quantity or quality.

Of course, most of this discussion has intentionally focused upon theoretical writings, not on state practice. In the real world, the acceptability of strategic prescriptions has often been determined more by political assessment of their impact on national economies, national prestige, service interest, or the balance of persuasive influence within the alliance. In the last resort most Europeans—with France the notable exception—have perceived the better part of wisdom in falling in with the preferences of the United States rather than in asserting the theoretical superiority of their own doctrine. Quite clearly, however, it would be exceedingly imprudent for Europeans to carry this ultimate deference to the point of suppressing all criticism and putting their faith in strategies which they thought so misguided that even their advocates would abandon them in crisis.

The more one moves to limited options, the more one may be driven into detailed reconciliation of foreign policy. In the seventies this reconciliation may require a greater concern with affairs outside the formal area of the North Atlantic alliance. For we must recall that, when the original debate on graduated deterrence took place, the great European powers were more accustomed than even the United States to maintaining and frequently applying a capacity for limited military action in Afro-Asia. The future efficacy and acceptability of limited options, both in Europe and elsewhere, will consequently be intimately related to the allies' capacity to agree not only on maintaining the potential but also on the application of limited military force. The likelihood of reaching some agreement would surely be enhanced if we could stimulate a thoroughgoing interallied debate, in which Europe's independent voice was heard more vigorously than in the past and in which the pattern of previous thought was both recalled and reassessed.

NOTES

1. B. H. Liddell Hart, *Deterrent or Defence: A Fresh Look at the West's Military Position* (London: Stevens & Sons, 1960), pp. 23, x.
2. Helmut Schmidt, *Defence or Retaliation: A German View* (London: Praeger, 1962), p. 16.

3. P. M. S. Blackett, "Nuclear Weapons and Defence," in *Studies of War* (Edinburgh: Oliver & Boyd, 1962), p. 57.
4. C. R. Attlee, "The Political Problem," *The Listener*, June 17, 1954, pp. 1035-36.
5. Denis Healey, "The Bomb That Didn't Go Off," *Encounter*, July 1955, p. 5.
6. John Strachey, *On the Prevention of War* (London: St. Martin's Press, 1962), p. 70.
7. Raymond Aron, *Le Grand Débat* (Paris: Calmann Levy, 1963), pp. 104, 169.
8. Peregrine Worsthorne, "How the Russians See It," *Encounter*, July 1958, p. 17.
9. R. H. S. Crossman, "The Nuclear Obsession," *Encounter*, July 1958, p. 4.
10. Michael Howard, *The Listener*, August 10, 1957.
11. The fullest single exposition of graduated deterrence was in R. Goold-Adams et al., *On Limiting Atomic War* (London: Royal Institute of International Affairs, 1956).
12. Denis Healey, *Hansard*, vol. 577, col. 416, November 7, 1957.
13. Sir Anthony Buzzard in Goold-Adams, op. cit., p. 12.
14. André Beaufre, *Deterrence and Strategy* (New York: Praeger, 1966), pp. 40 ff.
15. Aron, op cit., p. 48.
16. Sir Anthony Buzzard, "Massive Retaliation and Graduated Deterrence," *World Politics*, January 1956, pp. 229-30. See also his "The H-Bomb," *International Affairs*, April 1956, pp. 148-65.
17. See the works by these authors already cited.
18. "War without Sucide," The London *Times*, February 8, 1957, p. 9; Strachey, op. cit., p. 30; Charles Ailleret, "Opinion sur la Théorie Stratégique de la 'Flexible Response,'" *Revue de Défense Nationale*, August 1964, pp. 1323 ff., and "Armes Atomiques Stratégiques et Tactiques," *Revue Militaire Générale*, November 1957, p. 452; Blackett, op. cit., p. 59; Aron, op. cit., p. 49.
19. Richard Lowenthal, "The H-Bomb," *International Affairs*, April 1956.
20. "Graduated Deterrence," *The Economist*, November 5, 1955, pp. 457-58; Neville Brown, "Deterrence or Defense," *JRUSI*, November 1964, p. 319; Neville Brown, *Nuclear War: The Impending Strategic Deadlock* (New York: Praeger, 1964), pp. 218-19; Sir John Slessor, "The H-Bomb," *International Affairs*, April 1956, pp. 159, 162.
21. Buzzard, "Massive Retaliation . . . ," p. 229; Duncan Sandys, *Hansard*, vol. 583, col. 410, February 26, 1958.
22. Aron, ". . . *Débat*," p. 70, and *On War* (New York: W. W. Norton, 1968), p. 95; Schmidt, op. cit., pp. 18, 30; Solly Zuckerman, "Judgement and Control in Modern Warfare," *Foreign Affairs*, January 1962, pp. 196-98.

23. *The Observer,* April 1968.
24. Strachey, op. cit., p. 71; Blackett, op. cit., p. 59; Antony Head, *Hansard,* vol. 577, col. 401, November 7, 1957.
25. Buzzard, "Massive Retaliation . . . ," p. 233.
26. Crossman, op. cit., p. 8.
27. Schmidt, op. cit., p. 182.
28. Aron, *On War,* pp. 95 ff.; Aron, "Can War in the Atomic Age Be Limited?" *Confluence,* July 1956, p. 112; Strachey, op. cit., p. 96; Aron, ". . . Débat," p. 67: *"Peut-être, a partir d'un certain seuil, ces inégalites dans les capacités de destruction tendent-elles a s'effacer, mais il s'agit la d'un hypothese psychologique, non d'une vérité théorique."*
29. Helmut Schmidt, *The Balance of Power* (London: Kimber, 1971), p. 73.
30. Ibid., p. 196.
31. Pierre Gallois, "The Raison d'être of French Defense Policy," *International Affairs,* October 1963, p. 501. Whether a state would die or risk destruction even for itself is, of course, also a subject for debate.
32. Beaufre, op. cit., pp. 65 ff.
33. Pierre Gallois, *The Balance of Terror: Strategy for the Nuclear Age* (Boston: Houghton Mifflin, 1961), p. 138.
34. Denis Healey, "The Atom Bomb and the Alliance," *Confluence,* April 1956, pp. 75-76.

CHAPTER 4

Selective Nuclear Operations and Soviet Strategy

Benjamin S. Lambeth

In January 1974, Defense Secretary Schlesinger announced a major re-orientation of US nuclear targeting policy designed to supplement the "assured destruction" retaliatory strategy incorporated in the Single Integrated Operational Plan (SIOP)—the government's master contingency plan for implementing massive retaliation in the event of a general nuclear war—with an additional range of limited strike options suitable for deterring, or responding to, a Soviet attack below the spasm-war threshold.[1] This policy shift, which had previously been under intensive private deliberation within the U.S. government for some time and which was formalized by President Nixon in *NSDM 242*, was largely energized by two stimuli.[2] The first was the dramatic surge in Soviet advanced weapons development and deployment which became apparent in the aftermath of SALT I, a development which—with its prospective introduction of a large MIRVed ICBM inventory into the Soviet arsenal—portended an unprecedentedly rich Soviet menu of targeting options short of the all-out attack scenario envisaged by formal Soviet military doctrine and also threatened an eventual Soviet hard-target disarming capability against the US ICBM force. The second was a growing disenchantment throughout the national security community with the near-exclusive US reliance on the "assured destruction" formula and a growing perception of need within the government to provide the President with a greater breadth of nuclear targeting options than the rigid alternatives of implementing the SIOP or doing nothing.

Even in the absence of the massive development by the Soviet Union of its new generation of ICBMs, there would doubtless have been strong pressures within the US government to develop a capability for flexible nuclear employment. Throughout the Nixon administration, the President's annual foreign policy statements had contained repeated injunctions that the US National Command Authority (NCA) must not be saddled with the single option of retaliating reflexively against Soviet cities in response to any Soviet nuclear initiative against the Continental United States (CONUS). Moreover, the feelings had been mounting within the national security community that such an exclusive option would not only be dangerously inappropriate to a sub-SIOP Soviet attack, but also would lack credibility as a deterrent at precisely the time it was most needed, namely, during an intense nuclear crisis in which the Soviets had core values at stake and strong incentives to preempt against the US strategic posture. With the development and prospective deployment by the Soviet Union of its new MIRVed ICBMs, however, these perceived inadequacies of US strategic policy became forcefully underscored, and the development of an adaptable US strategic response capability increasingly departed the realm of the merely desirable and assumed the character of an urgent imperative.

As one might expect, this ongoing US policy shift has met with sustained and unqualified hostility in the Soviet Union, whose public pronouncements on the subject have alternately described the limited options strategy as anti-détente, contrary to the spirit of SALT, aimed at "legitimizing" the employment of nuclear weapons, and insensitive to the realities of nuclear warfare. Were these observations the sum total of Soviet commentary on the theme of targeting selectivity, the natural inclination would be to dismiss them as mere propaganda. Yet in broad effect if not precise content, similar attitudes are reflected throughout declaratory Soviet military doctrine, a highly institutionalized body of official precepts on the probable character of a future nuclear war essentially unconnected to the current East-West dialogue on détente and ostensibly designed to prescribe operational guidelines for employment by the Soviet armed forces in the event of such a war. This congruence of Soviet negative reactions to the new US strategy with many of the long-standing tenets of enunciated Soviet military philosophy makes it difficult to ignore the "Soviet factor" in the limited-options arena and warrants careful attention and consideration by US strategic planners.

THE SOVIET VARIABLE IN CURRENT US NUCLEAR PLANNING

Coming as it does at a time when the concept of limitation in strategic war remains largely anathema to known Soviet military thinking and practice, the current US effort to develop a capability for controlled and selective nuclear targeting raises a critical question of practical feasibility. Even accepting the proposition that the US NCA can maintain the cool self-discipline and organizational control necessary to implement a strategy of limited reprisal and fine-tuned diplomatic coercion under the heavy stresses of a deep nuclear crisis (a proposition which itself one must grant with considerable diffidence), to what end can such a strategy be put if the Soviet adversary has declared in advance that he will not be a party to any such doctrinal contrivance? Given the broad chasm which currently divides US and Soviet declaratory perspectives on the possibility and acceptability of restraint in central nuclear war, might not any such US efforts at controlled targeting be perilously analogous to sparring with an angered bear that would neither understand nor appreciate the fancy footwork and measured jabs, but instead would merely lash out with full force at the first available opening?

In the main, one can discern two opposing views on this question. One school, largely composed of supporters of the current US nuclear policy guidance, maintains that whatever the Soviets may say in their declaratory pronouncements, they remain governed by a keen instinct for self-preservation and, like all reasonable men, will unhesitatingly cast aside their avowed doctrinal preconceptions in favor of real-time improvisation if a nuclear crisis (and US behavior in it) should suggest that as an appropriate course of action. The opposite school, containing an admixture of hesistant sympathizers and outright critics of the limited options strategy, espouses a substantially gloomier view. Whatever the objective merits of limitation as an abstract strategic principle, its adherents assert, Soviet military doctrine is a fact of life that has to be accounted for. While it may not rigidly predetermine Soviet behavior in a crisis, they maintain, it is nonetheless an important indicator of general Soviet strategic dispositions, imbued as it is with a rich legacy of historical experience and practice. At best, this school maintains, a US strategy of calculated limited nuclear employment is likely to be provocative and induce the Soviets during a crisis into escalatory actions they might prefer to avoid. At worst, it risks misreading Soviet norms of strategic behavior and leading the US into a military cul-de-sac in which unrestrained nuclear devastation would be the inexorable result.[3]

Which of these two schools of thought is closer to the mark must obviously remain a moot question in the absence of an actual nuclear crisis against which to test the opposing hypotheses. A case can be made, however, that the nature of Soviet behavior in any confrontation in which US limited nuclear weapons employment might be exercised is far too complex a question to permit any single pat answer or categorical prediction, and that in fact both hypotheses contain important grains of truth. As we shall see in more detail presently, there is no doubt that Soviet military doctrine stands at almost total variance with the expressed concepts and intentions of the emerging US strategy, and that the US development of limited nuclear options has evoked uniformly negative reactions from Soviet commentators. Indeed, of all the conceptual and weaponry asymmetries that currently obtain in the US-Soviet strategic confrontation, the one which rests on the question of targeting limitation and intrawar "crisis management" seems to be the most dominant and irreconcilable.

At the same time, there is no doubt that the Soviet Union possesses an abundant and growing array of military capabilities, including the weapons systems and command-and-control wherewithal necessary for conducting nuclear operations below the spasm-war level. Moreover, notwithstanding the disdain reflected in Soviet military pronouncements regarding the admissibility and practicality of limitation in nuclear warfare, Soviet political leaders retain the intellectual capacity for improvisation in crisis, and in such circumstances in which they would have *incentives* for limitation, there is no prima facie reason for believing that they would be precommitted by—or feel obligated to follow—the rigid edicts of their publicly articulated nuclear doctrine.

The critical question for US nuclear planners, therefore, is not so much *how* Soviet doctrine differs from the current thrust of US policy as it is to what extent this doctrinal asymmetry has operational significance that might affect (and possibly limit) US options in a possible crisis. Obviously, how and to what degree Soviet doctrine would govern actual Soviet behavior in such a crisis is another thorny question that does not lend itself to pat answers in the abstract. Undoubtedly it would depend on the nature of the crisis, the relative stakes involved, the relative risk-taking propensities of the two sides, which side crossed the nuclear threshold first and against which targets and with what intensity, and a host of similar contingent circumstances. It bears noting at the outset, however, that Soviet military doctrine serves many functions besides prescribing war-waging strategies for the Soviet political-military leadership. Accordingly, it may not reflect a fully accurate picture of how the Soviets would actually comport themselves on the novel and bewildering terrain of a future nuclear contest of wills, where not only the integrity of Soviet military philosophy but also Soviet survival lay at stake.

In the discussion that follows, we cannot explore in detail the wide variety of force-application modalities available to the Soviet Union, nor probe deeply into the various conceivable escalation scenarios that could seriously challenge the validity of Soviet doctrine and induce the Soviet leadership to contemplate alternative options. We will, however, lay out some preliminary benchmarks for such an analysis by looking at various features of the Soviet military scene that suggest the Soviets may not be as firmly committed to SIOP-scale operations as one might gather from a superficial reading of their strategic literature. Before doing so, let us take a closer look at the Soviet doctrinal treatment of limitation in war as it has evolved over the past decade and at how Soviet military writings currently visualize the likely progression of a nuclear conflict with the US and NATO.

SOVIET DOCTRINAL VIEWS ON THE QUESTION OF TARGETING RESTRAINT

Soviet doctrinal commentary on the theme of limitation in modern warfare has origins running back to the early 1960s, when the United States under Secretary McNamara's tutelage was developing its flexible response policy for the NATO environment and experimenting with a strategy of city-avoidance for the contingency of central nuclear war.[4] At that time, Soviet military writings tended to be uncompromising and categorical in their insistence that any direct military collision between the superpowers would inevitably escalate rapidly to the level of global nuclear exchanges. In the case of a potential theater war in Europe, the Soviet position held that the pressures for crossing the nuclear threshold would be so compelling that any possibility of a carefully controlled conventional "pause" or an extended nonnuclear war of attrition was simply out of the question. On the matter of targeting restraint in intercontinental nuclear warfare, Soviet military commentary was even more adamant, not only in its rejection of the possibility of such restraint but also in its outright refusal even to countenance the idea of limitation as an acceptable concept in principle. Soviet political-military spokesmen took every opportunity to heap scorn on McNamara's "no-cities" strategy, variously depicting it as a cynical US ploy to "legalize" nuclear war and as a clever but hopeless effort to provide the United States with the key to a quick and easy victory. In a doctrinal refrain which left no doubt that the Soviets would have no part of any such scheme, Soviet military writings uniformly espoused the contrapuntal proposition that any global nuclear conflict would inevitably constitute the decisive clash between the opposing social systems, in which Soviet strategic power would be fully mobilized and employed with the ultimate goal of achieving total victory. The Soviet scenario for that conflict, in clear contrast to the stylized image of graduated reprisal reflected in the McNamara strategy, envisaged a massive Soviet preemptive blow simultaneously against US military and economic-administrative resources, with a view toward seizing and maintaining the initiative, "breaking up" and "frustrating" the US attack, and stunning the United States into incapacity and eventual surrender.[5]

Whether this image of nuclear war (and the inadmissibility of limitation in it) reflected real Soviet attitudes and planning assumptions or mere propaganda is not a question that lends itself to any simple and definitive answer. In all probability, it contained elements of both, along with a heavy sprinkling of genuine uncertainty about the sort of escalation dynamics which the still-embryonic nuclear-missile era actually portended. Certainly the Soviet declaratory repudiation of McNamara's city-avoidance notions had a substantial political-manipulative function, at least in effect if not design: by placing the United States on advance notice that it could not count on Soviet cooperation in observing its Marquis of Queensberry-like code of nuclear conduct, the Soviet doctrinal line served to heighten US uncertainty about the practicability of its strategy and thereby helped to enhance the deterrent value of the Soviet nuclear posture. The same could be said of the Soviet declaratory insistence on the near certainty of escalation to the nuclear level in a European theater engagement, a doctrinal stance which had the effect of throwing a monkey wrench into many of McNamara's more subtle calculations regarding the possibility of carefully controlled force application short of the nuclear firebreak and obliging US strategies to base their "worst-case" contingency plans on the least common denominator dictated by enunciated Soviet military intentions.

It is important to remember, however, that at the time these doctrinal themes were being given expression, Soviet conventional forces had been reduced to near austerity levels in the wake of Khrushchev's single-minded emphasis on building up the recently constituted Strategic Rocket Forces. Moreover, the Soviet strategic arsenal was not only vastly inferior numerically to that of the United States but also consisted of cumbersome and slow-reacting ICBMs and IRBMs deployed in highly vulnerable soft-site configurations. Given this primitive and inflexible strategic capability, the Soviets plainly lacked the wherewithal for underwriting the sort of sophisticated strategic targeting concepts envisaged by the McNamara policy and had every reason to refrain from attempting to compete with the United States on the latter's terms. Outnumbered and outclassed as they were by the emerging US Minuteman and Polaris inventory, and burdened as they were by a strategic force possessing virtually no prelaunch survivability, the Soviets probably genuinely believed that a preemptive strategy against US value resources represented the only credible option for deterrence available to them, for the simple reason that it constituted the only employment mode in which they could count on their force to perform with reasonable confidence.

By 1967, however, Soviet military writings had begun to move away from their rigid insistence on the impossibility of limitation and to reflect tentative signs of an emerging belief that, at least under some circumstances, a US-Soviet military conflict could remain restricted to nonnuclear exchanges. This was a time, it may be recalled, when the Soviet Union under the new Brezhnev-Kosygin regime was well along in a program of intensive strategic force improvement designed to eradicate once and for all the inadequacies of the nuclear posture bequeathed to it by Khrushchev. With their ongoing acquisition of silo-deployed SS-9 and SS-11 ICBMs in large numbers and their impending acquisition of an SLBM force incorporating the SS-N-6 in Yankee-class nuclear submarines, the Soviets had finally come to acquire a survivable nuclear arsenal which lacked the hair-trigger character of its predecessor and could conceivably be withheld for a time during a gradually intensifying US-Soviet crisis without running the risk of being destroyed by a sudden US disarming attempt. Moreover, by this time the United States had abandoned its brief flirtation with the city-avoidance strategy (along with its implicit counterforce first-strike underpinnings) and had retrenched largely to a deterrence-only policy based on the threat of "assured destruction" retaliation. Additionally, by 1967 the United States had become fully preoccupied with the Vietnam War and for all practical purposes indisposed to upgrade its strategic capabilities beyond the programmed force levels laid down in the early 1960s.

In this environment of essential strategic stalemate and US embroilment in Southeast Asia, further highlighted by disarray in NATO and growing Soviet conventional capabilities opposite Western Europe, Soviet military writing and pronouncements began to exude an unprecedented tone of self-confidence and tended to show a newfound willingness to embrace the possibility of restraint in direct superpower confrontations. Elaborations on the preemptive attack theme, while hardly dropped from the rhetoric of Soviet strategic discourse altogether, began to appear with sharply diminished insistence and came to be complemented by increasing Soviet commentary on the alternative theme of retaliation. More important, Soviet doctrinal writings began for the first time to suggest that a theater conflict need not "inevitably" escalate to the nuclear level and also to instruct the Soviet forces to prepare for contingencies involving solely the employment of nonnuclear weapons.

To be sure, this doctrinal shift came nowhere close to embracing the elaborate gradations of conflict envisaged by prevailing Western strategic thinking, and plainly did not constitute anything approaching a Soviet acceptance of the "conventional-emphasis" principle that dominated US theater-war planning. As far as the question of intercontinental nuclear war was concerned, Soviet military writings continued to assert that the engagement would represent the ultimate cataclysm for the West, in which no quarter would be given by the Soviet armed forces and in which all available nuclear forces would be brought to bear against the US homeland in a "crushing blow" that would result in resounding Soviet victory. Even at the lower level of theater warfare in Europe, Soviet doctrinal commentary continued to dwell predominantly on nuclear operations, with heavy stress on the themes of surprise, initiative, concentration of fire, and continuity of the offensive to victory. The overall tenor of these Soviet writings, to be sure, reflected little *expectation* that a superpower conflict could remain limited for long. Yet it represented all the same an important advance in its tentative intimations that such limitation lay within the realm of the possible, at least as long as the Soviet conventional campaign remained clearly on the offensive and the United States and NATO remained deterred from crossing the nuclear threshold.

With few modifications and only slight shifts in relative emphasis, these perspectives on nuclear war and associated questions of limitation continue to constitute the bulk of publicly articulated Soviet military doctrine today. Soviet writings now seem more disposed than before to admit threshold distinctions between theater and intercontinental nuclear war and between conventional and nuclear operations within the theater-war context. They also seem prepared to accept the possibility of threshold restraints within each of these categories so long as the Soviet side remains ahead and the United States has the good sense not to escalate. Yet within these three broad categories of conflict—theater nonnuclear war, theater nuclear war, and central nuclear war—the Soviets show no indication of endorsing any concept of restraint in the tempo and intensity of combat and no inclination to refrain from attacking certain target categories in the interests of collateral-damage avoidance or intrawar coercive diplomacy. Of course, the Soviet Union—no less than the United States— labors under an obvious constraint imposed by the determinate number of nuclear weapons and delivery systems it has available at any moment. Insofar as the disparity between that fixed number and the much larger array of potential aim points it might wish to cover obliges Soviet military planners to adhere to some set of targeting priorities, it naturally follows that Soviet force-application doctrine adheres, at least in a trivial and superficial sense, to a criterion of "selectivity." Yet it should be emphasized that this notion of "selectivity" bears no relationship whatever to the concepts of escalation control and crisis "reversibility" that lie at the heart of contemporary US nuclear planning. Soviet military writings continue to assert that in any nuclear engagement, theater or global, Soviet nuclear forces will strike simultaneously at the strategic capabilities, political-military command infrastructure, and economic-administrative centers of the adversary. Moreover, they reveal no trace of interest in the notions of intrawar bargaining, graduated escalation, and crisis management which play a heavy role in current US strategic theorizing. On the contrary, they tend to regard the business of psychopolitical coercion largely as a peacetime or precrisis function to be fulfilled—to the extent possible—by the passive threat implications of Soviet strategic forces in being. Once the nuclear threshold is crossed, Soviet military doctrine continues to posit—as it has throughout the past decade—that the role of nuclear weapons is the simple and unambiguous attainment of military victory, a task to be achieved not by slow-motion counterforce targeting, selective attacks on vital military or economic resources of the enemy, or any other limited schemes to in-

fluence his strategic behavior, but rather through the massive application of nuclear force on all targets necessary to destroy his war-waging
ability and his capacity for collective strategic action.[6]

THE SOVIET DOCTRINAL IMAGE OF A
FUTURE NUCLEAR WAR

Although the principal tenets of Soviet war-fighting doctrine have remained more or less constant since the early 1960s, there have been perceptible shifts in some of its relative emphases which seem to have been
direct responses to changed weapons technology, the emergence of US-
Soviet nuclear parity, and shifts in the threat system generated by modifications in US theater-war capabilities and concepts. Throughout the
Khrushchev era and during the initial years of the Brezhnev incum-
bency, Soviet doctrinal pronouncements tended to portray nuclear war
as most likely beginning with a massive US nuclear attack against the
Soviet Union without significant restraints and aimed at totalistic objectives (i.e., the annihilation of the USSR and the achievement of decisive
military victory). Informed by this image of nuclear war initiation,
Soviet doctrine proceeded to lay out several key themes and imperatives,
including (a) the need to maintain strategic forces that could be quickly
generated to a state of high combat readiness, (b) the achievement of
timely warning of an impending US attack, (c) the quick implementation of massive strategic counterstrikes aimed at breaking up the US
attack, (d) the simultaneous initiation of combined-arms offensive operations in the European theater, and ultimately (e) the occupation of
Europe and the destruction of the United States as a militarily potent
entity. This doctrinal perspective was heavily laced with implied en-
dorsement of preemption as a standard operating premise, and occasionally included explicit assertions that the Soviet strategic bomber and
missile force would be launched upon assessment of an incoming US
attack.[7]

In more recent years, this "spasm war" preoccupation of Soviet doctrinal writings has been supplemented and somewhat subordinated
(though not totally supplanted) by discussion of the character and requirements of nuclear war growing out of an escalatory process beginning with nonnuclear combat operations between NATO and Warsaw
Pact forces. One continues, of course, to find ritual statements in the
Soviet literature to the effect that strategic nuclear war would be un-
compromisingly destructive and that the Soviet side would ultimately

emerge "victorious." Yet both the burden of Soviet military planning and, increasingly, the tone of Soviet doctrinal commentary indicate that the Soviets, like ourselves, see a major strategic nuclear war—if it occurs at all—coming out of an expansion or eruption of theater warfare rather than "out of the blue" with no prior political-military hostilities.

At the same time, the current Soviet doctrinal image of nuclear war reveals noteworthy differences from prevailing US official thinking and planning. For one thing, US theater-war concepts tend to be essentially reactive and defensive in nature, aimed at (a) deterring a Soviet theater offensive if possible, (b) stopping it in place if it nonetheless occurs, (c) doing so with conventional weapons if possible, (d) using nuclear weapons initially only in support of conventional operations should the threshold have to be crossed, (e) studiously keeping the nuclear threshold as high as possible, and (f) endeavoring to revert the situation to something roughly like the status quo ante. Soviet thinking, while no less interested in seeking an economy of force and destruction, reflects quite different emphases and far fewer concerns. For one thing, it is explicitly and unhesitatingly offensive in nature, aimed at changing the European status quo rather than preserving it. Should a NATO/Warsaw Pact ground campaign for any reason get under way, Soviet doctrine clearly elevates the military defeat of the opposing side to a supreme level of importance. In the process, restraint is regarded far more as a convenience than as an imperative. There is considerably less stress placed on the importance of keeping the nuclear threshold high, and accordingly much less apparent hesitancy about using nuclear weapons. Finally, Soviet doctrine tends to regard nuclear operations not as carefully measured means of supporting the conventional campaign, but as independent means of decisively assuring the defeat of the enemy within the theater if possible and at the intercontinental war level if necessary. With some oversimplification, we can infer from the broad base of assorted Soviet military writings and statements an underlying (and uniquely "Soviet") concept of the escalation process which, in roughly reconstructed form, suggests the following planning logic:

Initiation of Theater-War Conventional Operations

Unlike American writings on strategy and crisis management, which dwell heavily on alternative ways a European theater war could be triggered, Soviet doctrinal writings are devoid of rumination over scenarios of war-initiation, and leave us at a loss to do much beyond speculating about Soviet thinking on this score. Occasionally one encounters passing references to the possibility that certain international flash points like the Middle East can lead to direct superpower clashes.[8] On the Central European front, however, where both US and Soviet military planning and forces are predominantly oriented and where the greatest security interests of the two powers lie, Soviet military commentary simply avoids discussion of the critical circumstances that could set the escalatory process in motion. Soviet doctrinal discussions of the theater-war contingency merely take it as given that a transition from the peacetime status quo to armed conflict has occurred and proceed directly to consideration of the sort of operations Soviet forces would be likely to undertake.

In general, the Soviet doctrinal calculus regarding the dynamics of a NATO/Warsaw Pact conflict (and the role of Soviet forces in it) seems to unfold something like this: the outbreak of war along the eastern flank of the NATO Center Region is first stipulated. (How it begins we are never explicitly told, though the implication is that it would stem from some provocation or ill-conceived adventurism on the part of the United States or its allies). Under such circumstances, the combined conventional land and air forces of the Warsaw Pact (presumably already in a state of advanced readiness based on previous political and tactical warning) would (a) contain and check the NATO ground operation, and (b) immediately launch into a massive armored and motorized infantry offensive across a broad front, with a view toward rolling back the NATO force, penetrating deep into NATO territory, defeating the opposing theater forces in the process, and consolidating a new status quo behind a newly established forward line of demarcation.

At this stage of the engagement, Soviet military thought displays full confidence that Soviet conventional forces could prevail and achieve their postulated objectives. Soviet doctrine also implicitly acknowledges that combat operations could cease at this threshold and become replaced by a postengagement US-NATO effort to salvage the situation as well as possible through diplomatic negotiations from a position of weakness. At the same time, Soviet writings are not sanguine about the *probability* that the war will remain conventional, and generally seem to assume that the United States and NATO, once pushed to the limit by the Soviet land offensive, will eventually be driven to transition over to nuclear operations in an eleventh-hour effort to save the day.

Threshold of Theater Nuclear Operations

Soviet planners undoubtedly recognize that the United States and NATO, if faced with an imminent rout at the conventional level, would have two basic nuclear escalation alternatives to choose from: (a) a highly selective and essentially symbolic use of nuclear weapons either within the theater or against the USSR itself, aimed at demonstrating US resolve and signaling the gravity with which the United States viewed the evolving situation; or (b) a more widespread employment of nuclear strikes throughout the theater, aimed not only at raising the stakes of the conflict but also at actually halting the Soviet offensive, attriting the Soviet conventional-force posture, destroying the Soviet theater nuclear forces, and regaining the initiative in the theater engagement.

Which of these two US nuclear employment modalities the Soviets believe would be more likely is not revealed in public Soviet military writings, and it is quite probable that Soviet contingency planners are genuinely not of a clear mind on the question. Logically, one would assume that the two alternative forms of transition to nuclear employment would present the Soviets with sharply divergent threat images and operational implications. Yet if such distinctions exist in the private calculations of Soviet military planners, they are not evidenced in the declaratory record of Soviet military policy. Rather, Soviet military doctrine seems to suggest that *any* US nuclear employment, whatever its form or purpose, would have the effect of fundamentally altering the "rules of the game" in a theater war and relieving the Soviets of any obligation to observe restraints on the use of nuclear weapons within the theater.

Soviet military literature is quite explicit in laying out the requirements for Soviet theater-war countermeasures once the nuclear threshold is breached. Colonel A. A. Sidorenko's *The Offensive* (1970), probably the most elaborate and detailed public exposition of Soviet theater-war doctrine and concepts to date, dwells heavily on theater nuclear operations and is unusually specific in explicating Soviet doctrinal views on such matters as targeting objectives, the timing and intensity of nuclear strikes, and the relationship of nuclear operations to the larger theater war effort. Although Sidorenko does not explicitly rule out symbolic strikes of the sort that have been prominently treated in Western strategic discussions, the tenor and focus of his commentary make overwhelmingly clear his view that the function of nuclear weapons in theater warfare is supremely military in nature. "In case of their employment," he points out, "nuclear weapons will become the main means for destroying the enemy in battle."[9] Citing the observation of tsarist General Suvorov that "a forest which has not been completely cut down grows up again," Sidorenko repeatedly stresses the central importance of seizing the initiative, implementing massive theater-wide nuclear strikes, shocking the enemy into disorganization and chaos, destroying his capacity for collective military action, and ultimately securing military victory in the shortest possible time. Strongly implied in his discussion is that anything short of maximum effort, such as isolated nuclear demonstrations and hesitant half-measures, would risk sacrificing the initiative, exposing Soviet forces to enemy nuclear operations, and possibly losing the prospect of victory altogether. In Sidorenko's words, "a delay in the destruction of the means of nuclear attack will permit the enemy to launch nuclear strikes first and may lead to heavy losses and even to the defeat of the offensive."[10]

On the question of preemption, Sidorenko leaves no room for ambiguity. Most Soviet writings have restricted themselves to veiled intimations that in the event of an imminent enemy nuclear initiative, Soviet forces would act promptly to "break up" the attack before it could be fully implemented. Sidorenko, however, categorically asserts that "preemption in launching a nuclear strike is the decisive condition for the attainment of superiority over [the enemy] and the seizure and retention of the initiative."[11] Similar stress is placed on the preeminence of the counterforce mission. Noting the presence of a large US inventory of theater nuclear forces in Europe, Sidorenko observes that "the successful conduct of the offensive is unthinkable without the timely and dependable neutralization and destruction of these means," and that "all tactical means of nuclear attack are area targets suitable for the launching of nuclear strikes of corresponding yield."[12] Such nuclear strikes, moreover, are not envisioned as a single-salvo operation followed by a pause to let the dust settle and allow an assessment of the results, but as a sustained effort waged day and night until all remaining and targetable objectives are destroyed. Soviet theater-targeting doctrine also stipulates the importance of distinguishing launch-ready nuclear forces from those delivery systems not mated with nuclear warheads, and stresses the necessity of striking the former on a time-urgent basis as the priority task of nuclear combat operations. In Sidorenko's formulation, "it is known . . . that US ground forces have a large number of means of nuclear attack. However, this does not mean that each launcher or gun can have and employ a nuclear weapon at each given moment. The enemy may have considerably fewer such weapons than guns or launchers capable of delivering these weapons to target. Therefore, it is very important to receive reliable data in good time not only about the location of the means of nuclear attack but also about the presence of nuclear ammunition with them."[13] Obviously this objective places a high premium on comprehensive tactical intelligence regarding the disposition of NATO's nuclear forces. While conceding that timely acquisition and processing of such intelligence constitutes a "difficult task," Sidorenko nonetheless asserts that its accomplishment is possible.

Threshold of Intercontinental Nuclear Operations

As in the case of theater nuclear war, Soviet doctrinal writings leave us with little feeling for how Soviet planners envisage the likely initiation of a central exchange between the superpowers' homelands. The dominant impression one gathers is that the Soviets see the problem of intercontinental nuclear war essentially as a variant of their theater-war model writ large, featuring the same emphasis on the familiar themes of preemption, initiative, continuity of the offensive, and massive force application for attriting the enemy's war-waging abilities. One notable difference is that while large-scale countermilitary operation remain heavily stressed, an important role is also assigned to countereconomic and counteradministrative targeting, with a view toward destroying US nonmilitary power resources, disrupting the functioning of US society, and eradicating the national leadership and political-military command infrastructure that would be required for the United States to pursue a coherent wartime strategy.

There is nothing in Soviet military doctrine that approximates the US "assured destruction" concept, and Soviet writings do not insist that a central function of nuclear operations is the decimation of the US population for its own sake. Yet the targeting criteria which those writings *do* specify leave no doubt that any implementation of declared Soviet nuclear strategy would feature high civilian fatalities as an inevitable by-product. Moreover, at this level of violence, Soviet doctrine shows no interest in any notion of limitation. Unlike US pronouncements, Soviet commentary on intercontinental nuclear war reveals no concern for minimizing collateral damage to value resources, either as a gesture of restraint or as a moral end in itself. Also, in contrast to the current US preoccupation with developing controlled targeting options for use as instruments of escalation control and intrawar bargaining, the Soviet Union continues to reject such ideas as being both impractical in principle and unattuned to the realities of modern war. Both the logic of Soviet military doctrine and the record of Soviet comportment in past crises suggest that Moscow's attitude toward nuclear war is instead akin to the age-old axiom that one does not hit a king unless one is determined to kill him. In operational terms, this implies that in any direct US-Soviet confrontation, the Soviets would tend initially to follow a policy of conservatism, studiously avoiding experimentation with nuclear demonstration attacks against CONUS and other resolve-testing ploys designed to intimidate the United States into diplomatic accommodation, and hoping instead that stern verbal warnings backed up by visible Soviet strategic power would suffice to move the crisis off the rails of escalation in a way congenial to Soviet political interests. It also implies, however, that once they became convinced a major strategic war was unavoidable, the Soviet military would want to move promptly and unwaveringly to large-scale countermilitary strikes against the United States, with no intervening half-measures against selected subsets of the American target array.[14] Such an operation, if the Soviets were to follow the edicts of their military doctrine to the letter, would presumably feature at the outset a massed and coordinated ICBM attack against US missile sites, alert bomber bases, and early warning facilities, followed closely by additional strikes against the US political-military command network and other war-supporting capabilities such as SLBM ports, troop-marshalling areas, airlift departure points, and possibly satellite surveillance systems.

Termination and Aftermath

On the important question of how a nuclear war would ultimately be settled, Soviet military writings and statements have conspicuously little to say. About the closest the Soviets have ever come to elaborating any specific image of what winning would actually involve has been to imply occasionally that the dislocations levied by a massive preemptive nuclear attack would so thoroughly destroy the US capacity for organized strategic action that the war could be settled on terms favorable to the Soviet Union forthwith. In this regard, Colonel General N. Lomov suggested some years ago (in a refrain that one continues to find in Soviet doctrinal writings) that massive nuclear-missile strikes can "at once, from the very beginning of the war, achieve results of great significance . . . by-passing the methodical, step-by-step development of tactical successes into operational, then strategic, and finally political results."[15] Another Soviet military spokesman writing in this same vein observed that successful implementation of a preemptive nuclear strike can "in almost an instant disorganize and demoralize the enemy's forces, obliging them to operate in uncoordinated and chaotic fashion, and even to cease resistance."[16] These intimations of an underlying Soviet "theory" of victory doubtless reflect a considerable measure of whistling in the dark on the part of the Soviet military, and certainly should not be read as expressions of Soviet confidence that things would actually work out so swimmingly. Nonetheless, they may indicate a guarded belief that if a Soviet preemptive attack succeeded in leaving the United States prostrate and the Soviet Union not only largely undamaged but in possession of a large residual force, the United States might opt for a diplomatic settlement rather than launch a punitive spasm response with its surviving retaliatory forces, which would only assure even greater US urban-industrial losses in reprisal.

POSSIBLE PRIVATE SOVIET THINKING AND PLANNING

States do not always mean what they say, say what they mean, or reveal all of their intentions and contingency plans. Given the closed and secretive nature of Soviet society, this observation applies to the Soviet Union with particular force. To be sure, it would be foolhardy to dismiss Soviet military doctrine and declaratory commentary out of hand as mere public posturing. While they may not represent a precise forecast of how the Soviets would actually behave in a nuclear war, and indeed may not even remotely reflect the way the Soviet leadership would react with its feet to the fire in a real nuclear crisis, they surely tell us something about the general strategic mind-set the Soviets would bring into such a situation and, as such, cast important light on the basic premises and planning assumptions they would use as a point of departure for whatever improvisation they might contemplate. It is important to bear in mind that Soviet military doctrine, whatever its apparent rigidities and ambiguities, is not primarily a propaganda contrivance designed to intimidate or deceive the West, but an important body of functional operating principles intended, along with other organizational and political determinants, to help lend coherence and direction to Soviet force-structure and contingency planning. Also, to the extent that it reflects a long tradition of actual Soviet military performance and style in past wars, it cannot help but contain some indicators, however fragmentary, of the way Soviet military leaders and planners actually think.

Having said this, however, we must take care to avoid indiscriminately accepting Soviet doctrinal and policy pronouncements at face value. As noted earlier, Soviet military doctrine has other purposes besides simply prescribing ground rules for observance by the Soviet armed forces in combat. It also has the functions, among other things, of (a) providing bureaucratic rationales for the various Soviet services to invoke in their quest for military budgetary allocations, (b) imparting a sense of continued mission, morale, and purpose to Soviet soldiers in an era of deterrence where wars are ideally supposed to be avoided rather than fought, and (c) projecting a credible external image of Soviet military prowess and toughness and thereby enhancing the deterrent and psychopolitical value of Soviet power in Western perceptions.[17] Moreover, while it doubtless constitutes an important conceptual framework for Soviet contingency planning (surely, for example, there must exist somewhere in the General Staff a Soviet equivalent of the US SIOP that accords with the principles of Soviet strategic doctrine), it neither represents necessarily the full range of Soviet military plans and options nor obligates the Soviet political leaders to adhere to its edicts dogmatically.

As for the published Soviet reactions to the US selective-targeting strategy, it should be noted that these have uniformly emanated from Soviet civilian publicists and commentators, not professional military officers, and have uniformly appeared in media that have substantial internal or external propaganda functions.[18] Moreover, they have typically employed the language and logic used by US critics of the strategy and, as one hypothesis, may perhaps be explained as an exercise in ventriloquy more than as a reflection of idiosyncratic Soviet thinking. Finally, they have focused exclusively on *American* strategic policy and have remained conspicuously mute regarding the possible existence of an evolving *Soviet* policy on the question of targeting selectivity. Soviet professional military writings, for their part, have followed a parallel track with similar effect: although they have not addressed the Schlesinger strategy at all, they have also maintained a

Sphinx-like silence on the theme of limited strategic nuclear options generally.

This silence as to the possible existence of a Soviet policy regarding controlled nuclear targeting should not automatically be interpreted as a sign of Soviet uninterest. Indeed, it may well be an indication of precisely the opposite. In their emphatic and prolific treatment of the massive-exchange variant of intercontinental nuclear war, Soviet strategic writings during the past several years have not, it should be pointed out, explicitly rejected all other possible variants but have merely slighted them (or appeared to slight them) through selective inattention. That is to say, rather than categorically foreclosing the possibility of targeting restraint by direct repudiation, they have simply elected to ignore the question altogether. If it is a valid hypothesis that the constraints of Soviet secrecy are likely to inhibit Soviet military spokesmen from discussing the fine details of their strategic concepts and planning assumptions with the volubility and candor that one finds, for example, in Secretary Schlesinger's last Defense Department posture statement, then there is a powerful presumptive case to be made that the public record of Soviet strategic doctrine is but the tip of a very large iceberg which we should only accept as a partial representation of the overall Soviet image of nuclear war.

What lies beneath the surface obviously is one of the central questions facing US strategic analysts and one whose answers will weigh heavily in determining the ultimate practicability of evolving US strategic concepts. It is equally obvious, however, that the question is an exceedingly difficult—if not practically impossible—one to resolve with confidence, for the twin reasons (a) that the Soviet leaders do not make it a habit to disclose the specifics of their contingency plans and nuclear force-application options, and, more important, (b) that the Soviet leaders themselves probably have no clear idea of what strategic decisions they would make in a future nuclear crisis.

All the same, notwithstanding the heavy-handed themes enunciated in open Soviet military writings, there are valid reasons for suspecting that in their private thinking and planning, Soviet political and military leaders are closely attuned to the issue of strategic targeting selectivity and are fully prepared, both intellectually and operationally, to wage less than insensate strategic offensive warfare should they conclude that the exigencies of the moment warranted it as a preferred course of action.

To begin with, there is the hard fact of the currently emerging Soviet force posture of fourth-generation MIRVed ICBMs, whose surfeit of potential reentry vehicle (RV) strength and prospective delivery accuracy and targeting flexibility promise to permit strategic operations far more sophisticated than anything presently discussed in published Soviet doctrinal writings.[19] To note only the most obvious of these potential targeting options, the Soviets are progressively moving toward the point where they may be able to implement a high-confidence disarming attack against the US Minuteman force solely with about 300 MIRVed SS-18s, leaving a residual force of 1,000 SS-17s and SS-19s (along with a fully alerted and undepleted SLBM fleet) for carrying out selective strikes against other targets in CONUS and elsewhere or for providing a credible intrawar deterrent against US countervalue retaliation with its surviving elements of the Triad. Indeed, it is in large measure an abiding concern with this specter of an *initiatory* Soviet selective nuclear attack that has sparked questioning of the appropriateness of the US SIOP in such a situation and driven the US defense community to develop an additional set of more flexible and purposeful strategic response options. Although there is no firm evidence that the Soviet military establishment is actively planning for such a contingency, the idea of withholding certain strategic forces for intrawar coercion has been tantalizingly suggested in an observation by the Soviet naval commander-in-chief, Admiral Gorshkov, that "missile-carrying submarines, owing to their great survivability in comparison to land-based launch installations, are an even more effective means of deterrence" than ICBMs.[20] There is also the reported fact, noted by Secretary Schlesinger in congressional testimony, that "in their exercises the Soviets have indicated far greater interest in the notions of controlled nuclear war and nonnuclear war than has ever before been reflected in Soviet doctrine."[21] Lastly, to mention only two more of a whole range of imaginable possibilities, the Soviets currently have the capability to wage a massive and rapid-tempo theater nuclear war against NATO while retaining their central strategic forces for deterring a US escalation to the intercontinental-war threshold, and are within reaching distance of acquiring (with their prospective ocean-surveillance satellite system SS-NX-13, anti-shipping SLBM, and Backfire bomber now entering Soviet naval air regiments) a weapons package capable of attacking and destroying US carrier task forces and other naval units at sea, either massively or through slow attrition, while withholding attacks against land-based military targets in CONUS and NATO.

At the conceptual level, there are also traces which suggest that Soviet military planners may be less firmly wedded to their enunciated doctrinal line than one might surmise from a superficial reading. Soviet General Staff Chief Kulikov not long ago lent his authority to a common refrain of the Soviet doctrinal literature that successful leadership and control in modern warfare call not only for "confidence and persistence, but also the clear substantiation of decisions and frequently boldness in making the necessary amendments in a rapidly changing situation."[22] More recently, Soviet Defense Minister Grechko added his own imprimatur to this proposition when he observed, during a disquisition on the contemporary relevance of Soviet experiences during World War II, that the supremacy of Soviet military art was "displayed by the fact that during the war the Soviet command implemented its plans increasingly flexibly and efficiently, and was more far-sighted in its plans and more facile and resolute in the means of implementing them."[23] In concluding his point, he went on to note that "the active, creative style of Soviet military thought was shown by innovation and the quest for forms and methods of conducting military operations according most fully with the conditions of the war. . . ." While such pronouncements tell us little about how the Soviet forces would translate these ideals of flexibility and innovation into action, they at least have the effect of conveying the impression that in the Soviet High Command's view, Soviet military doctrine is anything but doctrinaire.

What all this adds up to is extraordinarily difficult to say with certitude. Doubtless it would be premature to conclude, as some Western analysts seem to have done, that the Soviet leaders have fully adopted a strategy of flexible response roughly analogous to that of the United States and have assimilated it into their contingency planning and weapons acquisition criteria.[24] There are simply too many persistent stylistic differences between Soviet and American strategic philosophies to permit, at least yet, such a sweeping generalization. There is no evidence whatever, for example, to indicate that the Soviets have even the remotest sympathies for such US concepts as "threats that leave something to chance" and the symbolic employment of nuclear weapons as demonstrations of resolve and means of exerting psychopolitical leverage. For them, the idea of nuclear demonstration is most likely regarded as the height of strategic foolishness, since it implies a grave escalation in the *means* of inflicting violence without producing any tangible military gain, and further risks giving the other side every incentive to respond massively while it still has the strategic nuclear resources to do so. Nuclear crises, moreover, appear to be regarded by the Soviets as things to be avoided unless one seriously means business and has the most vital interests at stake, in which case they become not events to be played at with various sorts of nuclear "experimentation," but critical challenges to be decisively met by the most direct and forceful measures available.

At the same time, it is probably a fair presumption simply on grounds of logic that Soviet strategic thought and contingency planning are currently in a state of profound ferment and transition, even though visible signs of this may be few and far between. The Soviet Union is currently in the process of acquiring the most substantial and diversified strategic posture in its history as a nuclear power, and its leaders are scarcely likely to be unmindful of the rich potential for carrying out a wide variety of military operations. The following remark made by a senior Soviet military theoretician, while studiously ambiguous, may be highly relevant and instructive in this regard: "Military matters have marched sharply forward under the scientific and technical revolution, and the foreign policy functions of our armed forces have changed. All this has required, and continues to require, the introduction of the appropriate changes to the content of military doctrine and to the system of views on questions of war."[25]

Whatever these changes may be, we would probably be best advised to regard them not as emulative reactions to the US retargeting policy or as mirror images of contemporary American strategic concepts, but rather as uniquely "Soviet" responses to the changing potential of Soviet strategic power, conceived and formulated in a highly idiosyncratic Soviet frame of reference and heavily infused throughout with uniquely Soviet strategic perceptions and priorities. It is a time-worn axiom of military practice that one plays the game of war on one's own terms rather than on those of the adversary, however intellectually attractive they may appear, and that one tailors one's strategies and contingency plans in accordance with one's own strengths and interests rather than in conformity with some "objective" set of preferred military standards. It is highly unlikely that evolving Soviet strategic concepts bear any significant resemblance to those that currently inform US nuclear planning. The emerging Soviet image of a "limited nuclear operation," if it exists, may very well envisage a massive and rapidly executed preemptive theater nuclear blitz against NATO, coupled with a simultaneous countermilitary attack against all interesting targets in CONUS, while holding US cities as hostages with a large residual nuclear force to deter the United States from retaliating against the Soviet ZI. This is plainly a far cry from the sort of selectivity envisaged by the US limited-options strategy, but it is also a far cry from Soviet military doctrine as we presently know it, and constitutes a potential threat that is well worth worrying about.

In any event, whatever track contemporary Soviet military thinking may be running on, there is no question that the Soviet Union is acquiring the strategic nuclear wherewithal to do—or threaten to do—things far beyond anything presently addressed in the Soviet military literature. As a consequence, the evolving Soviet military scene warrants the most careful and reflective scrutiny by Western strategic analysts in the years ahead, with a view toward better understanding the diverse opportunities afforded by Soviet strategic power, the sort of situations that might provide a context for those opportunities to be tested, the conceptual and technical constraints that might act to inhibit Soviet flexibility, and perhaps most of all, the continued Soviet vulnerabilities that might usefully be exploited by countervailing US and NATO capabilities and strategies.

NOTES

1. John W. Finney, "U.S. Says It Is Retargeting Some Missiles under a New Strategic Concept," *The New York Times*, January 11, 1974. For a full official articulation of the new targeting policy and the concerns and assumptions underlying it, see Secretary of Defense James R. Schlesinger, *Annual Defense Department Report, FY 76*, February 5, 1975. For a balanced analysis of the policy and its role in the changing US-Soviet strategic balance, see William R. Van Cleave and Roger W. Barnett, "Strategic Adaptability," Orbis, vol. 22, no. 3 (Fall 1974), pp. 655-76.

2. For a brief discussion of the major planning milestones that led up to NSDM 242, see George Sherman, "Nuclear Strategy and Schlesinger," *Washington Star-News*, April 15, 1974. For a comprehensive survey and analysis of the US selective targeting strategy, and the way it evolved, see also Desmond Ball, *Deja Vu: The Return to Counterforce in the Nixon Administration* (Santa Monica, Calif.: California Seminar on Arms Control and Foreign Policy, 1974).

3. This concern has been succinctly stated by David Holloway in his observation that it takes two sides to play the game of limitation, and that recent Soviet negative reactions to the US retargeting policy raise serious questions as to whether we can count on Soviet compliance ("Soviet Strategists Attack Schlesinger," *The New Scientist,* November 5, 1974, p. 707). It is worth noting, however, that despite its attempt to develop a capability for flexible nuclear response, the United States still retains both the hardware requisites and SIOP-scale attack options to play the massive war game envisaged by Soviet military doctrine. A point frequently overlooked by doubters is that the development of strategic targeting selectivity in no way commits us to limited nuclear employment, nor requires an expectation on our part that the Soviets will comply with the norm of restraint. The purpose of the policy, rather, is to provide in advance the capability to cope with a nuclear shooting engagement that unexpectedly occurs and appears amenable to restraints aimed at turning the situation around before everything goes up in flames. It is definitely not intended, as many of the more outspoken critics have alleged, to allow us to go out on the warpath actively seeking opportunities for employing nuclear weapons, any more than life preservers aboard ocean liners are intended to allow passengers to jump overboard whenever the idea strikes their fancy.

4. Among the voluminous literature on this phase of US strategic policy, the standard work is William W. Kaufmann, *The McNamara Strategy* (New York: Harper and Row, 1965).

5. The most detailed compendium of Soviet doctrinal views on nuclear war during this period is Marshall V. D. Sokolovskii, *Soviet Military Strategy* (Englewood Cliffs, N.J.: Prentice-Hall, 1963).

6. For an unusually hard-hitting Soviet commentary which explicitly rejects the alleged impossibility of victory in nuclear war and confidently asserts that in such a war the Soviet Union would decisively prevail, see Rear Admiral V. Shelyag, "Two World Outlooks, Two Views on War," *Krasnaia zvezda,* February 7, 1974.

7. See, for example, the assertion that in the event of a nuclear war, the Soviet Union's missiles and bombers "would take off *even before the aggressor's first rockets, to say nothing of his bombers, reached their targets*" in I. Glagolev and V. Larionov, "Soviet Defense Might and Peaceful Coexistence," *International Affairs* (Moscow), no. 11 (December 1963), p. 32 (emphasis in the original).

8. See Lt. General P. Zhilin's several comments to this effect in "The Military Aspects of Détente," *International Affairs* (Moscow), No. 12 (December 1973), pp. 24-27.

9. Colonel A. A. Sidorenko, *The Offensive,* trans. by US Air Force (Washington, D.C.: U.S. Government Printing Office, 1970), p. 109.

10. Ibid., p. 134.

11. Ibid., p. 115.

12. Ibid., pp. 132-33.

13. Ibid., p. 135.

14. Even if the Soviets were to fall short of implementing a large-scale attack and could content themselves with more measured strikes while holding in reserve a larger force for deterring further US escalation, the Soviet General Staff would still probably be more inclined to counsel militarily purposeful operations than the clever targeting of bizarre aim points (like US oil refineries or key electric power generating facilities) simply because they happened to aggregate in a superficially neat "LNO target set." Albert Wohlstetter has observed that many of "the scenarios fantasized in discussing limited nuclear confrontation are totally devoid of political context. They ignore the fact that in the real world it is likely that each side would have powerful incentives to select targets for their military significance in relation to an ongoing conventional war. These targets would not be abstract counters to be exchanged in a game of nuclear checkers where each player demonstrates his 'resolve.'" "Threats and Promises of Peace," *Orbis*, vol. 28, no. 4 (Winter 1974), p. 1136. His point, intended to be instructive in the US nuclear planning context, also happens to be a concise statement of probable Soviet limited nuclear-targeting premises.

15. "The Influence of Soviet Military Doctrine on the Development of Military Art," *Kommunist Vooruzhennykh Sil*, no. 21 (November 1965), p. 21.

16. Colonel S. Tiushkevich, "Necessity and Chance in Modern Warfare," *Kommunist Vooruzhennykh Sil*, no. 10 (May 1964), p. 40.

17. For further discussion on the diverse origins and functions of Soviet doctrine, see Benjamin S. Lambeth, "The Sources of Soviet Military Doctrine," in F. B. Horton, A. C. Rogerson, and E. L. Warner, III, eds., *Comparative Defense Policy* (Baltimore: Johns Hopkins University Press, 1974), pp. 200-216.

18. A representative example of the Soviet media reaction to the US retargeting policy may be found in M. Milshtein and L. Semeiko, "The Problem of the Inadmissibility of a Nuclear Conflict: On New Approaches in the United States," *SShA: Ekonomika, Politika, Ideologiia*, no. 11 (October 1974). For a good capsule summary of the Soviet propaganda stance on the issue, see also Thomas W. Wolfe, *The SALT Experience: Its Impact on U.S. and Soviet Strategic Policy and Decision-making* (The Rand Corporation, R-1686-PR, forthcoming).

19. For elaboration, see Benjamin S. Lambeth, "The Evolving Soviet Strategic Threat," *Current History*, October 1975.

20. Quoted in E. T. Wooldridge, Jr., "The Gorshkov Papers: Soviet Naval

Doctrine for the Nuclear Age," *Orbis*, vol. 28, no. 4 (Winter 1975), p. 1167. As a cautionary note, however, it is worth pointing out the alternative possibility that Gorshkov's comment may have been principally motivated by his bureaucratic desire to justify a larger place for the SLBM force in the allocation of Soviet military missions and budgets.

21. Quoted in S. T. Cohen and W. C. Lyons, "A Comparison of US-Allied and Soviet Tactical Nuclear Force Capabilities and Policies," *Orbis*, vol. 19, no. 1 (Spring 1975), p. 91.

22. General V. Kulikov, "High Combat Readiness—The Most Important Condition for the Reliable Defense of the Motherland," *Kommunist Vooruzhennykh Sil*, no. 6 (March 1973), p. 20.

23. Marshall A. A. Grechko, "The Science and Art of Victory," *Pravda*, February 19, 1975.

24. For an argument which, despite its cautiousness, comes close to representing this view, see C. G. Jacobsen, "The Emergence of a Soviet Doctrine of Flexible Response?" *Atlantic Community Quarterly*, vol. 12, no. 2 (Summer 1974), pp. 233-38. For a more conservative approach to the subject which provides an excellent treatment of evolving Soviet strategic developments and options, yet reserves judgment on the question of where they may be pointing, see William R. Van Cleave, *Soviet Doctrine and Strategy: A Developing American View* (working paper prepared for a conference at the Stiftung Wissenschaft und Politik, Ebenhausen, West Germany, 1975).

25. Lt. General I. Zavialov, "The Creative Nature of Soviet Military Doctrine," *Krasnaia zvezda*, April 19, 1973.

III

PROMISES
OF TECHNOLOGY

CHAPTER 5

New Technologies: The Prospects

Cecil I. Hudson, Jr. and Peter H. Haas

This chapter is devoted to an explanation of a number of new technologies and a discussion of some of the implications of these technologies for the defense of Europe. The bulk of the discussion is concerned with what can be accomplished technically, but with some understanding and appreciation of practical political, military, and economic realities.

The phrase "new technologies" refers both to systems which are already in existence or development, but have not been widely deployed in NATO, and to conceptual systems which have a solid base in existing technology.

The key technologies include those which lead to improvements in delivery accuracy, target acquisition, delivery systems, and conventional and nuclear munitions. These technologies can be applied in developing new critical and cost-effective weapon systems which can lead to improved defense capability for Western Europe.

IMPROVED DELIVERY ACCURACY

The accuracy improvements possible with modern delivery systems have several major implications. Improved accuracy provides improved

The authors are particularly indebted to Dr. Donald A. Hicks for his collaboration in the preparation of this chapter.

delivery system effectiveness. This, in turn, leads to a requirement for significantly fewer weapons to achieve a given degree of target damage. Fewer tons of ordnance are required, thus greatly reducing the logistics load. The combination of improved accuracy and the requirement for fewer weapons greatly reduces the collateral damage potential. In addition to improved accuracy, there are improvements in munition technologies which can enhance their target damage capability. The net result is a major increase in military effectiveness with a consequent improvement in restraint, precision, and control. From a strictly technical standpoint, accurately delivered modern conventional munitions are competitive with nuclear munitions for some applications and are superior for others. This means that some operations which in the past were thought of as requiring nuclear munitions can, with modern technology, be conducted with nonnuclear munitions.

Precision-Guided Munitions

One of the major current weapon system needs is for guided munitions which are capable of being delivered in all-weather, high-attrition environments and despite enemy electronic countermeasures.

History of PGMs. PGMs actually have been evolving since World War II. Guided bombs of that era, such as TARZON and RAZON, used vacuum tubes. While they displayed some measures of success, they proved to be quite unreliable. During the 1950s, technology in air-to-air missiles brought forth the infrared and radar homing missiles of the Sidewinder, Falcon, and Sparrow class and had a profound impact on air combat tactics. Improvements in visually guided air-to-surface missiles were also brought into operational status, as typified by Bullpup. Unfortunately, the continuing constraint of having to fly the launching aircraft toward the target during guidance prevented obtaining, under operational conditions, the high degree of effectiveness demonstrable under test conditions.

However, two highly competitive environments over the past fifteen years or so have brought the necessary resources to bear to make major advances in the fundamental technologies essential to the achievement of highly accurate and reliable weapons. Both of these efforts depended on massive resources which are not available to all US European allies. One was the relatively peaceful competition between the United States and the USSR for dominance in manned space flights to the moon and the exploration of the planets. No one having experienced the amazement of seeing real-time television from the moon can doubt the ability of technically advanced countries to remotely control hardware on a real-time basis anywhere on earth as well.

The second competition was the US involvement in the conflict in Southeast Asia. There was a great incentive during that conflict for the United States to substitute advanced hardware, quickly developed from available technology, for manpower. Many extremely effective systems, such as the USAF "Gun Ship," came out of that activity. (Recently the capability, previously demonstrated in Vietnam, for the F-111 to deliver free-fall bombs in bad weather from low altitude with an accuracy of less than 100 meters in reference to a previously placed beacon, was shown in Europe.) The most significant impact, of course, was the phenomenal success of the various precision-guided munitions, particularly those using laser designation. (A laser beam is directed at the target, and the PGM tracks the reflected laser energy.)

Experience in Vietnam. This capability was not initially available in Vietnam, and so a comparison of the "old" and "new" side-by-side is quite convincing. Choke points, such as bridges and passes, were important to eliminate the surge of supplies from North to South Vietnam. Two examples are worth enumerating.

In order to block some of the passes along the Ho Chi Minh Trail, a large number of "dumb" bombs were dropped from B-52s with little lasting effect. Although passes were blocked or roads were cut, they were soon cleared or work-around networks were developed, requiring further extensive B-52 raids. However, when the pass area was laser designated, and precision-guided bombs were dropped by F-4s, the resulting slides blocked the pass. More importantly, the operational effort to continue to keep the pass or choke point blocked was greatly reduced. One of the most famous examples was the Thanh Hoa Bridge between Hanoi and Vinh, where thirty US aircraft were lost in repeated raids without ever closing the bridge. When laser-guided bombs became available, two raids of four aircraft each dropped the bridge without any loss of aircraft. Only one raid would have been required, but heavy clouds interferred with a view of the bridge on the first attack.[1]

Potential Use in Europe. Despite the successful use of PGMs in Southeast Asia, many observers still doubt that this development has increased our military effectiveness sufficiently to offset the massive Warsaw Pact threat, and believe that tactical nuclear weapons will be required. The usual areas of concern are frequent cloud coverage in

Europe, the possible inability of precision weapons to deal with large numbers of attacking armor (where area coverage may be needed), and the massive amount of military equipment that is expended quickly in modern conventional war, with the resulting critical resupply problem for NATO.

Of course, cloud cover is a major problem for electro-optical systems. North Vietnam also has considerable cloud cover, which did create operational problems. Also, the October War in the Middle East in 1973 showed that massive amounts of equipment are expended quickly even when unguided conventional munitions are used (most of the tanks killed were killed by other tanks). However, toward the end of that war there were a number of demonstrations of the effectiveness of guided munitions (e.g., 52 tanks killed by 58 Maverick air-to-surface missiles launched).

The very effectiveness of the PGMs will mean that despite the high use rate, the logistics problem will actually be less severe because they will be replacing large amounts of less effective ordnance. As has been pointed out,[2] this high use rate will cause a need for accessible stores which, because of the high value, will have to be smaller, more numerous, and separated. The same arguments hold for the various military platforms: they should be highly mobile, smaller, of lower cost, and more numerous. Many trades are possible among these quantities.

Countermeasures.   The capabilities of PGMs will create a strong incentive for the Warsaw Pact to develop new strategies and countermeasures against these weapons. Proposed systems should be evaluated for their sensitivity to simple countermeasures and should be designed with potential countermeasures in mind. However, the mere possibility of developing PGMs or PGM countermeasures by the Warsaw Pact should not be used as a reason for *not* developing these systems in the United States and NATO. There is a continuing need to improve our capabilities and system effectiveness by using technologies at hand or nearly at hand.

Cooperative Efforts.   The advantage of approaching this effort in a cooperative mode between the United States and NATO is obvious. A large number of precision-guided munition programs are being carried out by the United States and many of the countries of Europe. We have had sufficient experience in cooperative research and development and coproduction between us that a more united effort, allowing competition but stressing more standardization, can be achieved. The opportunity exists for common development and production of the necessary weapon systems to bring to reality the defense of Europe by conventional means, as a contribution to the NATO Triad.

Accurate Weapon Delivery

The preceding discussion referred primarily to a technique of accurately placing a weapon on target by "homing," that is, by using the target's own "signature," or target-reflected energy from a designator (laser or radar), to guide the weapon to the target. Beacons can also be used, and progress has been made in the last few years in developing sensors that can detect and track natural infrared (IR) and microwave emission from targets. While the use of infrared sensors is limited to clear air mass (between sensor and target), the microwave emissions can be detected through clouds as well.

Correlation Guidance. ⟩If the target itself does not have an adequate (high-contrast) signature, "correlation guidance" schemes can be developed to determine the instantaneous position of the weapon with respect to the target. The correlation scheme, which can use visual, IR, or microwave information, measures the mismatch between the sensed "picture" of the area surrounding the target and a stored (pre-flight) reference picture that represents the target view from the (ideal) "on-course" position. This mismatch generates steering signals to correct the weapon trajectory to produce a hit (or an acceptably small miss).

Terminal Guidance Schemes. Several homing schemes are part of an automatic terminal guidance system, whereby the weapon flies (or falls) toward the target untouched by human hands, after the weapon has been "locked on" by the pilot of the launching aircraft. If the weapon also contains a two-way radio (or data) link to the launch aircraft, the pilot can remotely control the weapon while viewing the target scene, even after target designation—perhaps to select a specific aim point on a larger target (such as a ship) or, if necessary, to abort the mission at the last moment.

Such data links must meet several specifications. They must be able to transmit in real-time "wide-band" information such as TV; they must function reliably despite terrain obstruction, interference from other friendly transmissions, and the level of jamming (or other countermeasures) that an enemy can reasonably be expected to use under realistic combat conditions; and they must be of sufficiently small size and cost to be compatible with the PGM delivery system. The state of the art of data link technology has advanced to the point where jamming and interference-resisting links can be developed using so-called spread-spectrum techniques (but with limited bandwidth). By applying recent dramatic improvements in microelectronics (i.e., Large-Scale Integration, or LSI)[3] it is hoped that the size and cost of data links, in production quantities, can be reduced to acceptable levels.

Position-Fixing Systems.   Besides "homing," there is another class of precision terminal guidance schemes called "position-fixing" systems, which use radio signals from synchronized friendly transmitters to accurately determine the existing position of the delivery system. These signals can also be used to correct the accumulated errors of an inertial guidance system. Thus, position-fixing systems can also be used for mid-course guidance to steer a longer-range PGM into a region where terminal guidance can commence.

The familiar OMEGA and LORAN low-frequency guidance systems have relatively low accuracies (approximately 2 km and 100 m). These schemes are primarily useful for long-range navigation and mid-course guidance. Several systems are currently in development which offer the greater precision needed for terminal guidance, by virtue of their higher frequency (GHz) of operation: DME (Distance Measuring Equipment) uses signals from two or more surveyed ground transmitters to locate a vehicle or weapon within 50 m; GPS (the Global Positioning System of multiple satellites in high altitude orbits) is expected to permit location of airborne or surface units within 10 m, when it becomes operational in about ten years. Thus GPS position fixing, which is an all-weather system, is expected to compare favorably in accuracy with laser-guided weapons currently in operation, which are limited to fair weather. The accuracy of laser-guided weapons is better than 10 m.

The above considerations for the jamming resistance of data links also apply to the operational reliability of radio position-fixing systems.

In summary, modern aircraft using computers and map-matching radars can provide all-weather delivery of conventional munitions (free fall bombs) against fixed targets with accuracies of less than 100 m. The same aircraft can be used in a close air-support role by offset aiming from a ground beacon. In this role, the delivery accuracy may be sufficient to attack mobile targets. This, however, would require a rapid transfer and receipt of the forward observer's information on target and azimuth relative to the beacon position, and the use of area-coverage weapons.

The sensors of current precision-guided munitions limit them to use in moderately good weather, in contrast to the all-weather capability permitted by radar. The delivery accuracy with PGMs is less than 10 m instead of the 100 m noted above. Such munitions can be used for direct attack of fixed or mobile targets. Figure 1 summarizes the presently available technology for precision guidance.

Type	*CEP (m)*	*Comments*
Electro-optical	<10	Daylight only
Laser-designated	<10	Fair weather
Infrared seeker	<10	Fair weather
Radar area correlation	<50	Prestored imagery
Time-of-arrival/ distance-measuring equipment (TOA/DME)	<50	Requires target and weapon coordinates
Home-on-beacon	<10	Preemplaced beacon
Map matching with aircraft	<100	All-weather
Offset aiming from beacon	<100	Requires forward observer

Figure 1
Presently Available Technology for Precision Guidance

Delivery Accuracy Required

The above discussion centered on what was achievable in improved delivery accuracy. This section deals with what is required to effectively attack military targets while minimizing unwanted collateral damage.

The Importance of Size. Three important parameters affect or influence the effectiveness of weapons for damaging targets: the dimensions of the target, the delivery system miss distance, and the effective damage range of the munition employed. Whether a target can be considered a "point" or "area" target depends on the relative size of these three parameters. For example, even with perfect accuracy (zero miss distance), if the target area is large compared to the weapon damage area, achieving a given level of target damage may require multiple rounds. Viewing the same case from another perspective, larger targets do not require perfect delivery accuracies. The area of the target dominates the problem. These considerations are important for both nuclear and conventional weapons whenever the weapon damage range, delivery accuracy, and target dimensions are comparable in magnitude. Matching point and area targets appropriately with point and area munitions can provide the best combination of target damage and reduced collateral harm.

Types of Targets.   Targets of interest include typical theater targets—combat units, logistics systems, command, control, and communication systems, and, to a minor extent, the industrial base which produces the war materiel. In order to avoid proliferating specific targets and specific weapons, it is useful to attempt some categorization and generalization. One useful distinction is between point targets and area targets. Area targets may be treated as uniform in value or as containing a number of critical and noncritical elements. Both area and point targets may be either "soft" or "hard." Some targets do not fall clearly into any simple category. One example is linear targets such as roads, railroads, or bridges, although the bridge piers can be considered as point targets. Other point targets include buried command posts or bunkers. A single tank may be considered a point target, but a dispersed tank company is an area target with discrete distributed hard points.

Whether or not we treat a target as being uniformly distributed over an area depends not only on the way the target functions, but on our knowledge about its elements and their disposition, and how accurately we can attack it.

Other area targets include troops in the field, air defense units such as an SA-2 site, logistics storage facilities, industrial buildings, and industrial facilities such as oil refineries. A logistics storage facility is a good example of a uniform value area target, assuming that no intelligence information is available concerning the location of items which are under cover. An oil refinery covers a large area, but contains few critical components—the distillation and cracking towers.

Target Damage—a Simple Example.   As an oversimplified but useful illustration, a generic target can be taken as an example. For mathematical simplicity, the target can be treated as circular, with a radius of about 300 m. Such a target, a little less than ⅓ km² in area, might represent a large logistics storage facility or a major industrial area.

For purposes of defining accuracy requirements, this target will be treated in three levels of detail. First, it will be treated as a uniform value area target, even though a small fraction of the total area may be occupied by critical target elements. At the next level of detail, it will be assumed that approximately one-fourth of the total area is occupied by buildings. Finally, a different type of target will be con-

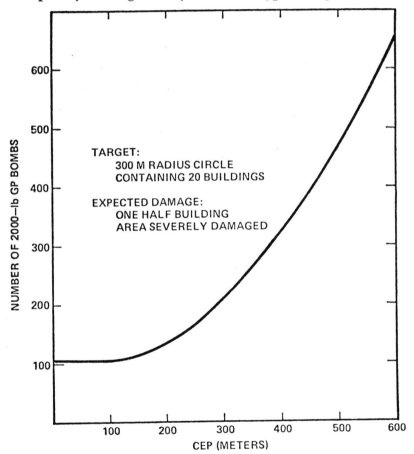

Figure 2
Number of Weapons Required to Damage One-Half of Twenty Randomly Spaced Buildings Within a 300-Meter Radius Circle

sidered, one with twenty critical elements within the same area, such as a small oil refinery or even a tank company dispersed within the same area.

Accuracy improvements can either increase the expected damage from a given number of weapons or reduce the number of weapons required to achieve a given level of damage. For illustrative purposes, consider a 2,000-lb General Purpose (GP) bomb and assume that the target area contains twenty large (say 3,700 m² or 40,000 ft²) single-story industrial buildings. Figure 2 shows the number of 2,000-lb GP bombs required to achieve a 50 percent fractional damage, as a function of delivery accuracy. The delivery accuracy is defined as the radius of a circle within which half the weapons impact, the radius being called the circular error probable or CEP. (Most delivery systems have noncircular error distributions, but this is a useful generalization for our purpose.) This figure assumes that the buildings are randomly distributed within the 300-m circle considered to be the target. Note the extremely rapid increase in weapon requirements as the delivery accuracy exceeds the target radius (300 m). Conversely, note that for this case a delivery accuracy of less than 150 m will not result in any reduction in the number of weapons required.

The mean area of effectiveness (MAE) for a 2,000-lb GP bomb against one class of such targets is 22,000 ft² (or roughly 2,000 m²).[4] The mean area of effectiveness may be defined by the relationship

$$f = 1 - \left(1 - \frac{M}{A}\right)^h$$

where f is the fraction of the total building area A damaged by h bomb hits, and M is the MAE. The term within the parentheses gives the means fraction of the total area which is not damaged by one bomb hit.

Since the actual targets assumed above only occupy about a quarter of the total space, we could achieve a factor of four reduction in weapons required by targeting the individual buildings. This would require additional improvements in accuracy to the point where the CEP is comparable to the building dimensions, to achieve the benefit of this potential fourfold reduction. The weapon requirements for this case are shown in Figure 3.

For the case in which the target area is assumed to contain only a few critical elements, the accuracy requirements are still more stringent and the weapon requirements less. If we assume a relatively hard target—say one for which the effective 2,000-lb bomb damage range is 10 m, and the goal is to obtain a 50 percent expected damage of 20 critical elements within the target—then Figure 4 shows the weapon requirements as a function of CEP.

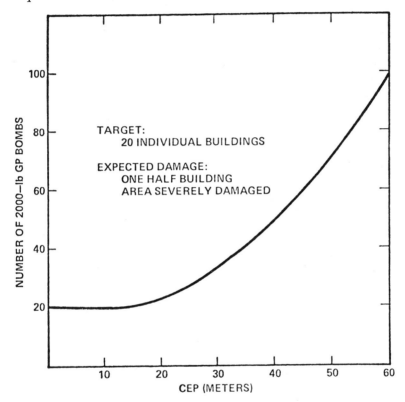

Figure 3
Number of Weapons Required to Damage Half of Twenty Buildings When the Individual Buildings Are Targeted

Another way of viewing the impact of accuracy is to estimate the total damage obtainable as the accuracy is improved for a fixed inventory of weapons. In the case of one thousand 2,000-lb GP bombs (1 kt of weapon weight), the total potential damage area for this type of target is 2 million m². The required accuracy is about half the building

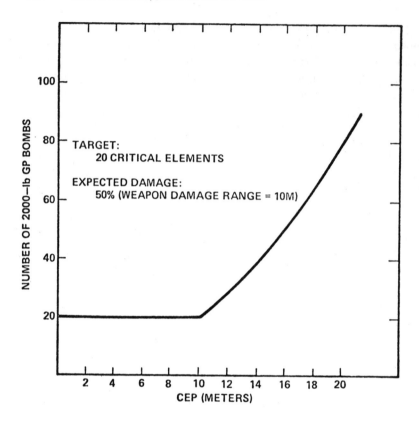

Figure 4
Number of Weapons Required to Damage Twenty Critical Elements

size, and roughly half the damage potential is obtained when the CEP is equal to the target radius. If the target is treated as a 300-m radius target containing twenty buildings, then three-quarters of the bombs landing within the circle will miss the target, so the damage potential is reduced to about one-fourth of 2 million m², but with a required accuracy of about 150 m.

An important point not considered in detail in the above discussion is the effect of overlap, which would reduce the expected total damage area. Achieving the total damage potential also requires some degree of patterning the impact points. (For example, in the 300-m radius target, perfect delivery accuracy would result in all weapons impacting in the same aim point, so that the expected damage area would be that from only one bomb.)

In all of the above examples, such fine points as detailed target shape, realistic bomb impact patterns, and weapon system reliability were not considered. The main point is to provide a feeling for the accuracy required and for the improvements in weapon effectiveness made possible by improving the delivery system accuracy for several different generic classes of targets.

Additional Benefits to Be Gained by Improved Delivery Accuracy

Reduced Logistics Requirements. Figures 2, 3, and 4 gave some indication of the total tonnage of ordnance of a given type which is required for attacking the targets considered. The drastic decrease in total tonnage with improved accuracy is quite remarkable. The point is finally reached where a minimum number of weapons is required. Typical World War II delivery accuracies were on the order of miles. A weapon planner would require thousands of tons of bombs to effectively attack a single large area target such as the one considered in the above example.

CEPs which are achievable with modern aircraft delivery of gravity weapons against fixed targets are more than sufficient for attacking the entire target area. In fact, accuracies of 100-m permit attacking individual buildings with comparable numbers of weapons. For PGMs with accuracies of less than 10 m, the critical elements within a large area could be effectively attacked, provided they can be acquired and identified. Even mobile targets may be effectively attacked by some PGMs.

Improved Military Effectiveness. Improved accuracy can also improve military effectiveness with nuclear weapons. Figure 5 shows along the horizontal axis some examples of targets of increasing hardness. The vertical axis shows the probability of destroying the target. The curves represent the variation of destruction probability with target hardness for several nuclear weapon yields for three levels of accuracy: 400-m, 30-m, and 3-m CEP. The gains in this probability with improvement in accuracy are readily apparent. For example, the probability of destroying military targets with a 1-kt airburst delivered accurately is greater than that of the same target with a 400-kt airburst delivered less accurately. For purposes of completeness, a hypothetical 1-kt earth penetrator is also shown.

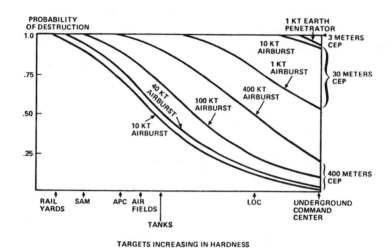

Figure 5
Accuracy and Military Effectiveness for Nuclear Weapons

Reduced Collateral Damage. Improved delivery also has a tremendous potential for reducing collateral damage. Traditional wisdom about conventional and nuclear weapons holds that nuclear weapons can destroy targets easily, but cause collateral damage problems which are essentially insoluable, and that nonnuclear weapons create no collateral damage, but have problems destroying hard and area targets. In either case, technical progress seems to lie in the direction of reducing collateral damage from nuclear weapons and increasing the target damage capability with conventional weapons.

However, conventional weapons have a tremendous capability for producing collateral damage. Any weapon which misses its target has the potential of causing unwanted collateral damage. In the strategic bombing of World War II this was not a serious problem since civilian casualties were usually considered an additional military advantage.

Considerations other than statistical fluctuations in an idealized impact distribution pattern are likely to lead to the impact of weapons outside the target area. These considerations include stray weapons and some aspects of weapon system reliability. Weapons which are prepared to detonate but suffer gross misses can create unwanted collateral damage, as can misidentification of the target. Unreliability factors of 5 percent to 1 percent are not unreasonable, but a figure as low as 1 percent would probably be difficult to achieve in practice. The collateral damage potential of stray weapons could be greatly reduced by some technological improvements, such as command and arming of a PGM (with a data link).

Figure 6 shows, on the left-hand scale, the fraction of weapons which impact outside the target area for a 300-m radius target as a function of CEP, assuming an idealized circular normal impact pattern. When this number reaches extremely small values, it tends to be limited by unreliability or the other factors noted above. The criteria assumed for collateral damage are of key importance. The collateral damage criteria should vary with the degree of population protection, but would probably be limited to levels which produce moderate to severe damage to civilian structures. For the 2,000-lb. GP bomb in the example considered above, the area of damage for light structures is about 7,000 m². The right-hand scale of Figure 6 shows the total potential collateral damage area as a function of delivery system accuracy, for 1,000 total weapons.

Other Methods for Reducing Collateral Damage. One possibility

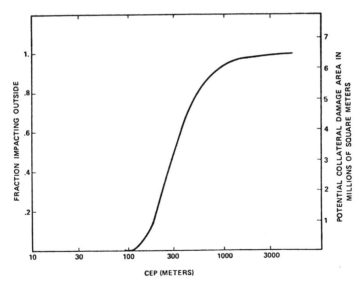

Figure 6
Fraction of Weapons Impacting Outside a 300-m Radius Target (Left Scale), and Potential Target Damage from 1,000 2,000-lb GP Bombs (Right Scale)

is to establish a buffer zone around the target area. In fact, such a buffer zone might be an explicitly designated exclusion area in which no targets would be attacked. The delivery system error and the collateral damage range of the weapon would determine the size of the buffer zone.

The improvement in technology which permits the greatest reduction in collateral damage is that in delivery system accuracy. Fewer weapons and/or less destructive weapons can achieve the same amount of target damage with improved accuracy.

Collateral damage may also be reduced by "microtargeting" or by considering the functional vulnerability of a target. In this type of targeting, an industrial installation is considered as a system. Critical elements or nodes are identified which, if damaged, would interrupt a critical function for a given time period. For precision-guided munitions, such microtargeting can greatly reduce the amount of ordnance required to achieve a given effect, compared to simply considering the target as an area a certain fraction of which must be destroyed. The simple examples in the preceding sections give some indication of how this approach can be applied.

Additional collateral damage reduction is possible by using the proper methodology for estimating target damage or weapon requirements. In many cases, simple point target damage formulas may either overestimate or underestimate the number of weapons required. A proper matching of types of weapons with types of targets can also reduce unwanted collateral damage. For example, area munitions used against fairly soft point targets create an unnecessarily large damage area.

Finally, improvements in munition technologies can reduce unwanted damage from both nuclear and nonnuclear munitions. A proper choice of weapon burst height or depth can minimize collateral damage from nuclear weapons, and offset aiming (away from nontarget areas) can give modest reductions.

TARGET ACQUISITION AND DESIGNATION

Since precise delivery capability requires an accurate determination of target position, reconnaissance and surveillance will become critical. Real-time surveillance for moving targets will be even more necessary in the future if mobility and concealment are adopted as a counter-measure to PGMs.

The United States has initiated a hardware program using a small, remotely piloted vehicle (RPV) which will send a real-time television display to a command center via a data link. The program will determine the feasibility of operating such a vehicle in the field and its ability to acquire targets. Eventually, such a vehicle could be used to laser-designate targets remotely and could operate up to 50 km into enemy territory (if it can survive the hostile environment). This laser designation capability could be used with laser-guided artillery shells as well as other PGMs. Other applications of remotely piloted vehicles are being studied, including deep reconnaissance strike vehicles.

An important program of particular interest to the European environment is a "mini"-RPV which could be launched by aircraft or by rocket booster. An aircraft such as the F-4 could launch the vehicle down to low altitude through the cloud cover, and could then remotely control the mini-RPV, acquire the desired target, laser-designate the target from the RPV, and then launch (from the aircraft) the PGM into the necessary "basket" for laser-homing on the target.

For an attrition level of around 0.01, it has been estimated[5] that a comparison of relative mission costs is: mini-RPV,1; high-performance RPV, 10-100; high-performance Aircraft, 200-1,000.

In order for an RPV to be successful, it is crucial that the data link be reliable, have low cost and weight, and be capable of operating despite some level of enemy electronic countermeasures. Since this is equally important for some precision guidance techniques, the discussion above on PGMs can also apply to RPVs. (In fact, placing a warhead in an RPV and diving it into the target converts it into a PGM).

SYSTEMS FOR INCREASED MOBILITY AND FIREPOWER

Consideration of conflict situations on NATO's flanks, in the Middle East, and elsewhere in the world all point up the need for highly effective lightweight forces which can deploy rapidly by air from CONUS bases. Within NATO's central region there is a strong need for increased force mobility in order to provide the firepower concentration needed to counter massed armor breakthroughs and concentrated air attacks against the most critically needed assets.

Multipurpose Rocket Systems

Large modern aircraft have made it possible to move troops great distances in a short time. People movement is no longer the obstacle to our ability to project ground forces rapidly and sustain them indefinitely using air lines of supply. Instead, the upper limit is set by the size and weight of our equipment and the amount of supplies needed to sustain ground units in combat. Substantially increasing our airlift capacity above its current level would be prohibitively costly; and it appears that considerably more can be gained by reducing the weight of the materiel to be transported. It is also necessary to gain and maintain air superiority during critical time periods, in order to realize the full potential of air mobility.

To make a large reduction in supply tons, a way has to be found to make major gains in weight efficiency of our indirect fire systems, such as mortars and tube artillery. Rocket systems used in place of tube artillery offer the prospect of substantial weight reduction while increasing mobility and possibilities for firepower concentration. In addition to the traditional mission of artillery to provide fire support to the force maneuver elements for harassment, interdiction, and counter-battery, there is increasing emphasis on the contribution which rockets might make toward suppressing hostile antitank and air defense weapons. The use of rocket-delivered scatterable mines to impede mobility is also of special interest, especially when used with the potentially highly synergistic combination of antitank precision-guided missile and terminal-homing rocket options. The mines slow down or stop the mechanized forces, and modern area munitions or direct hitting weapons destroy the quasi-stationary collection of targets.

A modular approach to warheads, terminal or command guidance options, and launchers would provide the flexibility needed for the various missions involved, in a manner analogous to the modular approach being applied by the United States to glide bombs and other precision-guided munitions. In fact, some of the same approaches and technology should carry over directly. The effective use of modularity requires a "threshold" for the supporting logistics systems.

High-Mobility Antitank Vehicles

Any effort to reduce the supply requirements of a force of ground units in combat should seek ways to lower the consumption of petroleum and ammunition. It appears that if consumption is to be lowered much, it will be as a result of lowering the weight of the things that are moved rather than as a result of technology advances in engines. We must, therefore, find ways of cutting the weight of our vehicles, but without diminishing their combat effectiveness. The high-low force mix offers a way to achieve this goal. Here the approach is to use special forces of highly mobile, lightweight antitank vehicles to provide rapidly deployable, concentrated firepower to counter enemy armored advances. Our own tanks would be used more for offensive operations, and consequently fewer tanks would be required. This force mix approach requires more resources than a single force, but provides a net gain in cost effectiveness.

These antitank vehicles could be jeep-sized or larger, depending upon the extent of firepower each carries. An upper limit might be an 8-ton vehicle carrying up to ten TOW missiles. Speed over moderately rough terrain should exceed the speed of tanks by 20 to 30 km/h. They should be air-droppable, lightly armored against small arms, and equipped for night operations. It should be possible to transport a company-sized unit including personnel in a single C-5 aircraft.

Air Threat Interception

Similarly, the formidable air threat facing NATO today imposes the requirement for extensive opposing firepower and for the ability to concentrate this firepower quickly in the attacking aircraft approach corridors. In the Central Region of NATO, for example, most of our critically important nuclear capabilities and command and control facilities are based a mere ten to fifteen minutes' flight time from the political border—close enough to Warsaw Pact air bases to permit penetration at low altitudes using low weather ceilings and rough terrain to aid survivability. Surface-to-air missile systems would weaken the attackers to some extent; however, a combination of terrain masking, extensive enemy jamming, and air strikes directed initially against these SAMs would limit the contribution they could make. Inherently, SAMs do not have the mobility needed to permit rapid deployment to concentrate firepower in the enemy's approach corridors.

Fighter aircraft do have the requisite mobility, but only the most expensive of these aircraft have been equipped with the kind of firepower needed to intercept the WP strike force and the maneuverability needed for self-defense while carrying out this prime mission. The trend in recent years toward higher and higher costs for these airplanes severely limits their force size well below what is needed to match the threat. While the "low-high" mix appears the only solution to the force constraint imposed by limited defense budgets, to date the small low-cost fighters have not carried the extensive firepower and the all-weather operational capability demanded by the nature of the threat and the European environment.

An important aspect of firepower has to do with the tactics required for its application. One-on-one dogfight engagements or conversions to co-altitude tail-chases for Sidewinder launching severely restrict the number of kills available per fighter sortie. When the attackers are exposed only ten to fifteen minutes before reaching their targets, such one-on-one tactics impose the requirement for a prohibitive number of aircraft. A major increase in kills per sortie should be gained by equipping these aircraft with the capability to shoot missiles down at the attackers as they approach, avoiding the time- and fuel-consuming tactic of flying the fighter down to meet them.

Pulse doppler radar technology recently has matured to the point where it can be used in even the lightest of fighter aircraft to give all-weather look-down acquisition and tracking of penetrating threat aircraft. Assisted by an airborne acquisition platform such as AWACS (Airborne Warning and Control System), these fighters can be vectored into position for the desired massing of defending firepower. What is needed at this point is a small, low-cost, air-to-air missile capable of being fired through cloud cover and down into ground (and sea) clutter target backgrounds—and capable of being carried in fairly large numbers, perhaps six or eight per aircraft. Once again, doppler radar technology can be exploited for the needed capability. Applied originally to the Sparrow and Phoenix missiles in the United States during the fifties and early sixties, this technology has advanced to the point where it can be applied to much smaller missile airframes, which is more consistent with the need.

IMPROVEMENTS POSSIBLE WITH NEW CONVENTIONAL MUNITION TECHNOLOGIES

This section is concerned primarily with the improvements which can be made in increasing target damage, assuming a weapon arrives at the target, is fused properly, and detonates. For some weapon systems, it is difficult to obtain a clear analytic or logical separation of the delivery system from the "front end," or explosive payload. Penetrating weapons are a good example. The kinetic energy imparted by the delivery system is an important factor for producing target damage. Nuclear munitions usually provide a clear distinction between the delivery system and the "warhead."

General-purpose blast fragmentation weapons have been the workhorse of recent military conflicts. Laser guidance kits provide a practical, low-cost method for attacking point targets with these types of weapons. Other types of conventional munitions such as incendiaries and firebombs have been widely used in past conflicts.

The history of conventional weapon development contains many examples of some of the concepts noted below. However, in many cases these technologies were not effective because of poor delivery accuracies or because of excessive cost per round. Many of the current improvements are in low-cost reliable production techniques for both the payload and the fusing system.

Improved Point Munitions

Point munitions require hitting the target or achieving a near miss to obtain the desired degree of damage. A bullet is an extreme example of a point munition. It relies on its kinetic energy and on hitting a vital area to achieve a kill. In general, point munitions have effective damage areas less than the total area of the target. Examples are penetrators (kinetic-energy or explosive), semi-armor-piercing munitions (SAP), and axial-shaped charges. Penetrators and SAP rounds must have near normal incidence to prevent ricochet. Harder media and lower impact velocities generally require higher impact angles. For example, for 300 m per second impact on concrete, the incidence angle must be within 30° of vertical to prevent ricochet. For soil, it could be within 75° of vertical.

Shaped charges can penetrate the target at almost any angle of incidence, but require some degree of standoff from the target at detonation to achieve maximum effectiveness. Axial shaped charges are well known for their damage capability against tanks and armored vehicles. A 1-kg shaped charge can defeat a tank if placed in the proper position, and warheads in the 3 to 4 kg range are used in the Sagger and TOW wire-guided antitank missiles.

Axial shaped charges may have a variety of liner shapes, materials, types of explosive initiation, and wave shaping. As one example, conical shaped charges can achieve penetration depths of about 4.5 cone diameters into mild steel or 10 to 12 diameters into reinforced concrete. For heavy shaped charges, a ʃ800 kg conical shaped charge (using modern wave-shaping techniques) would be 89 cm in diameter, 1 m long, and require a 1.8-m standoff at detonation for optimum penetration. Such a warhead with a steel liner would penetrate about 10 m of concrete.

Axial shaped charges use a variety of methods for initiating and shaping both the explosive wave and the liner. Both the shape of the liner and its material determine the type of jet created and its penetration characteristics. In some cases, the shaped charge produces more of a cannonball than an actual jet. The type of damage done by a shaped charge can vary widely. It depends not only on the characteristics of the shaped charge itself, but on the material which is being penetrated and the liner material which is doing the penetration. A typical conical-shaped charge will produce an "ice cream cone" shaped hole. This hole can be made smaller and deeper, or wider and shallower, by varying the shaped charge design.

Some shaped charge damage mechanisms depend upon secondary effects for target kill. For example, shaped charges which are optimized as antitank weapons often rely on spalled material from inside the tank for crew incapacitation and/or detonation of the ordnance. Shaped charges are an extremely versatile weapon and may be optimized for maximum effect against various types of point targets.

Improved Area Munitions

Many targets require large area coverage in order to obtain the necessary degree of damage. There are several methods for improving area munitions. One is to use a single warhead (such as a fuel air explosive) which is optimized for covering a large area. A second method, which was used in World War II, is to spread the available energy over a wide area by dividing the total explosive weight into a number of smaller packages. Such cluster bomb techniques are not new, but today's technology provides reliable and reproducible dispersal, low-cost fusing, and optimized damage mechanisms for various types of targets.

Fuel Air Explosives. One example of a modern munition is the fuel air explosive. Fuel air explosive research was begun in World War II, but the early experiments were only successful in enclosed areas. The first successful free air experiments were made in the United States in 1960. Fuel air explosives function by first dispersing an aerosol which mixes in proper proportion with the air, then is detonated with a burster charge. By spreading the energy over a large area, the fuel air explosive more closely approximates an ideal damage pattern (complete destruction inside the pattern and no damage outside the pattern). Not having to carry the oxidizer with the fuel provides an additional advantage.

Figure 7 shows the relative overpressure as a function of relative range for equal weights of TNT and a typical fuel air explosive. Note that the overpressure for TNT drops very sharply with range so that it tends to produce excessive damage near the burst point and insufficient damage beyond the effective weapon radius. The fuel air explosive (FAE) overpressure is essentially constant with range and begins to fall off near the edge of the cloud. The FAE cloud is essentially a volume rather than a point energy source. Approximately four times the TNT mass would be required to equal the long-range FAE overpressures, while more than ten times the TNT mass would be required to achieve the overpressure at the "knee" of the FAE curve.

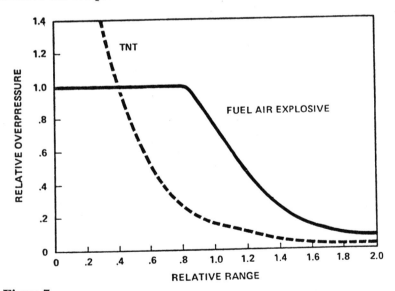

Figure 7

Comparison of Relative Overpressure as a Function of Relative Range for Equal Weights of TNT and a Typical Fuel Air Explosive

This comparison was based on overpressure only, whereas most targets are sensitive to the transmitted impulse. In terms of target damage effectiveness, a combination blast/fragmentation weapon may, in many cases, be more effective than a pure blast weapon. The effectiveness of FAEs against a number of targets relative to optimized blast/fragmentation warheads is still a subject of some debate.

Weapon-Tailoring Techniques. A variety of weapon-tailoring techniques are possible with conventional munitions. Case to explosive ratios can be varied to optimize fragment or blast damage or to provide a mix of both in a general-purpose munition. One weapon-tailoring technique is to alter the blast pulse in order to maximize the impulse produced. Figure 8 shows one example of the enhanced impulse possible by using a material such as aluminum mixed with explosive outside a standard cylindrical high-explosive charge. The aluminum flakes burn more slowly than the high explosive, giving an overpressure pulse which is no greater in magnitude, but longer in duration. This particular example is a 7/10 kg test charge. It is not known whether the same improvement in performance is possible for larger charge weights.

Combined Effects. Combined effects can be used against some types of targets. For targets containing volatile elements, an incendiary effect can be added to blast, fragments, or a shaped charge in order to increase the damage potential. The initial impact would expose the volatile elements to the air, where the incendiary effect could increase target damage. Fueled vehicles, POL storage, and refineries are examples of targets which could be damaged more effectively with such combined effects.

Cluster Munitions. All of the above types of weapons may be used as cluster munitions. Combined effects, shaped charges, or fuel air explosives can be used as clusters. As an example of the effectiveness of dividing a given payload into smaller and smaller packages, the use of munitions in the 20-kg weight class could be considered against the industrial buildings used as an earlier example. A weapon weighing about 2,000 lb (909 kg) could carry about forty of these submunitions. Each submunition is assumed to be a GP bomb with controlled fragments optimized for damaging industrial structures. An incendiary effect could also be added as an extra damage mechanism. The degree of effectiveness of incendiaries is, however, hard to quantify, since the effectiveness depends on the combustability of the building and its contents and on the effectiveness of fire control and firefighting measures. Figure 9 compares the effectiveness of such a cluster of 20-kg submunitions with a 909-kg bomb. Of course, practical problems of dispersal and pattern control remain. The example shown assumes a perfectly spaced pattern, and the CEP is the CEP of the centroid of the pattern.

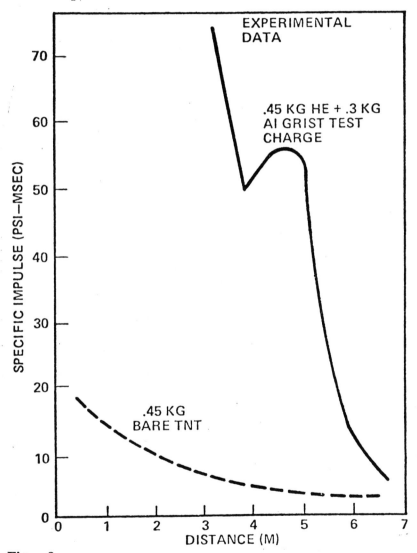

Figure 8

Example of Impulse Enhancement with Afterburning of Aluminum, Compared to a Standard High Explosive Charge

An even smaller class of submunitions (about 2 kg) might be considered against tank or armored targets. Such a weapon would have to hit the target in order to effectively damage it. In this case, the weapon effectiveness is dominated by the geometry of the target. Tanks and APCs are relatively large, about 20 m² (with some fraction of the total area being a vulnerable area which, if hit, would render the vehicle inoperable). The various degrees of damage include loss of mobility, loss of firepower, and essentially complete destruction. If such 2-kg submunitions were carried with a 1,000-kg store, somewhat less than 500 such munitions could be carried. If the total area of a tank is 20 m², then 1 weapon per 20 m² would give a reasonable probability of hitting the tank. Thus, the 500 weapons could be spread over a total area of 10,000 m². This is the area of a circle 56 m in radius. Gravity weapons could be delivered on-call by modern aircraft with a

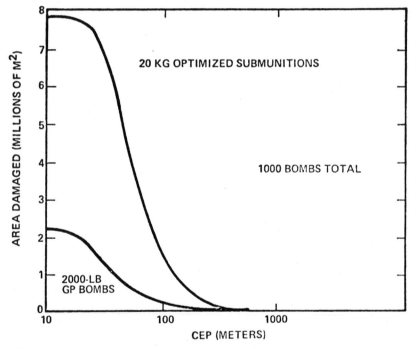

Figure 9
Total Expected Area Damaged as a Function of Delivery Accuracy, for a Pattern of 20-kg Submunitions (909 kg Total Weight) Compared with 2,000 lb GP Bombs

delivery accuracy of less than 100 m, so the capability of this type of weapon against mobile tanks would be marginal. A PGM such as Maverick has been demonstrated to be an effective antitank weapon, and can also be used to engage a moving tank. At a weight of about 200 kg, the Maverick would seem to be a better choice. Another potentially attractive antitank weapon is the Rockeye cluster munition.

Mines

Modern technology offers a number of potential improvements in mine warfare. The same technology which can place a remote vehicle on the moon, and provide a 100-step program in a hand-held computer, can produce mines capable of being directed remotely and of carrying internal logic.

Current technology can also provide mines which can be emplaced rapidly and remotely, and are capable of self-sterilization or self-destruction on command. Kill mechanisms can be optimized against a variety of targets, including personnel or materiel targets. Both land and sea mines can have improved capabilities.

Mines belong to a general class of "target-activated" munitions—munitions which depend on someone else taking action before they are brought into effect. Such munitions can, in principal, achieve improved effectiveness by firing on a target which has a particular signature when it enters the effective damage region of the munition. For example, a gun with a trip wire can be an effective antipersonnel weapon for a jungle path.

With the basic defensive position of NATO, mines offer an attractive method for delay, denial, or harassment of enemy forces. They are most effective when used in conjunction with other barrier or denial methods, and when covering fire can hamper an enemy's attempts at clearing the minefield.

Mines also offer the potential for very low collateral damage, since the locations are known and friendly forces and civilians can be warned to avoid them. Practical problems of reaction time and emplacement time limit the applicability of mines to some extent.

The Need for Proper Matching of Munitions and Targets

The proper matching of munitions and targets can increase damage effectiveness and reduce collateral damage. Of course, the number of possible targets is so great that an inordinate number of different types of munitions would be required to optimize a separate munition for each target. Examples where specialized munitions are worthwhile include antitank, antiaircraft, or antiship weapons. GP bombs are a good example of a compromise in weapon and munition design for achieving a fairly good damage effectiveness against a wide variety of targets.

Weapons such as penetrators and shaped charges can be used to good effect against such targets as bridge piers and hardened underground bunkers or command posts. Such targets cannot be effectively attacked by clusters of small munitions since each individual munition, even if it hit the target, would have only a small damage probability.

Dispersed troops in the field are best attacked by antipersonnel area weapons. Small cluster bomblets which are optimized as antipersonnel weapons can be quite effective compared to the same weight of GP bombs. One antipersonnel mine of World War II (the M2) had a lethal radius of 10 to 20 m and was dangerous to 50 m. Today's technology provides some improvements in optimizing fragment size and distribution patterns.

It should be clear from the earlier discussion that the distinction between an area target and a point target depends not only on the relative magnitudes of the target size and the weapon damage area, but also on the area of the expected weapon impact distribution. If the weapon damage area is small compared to the target area, then the target may be considered an area target. If the damage area is large compared to the target size, then the target may be considered a point target. If the weapon damage area and the target dimensions are comparable, then the target may be considered a point target if the delivery accuracy is sufficiently good to ensure a finite hit probability. Otherwise, mass bombing may be required to effectively damage the target.

From another vantage point, if a given damage effect is desired for a given target, then the accuracy required to achieve this effect can be estimated for different weapons. For area weapons against area targets, the accuracy required is slightly less than the dimensions of the target. (The probability of a hit is one-half when the CEP is equal to the target radius, for a circular target.) Point weapons are generally ineffective against area targets unless the targets contain critical point elements. If this is the case, then the accuracy requirement is determined either by the dimensions of the vulnerable area of the "point" or by the effective damage range of the weapon, whichever is larger.

Thus, if an area target is on the order of 100 m in its major dimensions, then a CEP on the order of 100 m can be quite effective when combined with munitions which have a large effective damage area. For targets with dimensions on the order of 10 m combined with weapons with damage ranges of about 10 m, delivery accuracies of about 10 m are sufficient to ensure a high degree of target damage.

IMPROVEMENTS POSSIBLE WITH NEW NUCLEAR MUNITION TECHNOLOGIES

Standard fission weapons make up the bulk of the current tactical nuclear weapon inventory. The unclassified literature describes the effects of these weapons fairly well. Modern technology has resulted in reductions in size and weight for a given yield. Weapons can be as small as the 155-mm nuclear artillery shell or as light as the old Davy Crockett warhead. Current technologies can provide additional improvements in available yield, in economy of special nuclear material use, and in weapon safety.

Tailored-effects nuclear warheads can select the particular nuclear effects which maximize target damage or which create the least amount of collateral damage. These different effects, along with various yields, can increase our military flexibility. Examples of US modernization programs currently in progress are shown in Figure 10. These include earth-penetrating weapons, warheads with increased radiation, and warheads with minimum residual radiation. Reduced-yield warheads are also possible with improved delivery accuracy.

Earth Penetrators

Earth penetrators and Atomic Demolition Munitions (ADMs) are useful primarily against ground motion or cratering sensitive targets. ADMs have been in the tactical weapon inventory for some years, with a primary utility for barrier or denial operations. The combination of improved delivery accuracy and modern earth-penetrating weapon technology may provide a similar capability without the need for prechambering or rapid hole-digging capability that the ADMs require for producing effective craters. Some features of earth penetrators are shown in Figure 11. Burial allows the use of lower yields to create a given-size crater, which provides a major reduction in collateral effects.

Nuclear Weapon Type	Advantages
Earth penetrators	Reduced yield possible Enhanced cratering efficiency compared to surface bursts
Increased radiation	Antipersonnel capability Minimizes blast collateral damage
Minimum residual radiation	Minimizes fallout
Smaller yields	Reduces collateral damage

Figure 10
Examples of Tactical Nuclear Modernization Programs

Penetrations of greater than 50 m have been achieved in wet soils. Penetration of 7 m of soil covered by ⅓ m of concrete has also been demonstrated. Earth penetrator tests in a dry lake bed in the western United States show that the vehicle survives penetration to 6 m at a high entry velocity. One shot penetrated extremely hard and compacted soil, almost as hard as a concrete runway. Tests have also been conducted in areas more typical of European soils.

A series of high-explosive cratering detonations were conducted in Louisiana during 1973 and 1974, which directly simulated a 20-ton ADM detonated in wet soil. The data can also be readily applied to low-yield penetrators. One detonation was at a depth of 6 m. An unmanned camera station was 200 m from the detonation, and ½-m clay chunks landed at this range. The crater dimensions, 48 m wide and four m deep, were affected by a high water table. That is, the crater was quite broad and shallow. A second crater, 36 m wide and 7 m deep, was produced by a detonation at a 12-m depth of burst. This is a typical crater shape for deeply buried detonations where there is no water table effect.

—Major reduction of fallout achieved through reduced yield

—Additional fallout reduction achieved due to deep burial

—Weapons designed to penetrate earth at high velocity

—Penetrations greater than 50 m achieved in wet soil

—Improved delivery accuracy makes possible remote delivery of earth penetrators (EP) for atomic demolition munition (ADM) role

Figure 11
Earth Penetrator Characteristics

Increased Radiation Weapons

A second example of possible weapon modernization is increased radiation warheads. Radiation has its greatest effect on targets involving people. The nuclear radiation lethality distance of a low-yield weapon

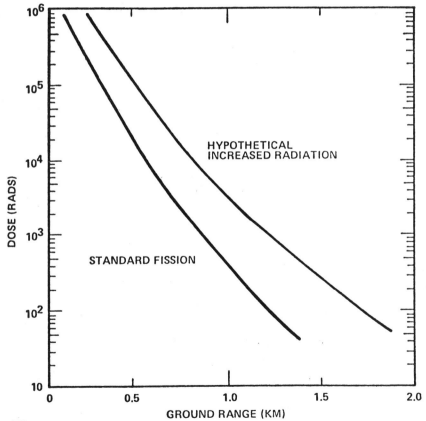

Figure 12
Variations of Dose with Range for 1-kt Weapons Burst at 61 m

with increased radiation is substantially larger than that of a low-yield normal fission weapon. Figure 12 is a graph of the radiation dose experienced by an unprotected person standing at the indicated horizontal distance from two nuclear bursts of 1 kt detonated 60 m above ground level. The lower curve represents a normal fission weapon. The upper curve applies to a hypothetical increased radiation weapon. Two features of the curves should be noted. First, for military targeting doses of interest, i.e., 500-10,000 rads, a rough rule of thumb is that the tailored weapon gives about ten times the dose at a given distance of the normal weapon. Conversely, the radiation effect from an increased-radiation weapon of 1 kt is equivalent to that from a fission weapon of 10 kt. For collateral damage (say 150 rads to an unprotected person) for the same yield (1 kt), the tailored weapon has a radius of 1,600 m while the normal weapon has about 1,150 m.

Figure 13 plots the lethal radius due to prompt radiation from hypo-

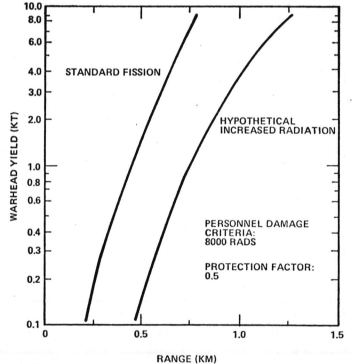

Figure 13

Lethal Radius of Warheads Against Tanks

thetical increased radiation and normal nuclear weapons parametrically for yields of 100 tons to 10 kt. The "lethality" criterion was set at 8,000 rads to crews inside the tanks. At a given distance from ground zero, the tailored effects weapon has the same lethal power as a normal weapon of ten times the yield, or alternatively, a tailored weapon of a given yield has a lethal radius about 300 to 500 m greater than a normal weapon of the same yield.

Figure 14 deals with collateral damage. It shows the comparative

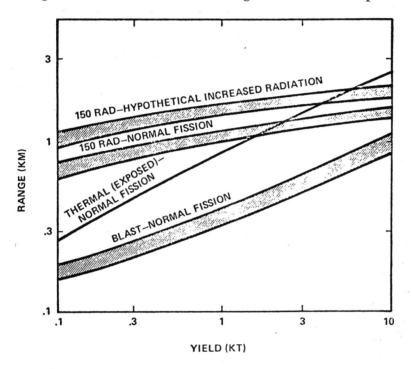

Figure 14

Variation of Collateral Damage Range with Yield

effects of hypothetical increased radiation and normal fission warheads against personnel. The width of the radiation and blast curves represent varying degrees of sheltering. The top of the radiation curve is for exposed personnel; the bottom, for people who are sheltered in home basements. The thermal curve applies to exposed personnel. The injury levels at the indicated ranges would be severe enough to require some degree of care for about half the people exposed at that range. For people in the open, nuclear radiation is the most important collateral damage mechanism for yields below about 2 kt (normal fission) or 6 kt (increased radiation).

As previously stated, a given military radiation lethality distance required an increased radiation warhead of only 1/10 the yield of a normal fission warhead. If the possible collateral effects from a 10-kt normal fission warhead are compared with those of a hypothetical 1-kt increased radiation warhead, we see that, for exposed personnel, the possible collateral damage ratio is about 2,500/7,600 in radius. Thus, for equal military lethality, the potential collateral damage area is reduced by a factor of 2.4. However, if some shelter against thermal radiation is available, then radiation would be the controlling factor in the 10-kt case, and the comparative collateral damage range is slightly greater for the increased radiation weapons. It should, therefore, not be considered a panacea for battlefield use, although in some situations, where civilians have been evacuated or are adequately sheltered, the increased radiation warhead could be of advantage from the point of view of significantly reduced blast collateral damage.

Of course, the data shown on these charts and the conclusions which followed them are conditional upon the collateral damage criteria used. If it is assumed that all civilians are behind some cover, then the effect would be to lower the "thermal" line, with radiation probably dominating throughout. Alternatively, if the population is in deep shelters, the radiation lines would be lowered and we would be concerned about fires or structural collapse of buildings. These are a few of the complexities associated with nuclear weapon planning and targeting.

Minimum Residual Radiation Weapons

A third modernization program we are working on is that of reducing radioactivity created from a surface burst. This is sometimes referred to as minimum residual radioactivity (MRR). MRR nuclear explosives were developed for the excavation program of project Plowshare. These devices have a low fission fraction and may also have a reduced neutron output compared to standard fission weapons, in order to reduce activation of soil. They provide an advantage in reducing collateral damage when employed in surface or subsurface burst modes against blast, ground motion, or cratering-sensitive targets. For a given yield they offer no improvement in damage effectiveness compared to normal fission weapons, but they do reduce collateral damage from fallout and to a lesser extent from prompt radiation. MRR effects cannot be achieved without some weight penalty, however, and weapon yields cannot always be reduced as much as might be desired.

Low-Yield Warheads

Finally, as already mentioned, precision-guidance developments permit the use of smaller yields to achieve desired military effects. The increased accuracy could also allow conventional warheads to replace nuclear warheads against some targets. Recent discussion of the possibility of replacing or renewing some of the current theater nuclear weapon stockpile with very low yield accurately delivered weapons has included nuclear weapons with yields of tens of tons to perhaps a few hundred tons. Aside from the political problems associated with such low-yield weapons, there are a number of technical and economic reasons why they do not appear particularly attractive. In the first place, they are uneconomical both from the standpoint of usage of fissile material and from that of delivery system requirements.

For example, in a lightweight weapon, the amount of plutonium or other fissile material required to achieve a 10-ton yield is not significantly less than that required to achieve a yield near a kiloton. One would not want to squander such a limited asset as fissile material by a proliferation of lightweight low-yield weapons. It is obvious that a certain mass of fissile material is required in order to achieve a critical mass in a nuclear weapon. It is also obvious that a somewhat smaller mass of fissile material may be used to achieve a given yield if the implosion system is made larger and heavier. If an attempt is made to improve the efficiency of the use of fissile material, it must be paid for by increased size and weight in the delivery system. Very low yield nuclear weapons do not appear technically attractive, either from the economics of the use of fissile material or from that of delivery system requirements.

From the standpoint of target damage, yields in the kiloton range have a sufficiently large damage area to be of interest for area targets such as dispersed troops or armored units. Ten-ton weapons have kill ranges so small that they may be useful only for attacking a single tank.

(Yields are illustrative; can be increased or decreased.)

Bombs or Air-to-Surface Missiles (ASM)

Yield	1 kt or 10 kt
Accuracy (CEP)	10 m or 50 m

Surface-to-Surface Missiles

Range	up to 700 km
Yield	1 kt or 10 kt
Accuracy (CEP)	50 m

Artillery

Range	up to 30 km
Yields	.1 kt, 1 kt

Figure 15
General Characteristics of New Weapons

A lower yield limit of about a kiloton for a standard nuclear weapon would provide a number of advantages. It would be fairly efficient from the standpoint of usage of fissile materials. It would also be efficient from the standpoint of delivery system requirements. It would provide a sufficiently large damage area for a number of military targets. And it would maintain a clear gap between the capabilities of nuclear and conventional weapons.

At the same time, improved delivery accuracy would permit current high-yield nuclear weapons to be replaced by weapons in the kiloton-yield range, which would greatly reduce the collateral damage potential of the current nuclear weapon stockpile, while maintaining its effectiveness for producing target damage. Thus it appears that improved tactical nuclear warheads with yields in the kiloton range would be desirable from a number of standpoints. The "mininukes" with tens of tons of yield do not appear to be particularly interesting from any technical standpoint.

Summary of New Nuclear Weapon Technology

These new technologies can be translated into weapons with the general characteristics and capabilities shown in Figure 15. These yields and accuracies could also: (1) apply to earth-penetrating warheads which would improve cratering (and reduce fallout due to reduced yield); (2) include MRR for laydown bombs which would reduce fallout; and (3) include increased radiation warheads which would provide anti-personnel weapons, minimize blast, and reduce collateral damage.

By improved accuracy and by tailoring of weapon effects, employing technology available, it is possible to effect significant changes in the characteristics of nuclear weapon systems.

NUCLEAR AND CONVENTIONAL MUNITIONS: SOME COMPARISONS

Nuclear and nonnuclear weapon comparisons are in general fairly difficult. One problem is the different effects involved. It is almost impossible to make a one-to-one comparison between fatalities produced by radiation and those produced by fragments and blast. In a limited number of cases, it is possible to make a comparison on the basis of the free field environments created by the two types of weapons. Whereas all neutrons can be characterized by their quantity and energy, a description of a fragment pattern or a shaped charge is much more complex.

The target damage capability of conventional weapons can be determined by conducting large numbers of tests. This has led to a proliferation of data describing the effectiveness of a given weapon when used in a given mode against a given target. The amount of nuclear weapons testing, on the other hand, has been very limited, making it necessary to use a different approach. The free field environments have been measured, calculated, or estimated, and the target response to these various environments has been separately calculated or estimated from the somewhat sparse test data base. The environments and target response are then coupled to estimate the degree of target damage.

A second method of comparison is possible in a few cases when the same types of damage are produced by both types of munitions; an example of this is cratering. A third comparison is in the target damage capability of the two types of weapons. The damage area for a nuclear weapon or the mean area of effectiveness for a conventional weapon can be compared as a function of nuclear yield or conventional warhead weight. More interesting is the effective target damage area per unit weight or per unit cost of munition. The latter is important for budgetary considerations and overall cost effectiveness. The former is more important from the standpoint of the number of sorties required or the number of rounds that must be fired to achieve a given effect. Effectiveness per unit weight also strongly impacts the logistics required to support a given operation. Yet another comparison is in the total military cost to achieve a given objective. For air-delivered weapons, this includes the attrition of the aircraft plus requirements for additional defense suppression aircraft in a heavy air defense environment.

Comparison of Effects

Air blast and cratering are two effects for which direct comparisons are possible based on explosive weight for conventional munitions and yield in TNT equivalent for nuclear munitions. Nuclear munitions are slightly less efficient than conventional weapons in producing air blast, because of the large fraction of the energy which is emitted as thermal radiation. Figure 16 shows the efficiency for producing craters of the

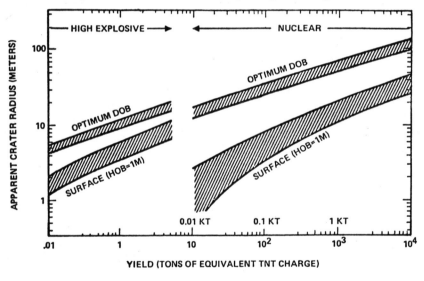

Figure 16
Comparison of Craters Produced by Nuclear and High-Explosive Warheads

two types of weapons. The width of the curves show the differences due to different media. This figure can be used to estimate the degree of damage produced in hard point targets, such as command posts, bunkers, or bridge piers, by a given weight or yield of explosive. This figure also illustrates the loss in cratering efficiency for surface burst nuclear weapons due to the energy lost as thermal radiation. High-explosive weapons can produce an equivalent size crater with almost a hundredfold decrease in explosive yield.

Collateral Damage Comparison

The collateral damage from nuclear weapons, like some conventional weapons, depends upon the criteria assumed and the degree of shelter-ing of the populace. For lightly sheltered populations and for yields less than about 10 kt, the initial radiation from a standard nuclear weapon provides a larger potential collateral damage area than blast or thermal radiation (see Figure 14). For comparison of collateral dam-age potential, the collateral damage area from a 1-kt air burst weapon is 3.9 km. Subtracting the 0.3 km^2 area of the 300-m radius area target considered earlier gives a net 3.6 km^2 of collateral damage potential. This is for a 150-rad dose inside an above-ground residence. For more heavily sheltered populations, the collateral damage would be limited by destruction of residences or by fires in urban areas.

Figure 6 indicated the potential collateral damage area for a thou-sand 2,000-lb GP bombs, which varied strongly with the delivery sys-tem accuracy, ranging from 65 km^2 with extremely poor delivery accu-racies (a factor of 18 worse than a 1-kt nuclear weapon) to about 0.6 km^2, depending on the unreliability factor (about a factor of 6 better than the nuclear case). By contrast, the nuclear potential collateral damage area is essentially independent of CEP. The effect of missing the target completely would be an increase from 3.6 to 3.9 km^2.

This comparison illustrates the tremendous collateral damage po-tential possible with conventional weapons, but is somewhat mislead-ing on several counts. First, a buffer zone of about 100 m could almost eliminate the collateral damage from accurately delivered conventional weapons, compared with a buffer zone of about 1,000 m for a 1-kt nu-clear weapon. Second, the two types of weapons should be considered from the standpoint of the dual criteria of target and collateral dam-age. If 10 psi is viewed as the target damage level for a 1-kt nuclear weapon, the damage area essentially fills the 300-m circle used in the example. By contrast, if properly placed on the right type of industrial targets, the 1,000-GP bombs could damage an area of 2 km^2—a factor of 7 larger than for the nuclear weapon. The conventional weapons can, of course, also be used in much smaller numbers in order to limit the intensity of the conflict.

Logistics Requirements

One advantage of nuclear munitions is the capability to package a large explosive yield in a lightweight package. A thousand tons of GP bombs weighs 1,000 tons. A 1-kt nuclear weapon may weigh between about 50 and 500 kg, depending on how it is packaged and on the extra weight required for the fusing system, structure, propulsion, or a parachute for retarded delivery. This immediately gives a benefit of a factor of 1,000 to 10,000 in explosive capability per unit weight. One way of demonstrating this graphically is shown in Figure 17, which is a plot

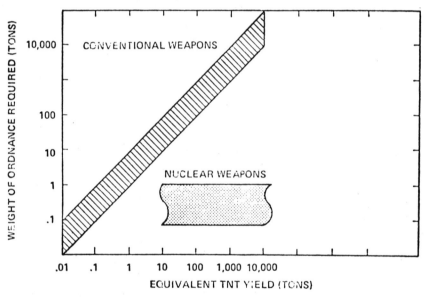

Figure 17
Weight of Ordnance Required as a Function of Equivalent TNT Yield, Conventional and Nuclear Weapons

of the weight of ordnance required as a function of the equivalent TNT yield. The bands indicate the range of variations possible with a number of different types of weapons and delivery systems. As an example of the number of sorties required to deliver a given weight of ordnance, modern aircraft can carry between about 8 and 30 tons of ordnance per plane (with less for longer ranges). A small attack (10 planes) could then deliver 80 to 300 tons. A large attack (100 planes) would be a major undertaking, delivering 800 to 3,000 tons. The large attack would be delivering a total explosive load comparable to a kiloton of nuclear yield equivalent. If accurately delivered, the conventional payload has the potential of producing much more target damage and much less collateral damage than the same explosive equivalent of nuclear yield.

Nuclear weapons do offer an advantage in providing much more explosive power per pound of ordnance, but part of this advantage is offset by the reduced effectiveness of this explosive power compared with conventional weapons.

Nuclear munitions are expensive per round, compared to conventional munitions. In 1964, the Atomic Energy Commission projected a charge of $350,000 for a 10-kt nuclear explosive,[6] although weaponized nuclear devices are much more sophisticated and therefore much more costly. By contrast, GP bombs cost in the range of $1 to $2 per pound. PGMs cost considerably more per round than GP bombs—tens to hundreds of thousands of dollars, depending on the size and complexity. One thousand 2,000-lb GP bombs would cost $1 million to $2 million. One thousand PGMs could cost at least $10 million. While these costs are greater than the cost of a kiloton nuclear explosive, the thousand conventional weapons can be more effective and can be used with more restraint.

NOTES

1. One obvious point can be made here about cost effectiveness. Precision-guided munitions in many cases are quite reasonable. More sophisticated standoff missiles can be relatively expensive. However, when the whole cost is added up for unguided munitions, the larger exposure of expensive military equipment, the tremendously higher support and logistics cost, to say nothing of the exposure of personnel, a comprehensive cost-effectiveness study has to favor precision-guided munitions.
2. See James F. Digby, *Precision Guided Munitions: Capabilities and Consequences,* Rand Paper Series P5257, June 1974.
3. The capability of integrated circuits is rapidly escalating. The number of devices per chip have gone from 50 to 10,000 in the past ten years. This not only leads to major reduction in cost, size, weight, and power con-

sumption, but reduces failure rate of the equipment ten to 100 times. The complexity continues to grow at a factor of two per chip per year. By the year 1980 we can expect to have Very Large Scale Integration (VLSI), which will allow 200,000 devices on a single 1 cm² chip.

4. Table 6B1, *Summary Technical Report of the National Defense Committee,* vol. I, "Effects of Impact and Explosion," 1946.

5. Kent Kresa and Col. William F. Kirlin, USAF, "The Mini-RPV, Big Potential . . . Small Cost," *Astronautics and Aeronautics (AIAA),* September 1974, pp. 48-62.

6. "Engineering with Nuclear Explosives," *Proceedings of the Third Plowshare Symposium* (U), TID 7695, April 1964.

CHAPTER 6

New Technologies: Some Requirements

Erik Klippenberg

Massive armies and tough soldiers are probably not the most important characteristics of the defense establishments in the Western democracies. Nor are further improvements in the standard of living and social welfare in our societies likely to increase the number of troops and their enthusiasm for necessary peacetime training for the hardships of war.

But the Western nations have been and continue to be in the forefront of technological evolution. Our strength has been our ability to take advantage of the opportunities offered by new technology and quickly turn these into equipment and weapons in the hands of our troops.

As described in Chapter 5, we are now in several technological sectors, witnessing rapid advances which already have had considerable influence on the battlefield. There can be no doubt that in the future these new technologies will have an even greater impact and that, if properly adopted, they could make a considerable contribution toward the maintenance of a credible defense.

Unjustified optimism about the extent to which new weapon technologies can solve our defense problems may, however, be just as harmful as failure to realize the advantages of well-chosen new weapons and equipment. The selection of materiel and the structuring of our defense must be based on careful studies not only of the effectiveness of new weapons, but also of their overall effect on our defense and their possible consequences, in the broadest sense of the word, for the forces we may have to face.

In the discussion of possible implications of new weapon technologies, such analyses seem, to some extent, to be lacking. Analyses of this type require both time and effort. The purpose of this chapter is to point out some of the factors which should be taken into account. Although some of the following discussion may apply equally well to nuclear weapon systems, it deals mainly with conventional weapon systems and conventional warfare.

EFFECTIVENESS OF WEAPONS AND EQUIPMENT BASED ON NEW TECHNOLOGIES

As discussed in Chapter 5, the primary sectors of technology offering significant improvements in weapon systems for conventional warfare are sensor technology and Large-Scale Integration of electronic circuits (LSI).

Electro-optical sensors working in visual, near-infrared, and far-infrared parts of the electromagnetic spectrum are now becoming available in sufficiently small and reliable versions to allow their use not only in vehicles and platforms for surveillance, but also in the seeker heads of quite small weapons. LSI now makes it possible to build considerable data-processing capacity into even small seeker heads and to increase the capability of the seeker or the surveillance equipment, electro-optical or radar, to discriminate between false and true targets and to handle several targets. Similarly, LSI makes it possible to reduce the cost and increase the reliability of telecommunication links, particulary data links.

The result of new seeker and guidance systems based on advanced sensors and LSI is greatly improved weapon delivery accuracy and the ability to deliver the weapon in darkness and under conditions of limited visibility. Chapter 5 has discussed the potential advantages of such weapons.

The crux of the greatly increased accuracy is the ability of these new weapons to make use of information received after launch, even up to the point of impact. Such information allows the weapon to derive relative positions and velocities of target and weapon and produce guidance orders for the control devices. The information is transmitted to the weapon from a weapon-control facility, from navigation stations, or from the target in the form of a radiated or reflected signal.

False signals can be injected into the receiver for purposes of deceiving or confusing the receiver or the guidance system. For example, an IR target seeker may be confused by decoys released from or positioned around the target. A radar may be deceived by similar means and by radar pulses transmitted from the target and designed to create a picture of several fictitious targets in the radar.

Signals in the form of noise can also be injected into the receiver, with the purpose of raising the threshold for detection of the wanted signals. A noise transmitter or jammer in the main lobe of a radar can deny the radar ability to measure range to the target. A sufficiently strong jammer may make it impossible for a radar even to see targets beyond a certain range.

In principle, the intensity of the interfering signal may be raised to such levels as to temporarily blind the receiver. For example, certain types of TV cameras can be temporarily blinded by directing a sufficiently strong source of light toward the camera in the nose of a missile or in a surveillance aircraft or remotely piloted vehicle.

Concentration of sufficient energy may even overload certain types of sensitive detector cells in the sensors to such an extent that they become permanently damaged. In principle, a laser may be used to burn out the IR detector cells in an IR seeker or in an IR surveillance device.

The ability of a seeker to detect and lock onto a target can also be impaired by measures intended to reduce the radiation from the target or the contrast between the target and its background. The IR radiation from jet engines on aircraft and helicopters may be reduced by shielding, and targets on the ground may be camouflaged to reduce their contrast, not only in the visual part of the spectrum of electromagnetic radiation, but in other parts of the spectrum as well.

As seekers and guidance systems become more intelligent through increased information-processing capacity aboard the weapons, weapon platforms, or surveillance vehicles, effective camouflage, deception, and disturbance will become more difficult. But if these new weapons and means of surveillance turn out to be as effective as it now appears, considerable effort must be expected from our opponents to curtail their performance.

The last thing we should do is base our defense planning on the assumption that performance in war will match peacetime performance at test ranges. There are several examples of systems which initially were sold on the basis of their peacetime performance, but which later turned out to be vulnerable to interference and had to have their expected wartime performance downgraded accordingly. This appears to have been the case with the troposcatter systems for military telecommunication. More recent examples may also be found in other fields.

It is also conceivable that the effectiveness of laser-guided weapons could be significantly reduced by installation on potential targets of suitable sensors which would provide warning of laser illumination and activate measures to interfere with the target picture as seen by the weapon seeker.

The threat of countermeasures in the broadest sense of the word, however, should not lead us to believe that the effectiveness of new and very accurate weapons will be completely nullified. Under special circumstances and for a short period this may happen to a small number of weapon systems. But there is no reason why we should let it happen to the majority of our systems.

The West has the necessary technological basis for developing modifications to reduce the effectiveness of countermeasures, and industrial and organizational capacity and flexibility to implement such improvements quickly. Given the political will to make use of these resources, and provided current efforts for standardization within the alliance do not burden us with an unwieldy bureaucracy incapable of reacting quickly to new countermeasure threats, we should be justified in expecting reasonable effectiveness of our new weapons and equipment, even though they do not perform as well in combat as on the test range.

EAST-WEST INTERACTIONS AS A CONSEQUENCE OF NEW TECHNOLOGY

The introduction of new and more effective weapon systems in NATO forces will, of course, influence the way the Warsaw Pact (WP) decides to equip and use their forces. The development, production, and equipment of operational forces with significant quantities of new weapons requires several years. Our potential adversaries will undoubtedly keep themselves reasonably well informed about this process and, if they deem it necessary, will take steps to equip their forces with similar weapons or weapons designed to reduce the effects of new weapons on our side.

Similarly, and with less delay, the WP may react to the introduction of new weapon systems in NATO forces with new tactics designed to reduce the effects of improvements on our side. For example, new guided antitank weapons in their basic versions seem to be quite vulnerable. New and more effective area weapons against soft targets such as antitank weapons and their crews may quickly cause sufficient attrition of antitank weapons to reduce their power considerably. Unless the new antitank weapons are given some form of physical protection, the endurance of antitank units may be quite limited. The same argument appears to hold for the new man-carried air defense missiles.

An assessment of the potential effect on NATO's defense posture must take into account these kinds of possible action-reaction relationships between NATO and WP forces. Any sound analysis of how NATO could best take advantage of new weapon technology would, of course, take into account technological and tactical options on both sides. It would probably not be unreasonable to expect that such two-sided analyses would moderate somewhat the expectations about the effects of new weapon technology.

LIMITED DEFENSE BUDGETS AND THE COST OF NEW WEAPONS

In spite of the fact that the Soviet Union continuously improves its force posture, defense budgets in most of the NATO nations do not show any significant increase in real terms. In some cases, there may even be a trend toward reduction in buying power.

At the same time, new weapons and equipment become increasingly more expensive, even after subtraction of cost increases normally ascribed to inflation. In consecutive generations of weapons designed to cover the same functions, the later generation has a tendency to become more sophisticated and therefore more expensive than its predecessor. For new weapon systems designed to take advantage of new technology and to cover broader functions than their predecessors, the increases in unit cost are even higher. Higher unit cost tends to reduce the numbers produced, which again increases the unit cost.

At the same time, operating costs for present defense forces, at least in some nations, seem to increase faster than the average inflation in the national economies. The reasons are perhaps not fully understood. One contributing factor may be the increased standard of living of our societies, which brings about pressures for better quarters for officers and men, better recreational options, shorter working hours, and so on. Another factor is increased maintenance costs as a result of more sophisticated equipment.

The unavoidable result is that the number of units of next-generation weapons which can be acquired has to be smaller than for the present generation. As long as the number of units can be maintained above a certain minimum, such reductions may be quite acceptable because the increased effectiveness outweighs the effect of smaller numbers.

However, the extent of the geography to be defended sets a certain lower limit to the number of units which are required. If the quantity of a certain weapon system which can be accommodated within the defense budget becomes less than the critical threshold set by geography, simple cost/effectiveness arguments become meaningless. Assessments of new weapon systems then have to be undertaken in a broader context, and the outcome is likely to be a preference for the less sophisticated systems, which have more limited performance, but can be acquired in meaningful quantities.

It would appear that unless defense budgets can be increased, several NATO nations would be well advised to examine carefully not only the direct cost/effectiveness ratios for new weapon systems, but also the question of whether a sufficient number of the new systems can be acquired to exceed the geographical threshold. If not, the "less sophisticated and more numerous" concept is probably to be preferred.

CHAPTER 7

Precision Weapons: Lowering the Risks with Aimed Shots and Aimed Tactics

James Digby

This chapter deals with the implications of precision weapons being widely available and with the opportunities for greater security opened up by these weapons. It deals both with how each superpower might project its power by the threat of using weapons of precisely controlled effects against the forces or homeland of the other—including threats of nuclear use—and with how precision weapons could be used in wars removed from those homelands, especially nonnuclear wars. It will say more on the second kind of use—with special reference to NATO's Central Front—than on the first. It also discusses the use of these weapons by the smaller countries, current trends in arms transfers, and some ideas for arms control which the new weapons suggest. The theme of the discussion is that strategies must be developed which cut risks by seeking carefully delimited goals, by trying for anticipated responses by the opponent—and that technology now facilitates these strategies by permitting military power to be applied precisely.

HAS THE HIGH-WATER MARK OF UNAIMED WEAPONS AND VAGUE WAR GOALS PASSED?

"Every bullet has its billet." When William III said that, he was undoubtedly thinking more of the workings of Almighty Providence than of the perfection of aiming mechanisms. In fact, in the ensuing two and a half centuries, military men came to regard their projectiles and bombs as so cheap and so plentiful that a large fraction of them were sent out without aiming at specific targets. Tactics grew up around the notion of aiming at areas which contained hidden targets, where movement could be inhibited, or where opponents might be frightened into submissiveness.

Our century has seen a great intensification of such tactics: the 1916 devastation of the approaches to Verdun as soldiers lay hidden in trenches, the terror bombings of English cities in 1940, the Hamburg raids of 1943, and the bombings from high-flying B-52s against guerillas hidden by the vegetation of Vietnam. Moreover, the development of the atomic bomb soon led to the ultimate in the strategy of threatening generalized destruction—as opposed to threats or use of weapons to gain specific advantages—and we now have the doctrine of mutual assured destruction of unnamed Soviet and American population centers as the paradoxical central (or overhanging) feature of every major military plan.[1]

But the high-water stage of the unspecific munition and of the corresponding generalized threat may have passed. The reader can consider this possibility as he reads the more detailed discussions in this chapter and elsewhere in this book. The decade of the seventies has already given several signals. There were the sensational results of using laser-guided bombs in Vietnam in 1972, where difficult targets were hit in one or two sorties—by forces who had been given strong injunctions against damage to nontargets—where dozens of sorties and hundreds of bombs would have been required without the precision (of the order of 10 m) of the "smart bombs." The reports of these bombings were coming in just as more precise war aims of the combatants were being laboriously, if ambiguously, codified in the Paris talks. Then, the Middle East war of October 1973 showed the importance of precision-guided antitank and antiaircraft weapons (and also the importance of taking their crews under fire). As to the war aims of the two sides, the removed observer sees the tragic difficulty of negotiating between Israel, whose government—if not all its masses—has mainly specific aims, and the Arabs, whose governments—impelled by the masses—seek mainly the nonspecific aims of restoring self-respect and national glory. But some observers believe the Egyptian *military*, by contrast, used its new weapons to achieve quite precise territorial aims;[2] otherwise, matters might have become even more hopelessly snarled.

It was also in the seventies that we saw precision-guided munitions mass-produced by the thousands, many at prices between $1,000 and $10,000. For some of these, only modest training and a minimum of maintenance are required. And for NATO, the last few years have seen a wave of hope—suitably cautious—that the new weapons might, if imbedded in a suitably structured force, be able to stand off the masses of Soviet armor without resort to nuclear weapons (see Chapter 12).

The seventies have also brought developments in the intercontinental nuclear confrontation. The adequacy of the generalized threat of destruction was questioned in Fred C. Iklé's paper, "Can Nuclear Deterrence Last Out the Century?"[3] and then, officially, by Secretary Schlesinger, who, after observing that the Soviet Union had sufficient forces to reinforce its political ambitions with selective strikes, and noting that threats against our nuclear forces might call for an option to respond in kind against military forces, suggested:[4]

> To the extent that we have selective response options—smaller and more precisely focused than in the past—we should be able to deter such challenges.

At the same time, technical developments promise to give the superpowers the means to carry out precisely controlled and highly specific operations against the opponent's homeland: cruise missiles that could go 1,000 miles or more and be guided accurately by terrain contour matching; map matching which might guide ICBM warheads to within tens of feet; maneuverable reentry vehicles (presumably the Soviet SS-NX-13 has this ability); and quick retargeting devices (such as the Minuteman III Command Data Buffer).

About all these developments—both for nuclear and for nonnuclear conflicts—we must ask:

1. How well do the new weapons work? Will their use by a defense which is suitably structured contain an offense without substantially expanding the level of violence or scope of conflict? For example, if WP armor moves on a NATO objective with no use of nuclear weapons, distant sea power, space warfare, or out-of-the-area bombing, can NATO repel the thrust with similarly limited means? Will pre-

cision nonnuclear weapons be on hand in sufficient strength to reduce the temptation to escalate to nuclear conflict?

2. Some military incidents involving the NATO and WP powers may be inevitable, given many years of confrontation. But can the major powers devise strategies which are to the interest of both parties to a confrontation, but which inhibit the widening of conflicts? To what extent can the two superpowers make their military forces usable, when great pressures demand, while retaining mutually understood firebreaks?

3. If limitations are indeed observed, can the military confrontations be resolved without great damage to nonmilitary targets? Without attempts to "break the enemy's will to resist"? This question is of interest, for example, both with respect to a large-scale nonnuclear war in Europe and with respect to limited nuclear attacks on the United States and Soviet Union.

4. Will the physical effects of the weapons used convey the intended message clearly—or will their failure to bring about all the planned damage and their inadvertent unplanned damage blur the true intent of their user? This question is of particular importance in considering limited nuclear conflict.

These are some of the criteria to consider in thinking of tactics which use weapons of the kinds described in the next section.

WHAT ARE PRECISION-GUIDED MUNITIONS?

The original laser-guided bombs, along with similar TV-guided bombs, were informally called "smart bombs." Pentagon officials soon decided to include them in a larger class of "Precision-Guided Munitions" (PGMs) and included rocket-powered and gun-launched rounds as well as bombs, with the word "munitions" implying a detonation at the target. In a recent Adelphi Paper[5] I put forward (rather hesitantly) a definition of a PGM which I modify slightly here:

> A guided munition whose probability of making a direct hit on its target at full range (when unopposed) is greater than a half. According to the type of PGM, the target may be a tank, ship, radar, bridge, airplane, or other concentration of value.[6]

Perhaps the term can be further defined by citing examples of weapons which most analysts would agree are PGMs, although the one-half hit probability may be obtained only by select crews operating under ideal conditions for some of these. You will notice that a very wide scope is included.[7]

Grail and SA-7 are NATO designations for a Soviet antiaircraft missile that can be fired from the shoulder. It has an infrared seeker and probably works best against subsonic aircraft flying lower than 1,500 meters (though improved versions are said to be effective against faster and higher aircraft).

TOW BGM-71A is an American-made antitank missile of either 3,000 or 3,750 m maximum range. It is launched from a tripod on the ground, or (usually) from a vehicle, and guided semiautomatically by signals sent along two thin wires reeled off bobbins; these signals make it steer toward a line of sight created as its gunner simply follows his target through a telescope. The Soviet Sagger AT-3 is similar in purpose, but requires more training, since its gunner must follow both missile and target, and must fly the missile into the target.

SA-6 (Gainful) is a larger, vehicle-mounted Soviet antiaircraft missile guided by a dual-frequency radar, with guidance commands transmitted by radio.[8] Egypt, Syria, and North Vietnam also operate SA-6s.

Sidewinder AIM-9 is the family name of an air-to-air missile developed by the US Naval Weapons Center. The AIM-9L is currently nearing production. It has an infrared seeker cooled by a blow-down gas bottle, weighs about 84 kg, and has an extended effective range. Many Western countries use various versions of the Sidewinder.

Maverick AGM-65A is an antitank missile now carried by USAF close-support aircraft. It is guided by a television camera in the missile's nose; once the flight crew lines up the cross hairs of the sight, they can actuate a lock-on switch and the circuits on board the missile automatically track the target. After launch, the aircraft can leave or take on other targets. This not only speeds up the aircraft's rate of fire, but permits it to avoid close-in air defenses. A developmental version uses a laser seeker instead of television.

CLGP—Cannon-Launched Guided Projectile is a US Army developmental project for guiding a 155-mm howitzer round; the projectile carries a laser receiver which provides steering. The projectile is made to home on a spot from a laser illuminator (or designator) which could be operated by a nearby ground or air observer.[9]

GBU-15—Modular Glide Weapons System is a USAF development built around a winged 2,000-lb bomb. As the name implies, its guidance modules can be switched according to the situation. The GBU-15 would use both DME guidance and the laser seeker devised for Maverick to steer an unpowered winged bomb to a target up to 60 miles away. Improved warheads would permit destroying hard concrete structures or runways.[10]

HARM—High-Speed Anti-Radiation Missile AGM-88A is a rocket-powered missile which homes on targets (like missile radars) that emit radio-frequency signals. It is a joint development of the US Air Force and US Navy.

Condor AGM-53A is a rocket-powered US Navy antiship missile, now in pilot production. It can be guided in its terminal phase as a remotely piloted vehicle (RPV) by an operator on the mother aircraft, who sees a relayed television picture from the missile's camera. (Other guidance options are also being developed.)

Shaddock SS-N-3 is the NATO designation for a Soviet antiship cruise missile; Shaddock and its derivatives can be launched from surfaced submarines or from surface vessels. Originally one saw estimates of 200 n mi range, but improved technology would seem to permit much longer aerodynamic ranges. *Jane's*[11] notes that this missile, in some cases, requires aid in guidance from an aircraft, and that "there is evidence that the missile may be programmed for shorter ranges and have an active radar terminal homing capability." It is said to carry either an HE or a nuclear warhead.

Pershing II is a US Army nuclear ballistic missile, with a range of 400 n mi, in development. Its inertial guidance system can be supplemented by a terminal homing reentry vehicle which uses a radar map-matching technique. An option will be a low-yield earth penetrator warhead for use against hard targets. Secretary Schlesinger pointed out its possibilities for reducing collateral damage and for replacing the more vulnerable QRA aircraft.[12]

SLCM—Sea Launched Cruise Missile YBGM-109 is a US Navy developmental program which includes a tactical antiship version and a longer-range strategic version. The tactical SLCM uses radar-seeker guidance from the earlier Harpoon, but extends Harpoon's 60-plus n mi range to about 300 n mi. The strategic version would have the even greater range of 1,300 to 2,000 n mi; it would supplement carrier-based strike aircraft. It carries an inertial guidance system which is corrected periodically by a terrain contour matching device. This permits great accuracy in attacking targets whose location is known with respect to known terrain, even though they may be quite distant from the launch point.[13]

Terminally Guided ICBMs are presaged by the US maneuverable reentry vehicle developments and the Soviet SS-NX-13.[14] These could lead to reentry vehicles steered by terrain contour matching or map matching which might be accurate to less than 100 ft. Since payloads of advanced HE warheads weighing 2,000 lbs or so could be carried, even moderately hard targets could be destroyed without using nuclear weapons.

Thus the variety of precision-guided munitions is great. Some—like the surface-to-air and air-to-air types—have been around for years. For others, the novelty is their simplicity or their producibility. RPVs are included in the category if they are intended to hit a target, and these seem to be of increasing military importance.

Let me repeat here two statements (slightly revised) I have made previously about PGMs:

> Accuracy is no longer a strong function of range; if a target can be acquired and followed during the required aiming process, it can usually be hit. For many targets hitting is equivalent to destroying.

The second statement may be just as important:

> Precision-guided munitions can now be mass-produced in great quantity; for many of these the cost per round ranges from the order of $2,000 to the order of $20,000. Moreover, many can be operated by ordinary soldiers.

Examination of the properties of PGMs gives an interesting insight into the obsolescence of some familiar ways of categorizing weapons and missions. In Chapter 11, Henry Rowen and Albert Wohlstetter tell why they believe the familiar labels "strategic missions" and "tactical missions" impede thought more than they help it. Contemplation of the variety of jobs that can be done by such types as Shaddock, Condor, the SLCM, and terminally guided ICBM confirms this view. As mentioned, munitions which can be terminally guided can be nearly as accurate at great ranges as at short ranges. They are quite indifferent to the means of transport that brought them to the launch point. Quite similar 1,000-mi cruise missiles could be launched from a land vehicle, a small ship, a "strategic" SSBN, or a B-52. Moreover, identical vehicles

162   *James Digby*

could carry nuclear payloads or enough nonnuclear explosives of modern design to do many of the more precisely defined military jobs. There would seem to be a strong suggestion in all this that future military forces will be designed not around their means of transport—air, land, or sea—nor around the old designations of strategic forces and tactical forces, but rather around the kind of targets to be found and attacked, the numbers of those targets, how they are located, and the problems of reaching them. For example, the job of attacking airbases might be handled by PGMs launched from the land or the sea as well as the air, and one can see that it might be institutionally efficient to allocate funds for these systems from a common task-oriented budget.

In the next section I shall discuss briefly the implications of modern weapon systems for use in conflicts directly involving the two superpowers, but where only a few, or a few dozen, targets are attacked; to identify this kind of war I shall revive the label *limited central war*. Later I discuss their implications for *large-scale nonnuclear war*, especially one which is regionally limited. Much of the real interest in this discussion is in the *potential* of the weapon systems and postures: how does their possession permit the projection of power or the calling of bluffs? It is less my intent here to contemplate these systems' actual use.

PRECISION WEAPONS FOR LIMITED CENTRAL WAR— NUCLEAR OR NONNUCLEAR

Later in this book Rowen and Wohlstetter discuss several classes of mission where response is matched to circumstances. Consider from their category "cross-border responses countrywide" two hypothetical examples: (1) a Soviet Union (SU) attack in 1980 by submarine-launched terminally guided cruise missiles on ten US naval bases, including SSBN facilities, and (2) a US attack in the same year by ICBMs on ten Soviet industrial plants supplying critical military needs. The important considerations of context, probable response, etc., are beyond the scope of this chapter. Here we assume that these considerations have led the national command authorities of each side to conclude that the destruction of just those ten targets and nothing else is the best way to terminate or de-escalate a conflict and at the same time to serve their national interest. Our question here is: What properties of weapon systems are desired?

1. Each weapon must have a high probability of damaging its target.

2. Each weapon must have a low probability of damaging non-targets. (Rowen and Wohlstetter call 1 and 2 the "dual criteria" and relate it to making a mission's intent precise and clear. The weapon properties implied are high accuracy, high reliability, and low bias (or systematic) errors in weapon guidance. The warhead should be well tailored to its job in explosive power, height of burst, etc. Additionally, it would be useful to be able to know just what damage was done.)
3. It would be desirable to monitor the weapon en route and to be able to divert or recall it if it goes astray or if the national authorities decided at the last minute to cancel the attack.
4. Preferably the attack itself should not generate serious new political problems. For example, it should not require overflying noninvolved countries or using en route bases in such countries.
5. The attack should not, in effect, suggest that the opponent lop off an arm in retaliation for the loss of a finger. For example, the United States would be lowering inhibitions against nuclear attacks on carriers all over the world if it had obviously launched a limited nuclear attack from a single carrier.

Consider the application of criteria 1 through 5 to a 2,000-mile cruise missile, US or SU, with guidance equal to the US SLCM (but with a command override), in the previously mentioned attack on ten targets. First one must ask if an appropriate target set far enough removed from population centers can be found within the missile's range. The missile system performance would be examined in terms of its surviving the air defenses and maintaining—without being jammed or deceived—its data link connection to its controller, two of the most difficult features to ensure. On the other hand, its accuracy should be good, it could be monitored en route, and, if sea-launched it need not generate political side effects. Its launcher could probably be reloaded; if it were an SLCM its launching platform could not easily be targeted.

What are some of the implications for overall force designs which encompass the weapons for limited nuclear and nonnuclear options (LNOs and LNNOs) for limited central war? Some ideas can be put forward on a very speculative basis—not as conclusions.

First, for some years to come, these forces may be drawn from existing forces by providing special plans, special training, and relatively low-cost extra gear (communications gear, for example). There may be designated elite units prepared to accept the unexpected. At the least these units must be relatively invulnerable to attack, and capable of being withheld for days or weeks.

Second, provisions for weapon reloading will be important. The employer of an LNO or LNNO does not want to appear weaker for very long because of the drawdown of his forces. This could militate against using SLBMs and in favor of cold-launched ICBMs (which do not do much damage to silos).

Third, the provision of a survivable and quick reacting intelligence, command, and control system tied in to the political authorities must be an integral part of the LNO-LNNO force. It will probably be impossible to keep a full staff of experts on tap for all likely limited options. But it will not be too hard to plan the physical facilities for a battle control room, to plan the communications circuits to task forces, and to plan how to provide it with near-real-time intelligence and reconnaissance.

IMPLICATIONS OF PRECISION WEAPONS FOR A LARGE-SCALE NONNUCLEAR WAR

Earlier, I put forward two statements about PGMs—that their accuracy is not a strong function of range, and that they can be produced and used in great quantity. Here I will set forth some implications of those statements for large-scale nonnuclear war. To begin with, these implications will be stated in simple terms, and as if PGMs would work about the way their designers intended. Then some complications will be mentioned, and some comments on the degree to which the simple ideas apply in the practical world.

First, it will probably become much less desirable to concentrate a great deal of military value in one place or in one vehicle. For instance, a combatant would be less likely to want to place a large fraction of his capability at risk as he exposes a single transport airplane, or a single surface vessel in the Mediterranean. He would probably prefer to have *many* inexpensive lightly armored vehicles instead of *fewer* more expensive tanks. Consider that the attacker has a limited number of PGMs, any one of which has a high probability of destroying either a valuable or less valuable target.[15] It is better to force him to spread his PGMs over many targets: he will strain *his* supply more and will face the difficulties of target acquisition more times.

Second, concealment will become much more important, and thus concentrations of many vehicles or men will be less practical. Concentrations will usually be easier to see and to keep track of than a larger number of independently moving targets. This is critical, because with PGMs, seeing a target can usually lead to its destruction. Smallness and mobility will make hiding easier, and both these qualities are consistent with the thrust of the first point. However, before arriving at a final judgment, one must consider the degree to which the concentration can be sheltered, or protected by active defenses, by comparison with sheltering or protecting dispersed elements.

This is a point of major importance in assessing the balance between an offense and a defense because a classical offensive tactic is to attempt overwhelming superiority in a narrow sector by concentrating forces there.

There have always been reasons why a commander should worry about having great force concentrations, but even the availability of tactical nuclear weapons did not, in practice, result in a full set of corresponding actions to decrease vulnerability. The tactical planner may have had some excuse for inaction because of the uncertainty about whether tactical nuclear weapons would be used. For PGMs, though, there is no question of their being used, given fighting, and no planner can any longer responsibly pass over their effect on his vulnerabilities.

Third, even small units can be very powerful when equipped with PGMs or designators that can call in and guide remote PGMs; these units might carry air defense weapons as well. In land warfare the natural size of many independently mobile squads might be three or four men, and these squads might get around by walking or by using inexpensive vehicles, *not* expensive tanks.[16] There would be a problem of protecting such units from conventional overrunning attacks by infantry, but their mobility and their ability to call in PGM firepower—or remotely launched missiles with area coverage—would help.

Fourth, a fraction of the munitions used need not be hauled all the way to the FEBA in systems where the units up front serve as spotters and designators; the munitions they call in might be ground- or air-launched from tens of kilometers farther back. Over a wide range of types of conflict, the weight of munitions delivered to the launch point *for a given effect* on enemy forces need not be nearly as great as in the past, because each round fired has a high probability of killing its targets.

Fifth, and relevant to the ideas at the start of this chapter, a natural consequence of having a high hit probability is that collateral damage to civil populations and economies is likely to be much less with precision munitions. In the NATO case, this prospect may have substantial consequences over the long run for German attitudes toward preparations for actual fighting on German territory in contrast to preparations that are part of a trip wire strategy. But a German concession would be much less likely if precision-guided "mininukes" were under consideration, a factor which is in addition to the negative aspects of mininukes in blurring the firebreak, as mentioned below.

Sixth, ground-based antiaircraft defenses have become extremely lethal. The Soviet SA-6 is an example of a powerful way to keep air off the backs of mobile units, and proves the operational feasibility of this class of weapons. The October War showed how such air defenses, as well as systems like the ZSU-23-4 four-barrel gun and the hand-held SA-7, are likely to be proliferated in great numbers over the area occupied by ground troops.

The lighter of these classes of weapons may well be added to the mobile squads mentioned above, and the heavier may travel with them, along with the antitank weapons. The end result of this trend may be a shift in how ground forces are protected against enemy air. More of the protection is likely to come from ground-based antiaircraft defenses, and less from attacks on enemy air bases and air-to-air duels.

These six trends will clearly have a major effect on forces and tactics for nonnuclear war. But the consequences of PGMs are too important for an opponent to permit them to be used as their owners wish; in addition, there are a number of practical complications.

To begin with, the technology for accurate guidance that is most fully developed requires transmission through the atmosphere in or near the visible spectrum. Simple radar guidance is not sufficiently accurate. Thus many present systems do not work at night or through smoke, clouds, or heavy dust. Systems using long-wave infrared will be in widespread use by 1980. These will be useful at night and will do fairly well through smoke, dust, and haze, but they will be fairly expensive and may be significantly harder to maintain in the field. Nevertheless, the majority of PGMs will require clear daylight for many years.

Another problem is command and control. In past wars, commanders tens of miles behind the front concerned themselves with entire enemy divisions or, at the smallest, battalions. With PGMs a division may consist of 500 separately targetable, individually moving objects. Rather than succumb to the temptation to handle this problem with data-processing technology from a centralized operations room, my own judgment is that much of the solution should be found in the delegation of authority and the use of standing procedures, even though the officers doing the detailed weapon control may well be many kilometers away from the target.

A third complication is that if the units near the FEBA become too small, or too mobile, or too well-hidden to target, then the natural tendency will be to target depots and other valuable concentrations in the rear-area support structure. Thus, there is likely to be a shift to targets farther and farther back as the missiles able to handle this job become more practical; *finding* the targets is a crucial part of the job. Let us consider this with special reference to NATO.

For some years this shift might find NATO at a relative disadvantage, since it has been the NATO style, and especially the American style, to build great depots and to rely on a much larger support structure than the Warsaw Pact forces use. Quite apart from any argument for making forward forces less vulnerable, the simple fact is that, as stand-off missiles get better and more practical, there must be actions to reduce the vulnerability of rear-area concentrations, even those several hundred kilometers back and formerly thought safe from any but the most determined air attack. Like several other moves to become better prepared for PGMs, this would also make NATO less vulnerable to nuclear attack, and thus help make a nuclear attack less attractive.

A further consequence of shifting attacks to targets farther back will be some new attitudes toward sanctuaries. For example, the vulnerability of hardly any of NATO's rear-area targets (except atomic-capable aircraft) has been a major subject of concern. Now those concerns must be extended, and priorities for protection calculated, for *any* concentration of military forces or equipment targetable by stand-off weapons.

As noted, counters to PGMs will take on a very high priority. Concealment and camouflage may work very well against present PGMs. When this is the case, the attacker might logically revert to area barrage fire or area bombing. Second, crews of most present PGMs are vulnerable (as are airborne platforms) and will be the focus of counterattacks. And third, new designs of armor may force up warhead sizes—which with shaped charges can now be quite small.

Consider again the first point of this section: there are complex questions of balance raised in the choice of "many inexpensive" instead of "fewer more expensive" vehicles. One has to ask about whether the inexpensive vehicles will have the needed speed, range, and payload. Will the operating manpower required make the "many" less desirable?

Will only the "few" be able to mount effective countermeasures devices?

And there are problems with the avoiding of concentrations. Dispersed forces may be inefficient to operate. As to the value to the offense of "overwhelming superiority in a narrow sector," can this be done by calling in offensive PGMs from far away and concentrating the firepower, if not the forces?

More reasons could be given why PGMs might not work as their users hope, or why their consequences are more complicated than the six trends I have listed. Simple analyses will not tell all we need to know to answer some very important questions. From the point of view of NATO, some thoughtful and rather complex analyses need to be made, preferably on a joint basis between Europeans and Americans. (This book records many of the points which are being so discussed, and may provide a foundation for more detailed analyses.) These analyses need to consider force-on-force, not just one-on-one. They need to consider how the new-style forces might affect plans and intentions—as well as conflict outcomes. They need to treat some exceedingly important questions about Soviet strategy with respect to the West, and NATO's ability to defend itself and to deter attack: Is the present design of the Red Army appropriate to the task of an anti-NATO offensive? Would prudent Soviet military judgment call for a less tank-heavy posture—a ponderous move—before certifying readiness to attack? Will NATO defense be adequate without resorting to nuclear weapons? These are among the most important questions to bear in mind while considering the relation of PGMs to nuclear warfare in the next section.[17]

PGMs AND THEATER NUCLEAR WARFARE

From the US point of view, a major value to be derived from NATO is that its solidarity appears sufficient to the Soviets to deter an attack which might lead to a theater nuclear conflict, and, in turn, to an intercontinental nuclear war. The latter, so improbable that war gamers often apologize for those elements of their scenarios which lead there, has two properties of interest here: it has such terrible potential that even improbable triggers deserve careful attention; and, second, intercontinental nuclear war could seem much more likely if there had been a major exchange in Europe, especially if most of the European Allies were going under and US forces had suffered heavy casualties. This chain of events could be the more dangerous if communications were unclear, if bluffs were misunderstood, or if leaders were inept.

There is, I believe, a new element of risk. Near the end of this paper I discuss how modern weapons—which are both numerous and releasable—are likely to speed up the rate of destruction in nonnuclear war, as well as the dollar rate of munitions consumption. This faster rate could lead to sudden surprises or to a pause—at which time there might be a heightened temptation to escalate to nuclear use. But if we anticipate this pause, and especially if both sides have observed limitations, the pause could lead to de-escalation and negotiation.

It is distressing, in a time when both Soviet and US forces possess huge theater nuclear forces, that the strategy for their contingent use has not been fully thought through, and that there is no general agreement on the specific purposes many of these weapons should serve.

Laurence Martin has suggested how this came about:[18]

Tactical nuclear weapons fell into disrepute with those who governed American strategy. This helped to inhibit the emergence of a coherent doctrine for their use and halted the development of new tactical systems specifically designed to execute well-defined tasks. Nevertheless, the demands of the armed services and the political need to reassure allies who had been taught that the stationing of tactical nuclear weapons in Europe was necessary to link them to the American deterrent ensured that the deployment of nuclear weapons continued energetically until NATO reached the legendary figure of about 7,000 for local use. In this haphazard way the present huge arsenal was deployed in Europe, unrelated to any well-accepted strategic doctrine and in many respects ill-adapted, even technically, to the execution of such military tasks as have been defined for it.

In 1974 Congressional concern over this same point was shown by the Nunn Amendment,[19] which:

prohibits any increase in the number of US tactical warheads in Europe except in the event of imminent hostilities and directs the Secretary of Defense to study our tactical nuclear policy and posture to ensure that it is coordinated within the alliance and is fully consistent with a strong conventional defense. The study must also consider the numbers and types of weapons that could be reduced.

The present US posture on tactical nuclear weapons in Europe does not appear to reflect current and comprehensive policy determinations; it seems to be more of an accumulation of kinds and numbers of weapons over a long period of time. The number, dispersal, and variety of tactical weapons and the high alert status we maintain is probably a destabilizing factor lowering the nuclear threshold. The committee believes that NATO needs a convincing nuclear deterrent but that we cannot afford the unnecessary risk of too many nuclear weapons in Europe or too great a readiness to use them.

The matter to be discussed in this paper, though, is the interrelation between PGMs and nuclear warfare. The situation just surveyed leads me to suggest three points for examination:

1. What effect will PGMs have on the nuclear threshold? Is the conventional defense of NATO now credible? It appears that nonnuclear PGMs are effective enough to do many of the jobs now assigned to nuclear weapons. Just which jobs?
2. Where nuclear weapons are used, precise delivery will permit smaller yield warheads. Damage will be more calculable. What effect will this have on the stockpiles of the nuclear powers, on their rules for control, and on their strategies?
3. Given the major changes in stockpiles and posture implied by these adjustments and by the new technology, and given the inconsistent and vague basis of current US and NATO theater nuclear strategy, what can be done to formulate a new strategy? Can clarity of purpose reduce the dangers?

Consider the first question: Will PGMs raise the nuclear threshold? Preliminary studies have shown that PGMs have a good chance of stopping a tank thrust without resorting to nuclear weapons. Future types, especially RPVs, can be quite potent in attacking targets in rear areas, and may be adequate substitutes for many middle-range nuclear strikes by QRA aircraft.[20] Nuclear-tipped air defense missiles are likely to account for a decreasing share of kills as weapons like Grail, Gainful, Stinger, and Roland are proliferated. New types of nonnuclear mines could replace atomic mines in many spots. But these are impressions, and it would be useful to see more specific studies comparing each of the theater nuclear weapons with the most effective nonnuclear alternative. Nonetheless, it seems abundantly clear that these developments will result in a higher nuclear threshold.

Second, if nuclear weapons are to be used, can yields be lower? Military forces might use nuclear warheads for four reasons: (1) they compensate for inaccurate delivery or uncertain target location; (2) they can destroy soft targets over a wide area; (3) they can damage hard targets; and (4) they would have a tremendous, but unpredictable, political effect. It is my own view that military conservatism, applied in several layers, has resulted in higher-than-necessary yields because of (1) above; with the new technology for both guidance and recon-naissance, yields could be brought down. As to (2), the new nonnuclear PGMs are available in such large quantities that they could reasonably substitute for smaller numbers of nuclear weapons in many cases. On the other hand, the dispersal of forces that PGM use encourages may increase the incentives to use multikiloton nuclear warheads for area coverage, especially if there is a time urgency.

Citing both military and political values, some planners have pro-posed the use of mininukes—weapons with very low-yield warheads, so low as to be nearly interchangeable with nonnuclear warheads. Ad-vocates of mininukes believe that any American nuclear contribution should be designed to repel an attack at its outset, and that the early release of small yields would be more credible and would result in less collateral damage. Opponents of this view question the military effec-tiveness of such a posture[21] and point to the problems of release and control if very early use is entailed. They also question whether the Soviet Union, which seems to be planning nuclear use on a large scale, indiscriminate basis, would be deterred by NATO mininukes. But, most of all, they point out the grave uncertainties as to where nuclear use, even though limited, might lead. In any event, the United States has stated that it does not intend to develop mininukes.[22]

Now to the third point: what can be done to formulate a new theater nuclear strategy in these times of changing postures and changing tech-nology? I believe that there will never be a better time. The new tech-nology has given us the ability to avoid collateral damage while effectively executing precise combat operations whose intent can be clearly understood. We need to design a strategy aimed at terminating or de-escalating conflict. To make our intent clear, we should have the previously mentioned dual criteria with respect to damage: damage to intended targets must be maximized and damage to nontargets mini-mized.[23] Nonnuclear PGMs meet these requirements and serve a con-flict-limiting strategy well. But the consequences of even the most limited use of nuclear weapons are unknowable (given the unknowable Soviet reaction) and this makes their use undesirable if the goal is to limit conflict.

But as long as NATO must count on the deterrent effect of theater nuclear forces, the previously cited article by Professor Martin[24] gives some criteria:

> This force must match, and therefore attempt to deter, the introduction of the Soviet Union's own theater nuclear weapons and, if need arises, must be used in a conspicuous, deliberate fashion. . . . Such a NATO nuclear force must attempt both to halt the aggressor's advance and to issue such a warning of dire prospects that the combination of momentary defeat and prospective disaster will impel him to terminate hostilities on terms acceptable to the West. To be satisfactory, the forces providing such an option to NATO must be quickly responsive, fully subject to the highest possible level of political and military control, and impervious to seizure or sabotage in peace or war.

In the present discussion, the question to ask is what effect precision delivery has in meeting Martin's criteria, and to note that the property of good accuracy at full range facilitates the centrally controlled covering force which Martin proposes. Remote nuclear PGMs would be easier to protect from sabotage or attack.

In sum, it is my view that PGMs reduce the need for theater use of nuclear weapons, that precision guidance of *any* weapon permits precision in what is destroyed, and that as long as we need theater nuclear forces, a shift to less vulnerable delivery means, to central control, and to a clear and mutually understood strategy, can reduce dangers for NATO and for the United States.

NONNUCLEAR PGMs AND THE SMALLER STATES

Some years ago it would have been out of the question for most small countries to do much about repelling enemy air attacks. Nor would those in exposed locations have had much chance of stopping a thrust of armored units. But the new style of arming goes a long way toward making small countries more defensible against those kinds of attacks.

Because many of the new weapons have a relatively short range, local geography and climate will have much to do with how well they work. For example, it is particularly relevant to study the canalization of attacks in considering the use of antitank PGMs in halting attacks on Northern Norway and on Iran. The clear weather and open spaces of the Arabian Peninsula make reconnaissance, perhaps by RPV, more important to its defense than in the case of Norway. Quite a different problem would be faced by the Philippines should it feel threatened by a mainland force: it would need antiaircraft PGMs and a combination of overwater reconnaissance and antiship PGMs (or RPVs). But the important point here is that even modest military establishments could support useful defensive forces in all these cases.

But could these, or similar, weapons be used to support an offense? Most of the present generation of PGMs are specifically designed for defensive uses, but some future longer-range weapons are likely to be useful to the offense when one small country attacks a neighbor, particularly a neighbor whose forces or valuable resources are located in only a few places. Another offensive use may be found where the local geography is suitable for leapfrog tactics. In a surprise move the attacker might suppress defenses, then seize and hold a key point, defending it heavily with antitank and antiaircraft PGMs. Thus, for the small countries, where the averaging effect of large numbers is less important, clever tacticians may eventually put the new weapons to offensive use.

❖   ❖   ❖

Subject to the several qualifications and omissions which have been pointed out, five main conclusions emerge.

First, the prospects for increased stability over the short run, as nonnuclear PGMs make both smaller states and NATO more defensible, seem encouraging.

Second, an important consequence of the dispersal of so much destructive power down to small units, and the natural delegation of authority to use it, is that the pace of war will be faster. In places with large concentrations of forces there will be an unprecedented intensity of nonnuclear conflict. Even though, as noted earlier, the total weight of munitions to do a job may decrease over the entire time of the conflict, the *rate* of use—in terms of fraction of stocks[25] consumed—is likely to go up. The material destroyed on both sides *per day of fighting* is likely to be an order of magnitude greater than we have been thinking about for nonnuclear war. We had a glimpse of this in the sudden logistic demands of the 1973 October War; a war in Europe could dwarf those consumption rates. Will this pace lead to escalation or to negotiation, as forces find munitions and equipment largely spent after three or four days of conflict?

Third, there is a hopeful sign that the trend of the first part of this century toward the inclusion of nonmilitary target systems and civilian populations in military campaigns will be reversed. Precision delivery means that military targets can be destroyed with less total explosive power and less collateral damage to nonmilitary targets. The faster pace discussed above means that tactical forces-in-being, as well as strategic forces, count more, and the general economy less, in achieving a favorable outcome.

Fourth, the pervasive changes in posture which PGMs are bringing about among the major powers suggest that this is a good time to revise theater nuclear policies—which are now so vague as to be dangerous. Precision delivery of nuclear weapons is conducive to their better protection and closer control, while the effectiveness of precisely delivered nonnuclear weapons makes the uncertainties of nuclear use much more avoidable.

Fifth, and finally, dissatisfaction with the central role in strategy of an almost unbelievable threat of assured nuclear destruction has been growing in the West, while Soviet capabilities to make limited use of nuclear force have increased. Precision weapons will clearly play an important part in making, or countering, a threat to use nuclear force in a limited way. Analysts are beginning to understand the mechanics of these new ways to use force, which may be very important for years to come. But no one understands well how to forecast the sequences of moves that may result from actual nuclear use.

NOTES

1. Approaching this matter from a different, but complementary, point of view, Raymond Aron said: "Defeat must be made to appear catastrophic, victory an unmixed blessing. In other words, the stake at issue escaped definition by the rules and regulations of diplomacy. It was no longer a question of shifting frontier posts a few miles. Only sublime—and vague —principles, such as the right of peoples to self-determination or the war to end war, seemed commensurate with such violence, sacrifice, and heroism. It was technical excess that gradually introduced ideologies in place of war aims. Both sides claimed to know what they were fighting *about*, but neither said what it was fighting *for*." In *The Century of Total War* (New York: Doubleday and Company, 1954).
2. In this case, securing the East Bank of the Suez Canal.
3. California Seminar on Arms Control and Foreign Policy, January 1973; abridged in *Foreign Affairs*, January 1973, pp. 267 ff.
4. James R. Schlesinger, *Annual Defense Department Report FY 1975*, p. 38.

5. James Digby, *Precision-Guided Weapons*, Adelphi Paper 118 (London: The International Institute for Strategic Studies, Summer 1975).

6. By this definition, the Japanese kamikazes of 1945 operated functionally as PGMs. A less well known and rather bizarre example is given in a recent Soviet book: "During the Great Patriotic War dogs were used to destroy tanks. They usually attacked tanks from a distance of 150-200 m. As a dog dashed under a tank frontally or at a 45° angle the trigger of the explosive charge caught on the bottom of the tank and set off the fuse. Thus in the sector of the 160th Infantry Division in the vicinity of Glukhovo six dogs destroyed five enemy tanks.

   "At Stalingrad, in the vicinity of the airfield, a squad of tank-destroyer dogs destroyed 13 tanks. At Kursk, in the zone of the 6th Guards Army, 16 dogs destroyed 12 tanks that had broken through into the depth of the Soviet defenses in the area of Tamarovka, Bykovo, Hill 244.5." In C. Biryukov and G. Melnikov, *Antitank Warfare* (Moscow: Progress Publishers, 1972), p. 91.

7. For a few more technical details on these, see Adelphi Paper, above. For greater detail, See *Flight International's* "World Missile Survey," *Jane's Yearbooks*, and *Aviation Week*. Unless otherwise noted, the data which follow are from the "World Missile Survey" of May 8, 1975.

8. For a better feel for how the SA-6 works as part of a system of guns and other missile types of complementary capabilities, see *International Defense Review*, no. 4, 1974, p. 450, for the chart, "The Antiaircraft Threat in Central Europe."

9. James R. Schlesinger, *Annual Defense Department Report FY 1976 and FY 197T*, p. III-69.

10. Malcolm R. Currie, *DOD Program of RDT&E, FY 1975*, p. 4-44 and 4-45. See also *Aviation Week*, December 10, 1973, p. 14, January 27, 1975, pp. 107 ff.

11. *Jane's Fighting Ships 1974-1975* (London: Macdonald and Jane's Publishers, 1975), p. 531.

12. Schlesinger, *FY 1976*, pp. III-66 and III-67; Malcolm R. Currie, *DOD Program of RDT&E, FY 1976*, pp. VI-24–VI-27.

13. See *Hearings on S. 920*, Part 10, Committee on Armed Services, United States Senate, April 1975, pp. 5130 ff.

14. *Soviet Aerospace*, November 18, 1974, p. 85, quotes Dr. Malcolm Currie as saying that this is a ballistic missile which may have a radar seeker that lets it home on surface ships.

15. This is not meant to imply that, for example, NATO defenders would, overall, have more PGMs than WP attackers. In fact, the reverse may turn out to be true.

16. The author first encountered this and a number of related ideas in discussions with T. F. Burke of the Rand Corporation in 1972. Burke has

developed this and a number of related ideas in lectures at the Army War College and other service schools; no published version is available.

17. In the previously cited Adelphi Paper I treat several implications of PGMs omitted here: the large numbers of highly portable antitank and antiaircraft weapons likely by 1980, the war of seeing and hiding on NATO battlefields, and the priority that will be given to attacking PGM crews. Some deficiencies of PGMs over the near term are listed, and possibilities for overcoming these deficiencies suggested.

18. In his "Theatre Nuclear Weapons and Europe," *Survival*, November/December 1974, p. 268.

19. *Report on S. 3000*, Committee on Armed Services, United States Senate, May 29, 1974. For the Defense Department's response, see *Survival*, Sept./Oct. 1975, pp. 235-41.

20. A fraction of the NATO-assigned nuclear-capable aircraft are kept on QRA, ready for nuclear strike missions.

21. For example, it would take kilotons to deal effectively in one burst with a typical area target like an armored regiment. "Mininuke" usually means a subkiloton weapon.

22. On May 23, 1974, the United States made a statement to the Geneva Disarmament Conference which "gave assurance . . . that it would not develop a new generation of miniaturized nuclear weapons that could be used interchangeably with conventional weapons on the battlefield." In an interview, Dr. Fred C. Iklé, director of ACDA, said, "We have no intention to move in a direction that could blur the distinction between nuclear and conventional arms" (*New York Times*, May 24, 1974).

23. See the section on "Progressive Technical Change and Continuity in NATO Doctrine" in Chapter 11.

24. *Survival*, November/December 1974, p. 272.

25. The assumption made here is that the initial stock level of PGMs was fairly well matched to the task at hand in the sector under consideration.

IV

CHANGING
THE ALLIANCE POSTURE:

Some Constraints

CHAPTER 8

Technological Change and Arms Control: The Cruise Missile Case

Richard Burt

The emergence of a new range of technological options raises important questions for defense planners in the West, which involve a host of operational, political, and budgetary issues. If, during the coming decade, these questions are resolved and the appropriate institutional and conceptual adjustments are undertaken, it is likely that precision guidance, target acquisition, command and control, and munitions technologies will enable NATO forces to carry out military tasks with more flexibility and greater discrimination. As new systems are introduced into Western inventories, it may also be possible to inject greater doctrinal flexibility into the Western defense posture, by giving the alliance, in the event of conflict, greater discretion in determining when, where, and how the use of nuclear weapons would be threatened and, in the event of conflict, actually applied.

In the process of creating intriguing new options for Western military forces, new technologies could also create profound new difficulties for existing institutions for East-West arms control. In this chapter, the nature of these difficulties—and their implications for existing approaches to arms control—will be examined by focusing on the impact of the American cruise missile on the US-Soviet negotiations at the Strategic Arms Limitation Talks (SALT). As the SALT record over 1975-76 attests, the US programs to develop long-range air-launched and sea-launched cruise missiles for deployment in the early 1980s introduced severe complications into efforts to translate the terms

of the so-called Vladivostok guidelines for a new ten-year SALT regime.* The issue was, in part, whether once deployed, US long-range
cruise missiles were to be constrained by a new SALT accord and, if so,
how this was to be brought about.

It is possible to view the cruise missile question as a procedural one,
a problem of interpretation similar to the difficulty of determining
which Soviet ICBMs were to be considered "heavy" missiles. But to
understand the problem in this fashion is to ignore the important
questions raised for defense planning and arms control by a new generation of technology that is embodied in the US cruise missile program. To appreciate this problem, three facets of the cruise missile
dilemma will be addressed: first, the character of a new technology and
its impact on mission performance and national and bureaucratic interests; second, how negotiation sought, but failed, to deal adequately
with the cruise missile following the Vladivostok accord; and third,
why the cruise missile, in addition to other developments, calls into
question some common, but perhaps no longer valid, assumptions about
East-West arms control.

THE CRUISE MISSILE

The term "cruise missile" is by no means new. It has been used for
twenty-five years to describe a large, but mixed, class of guided missiles
that have several performance characteristics in common: unlike ballistic missiles, they are continuously propelled, mostly air-breathing
vehicles, which resemble manned aircraft in their flight profiles. Perhaps the simplest and best-known cruise missile is the World War
II-vintage German V-1 buzz bomb (or "doodlebug"), a jet-powered
flying bomb which traversed the English Channel to strike targets in
Britain in 1944. The German experience is interesting because it reveals two important aspects of cruise missiles. The first is that the basic
components of the system are relatively simple: Germany was able
to develop and deploy the V-1 earlier than the much more sophisticated

---

* The agreement proposed an overall ceiling for three categories of strategic launchers—land-based intercontinental ballistic missiles (ICBM), submarine-launched
ballistic missiles (SLBM), and long-range, so-called "heavy" bombers. The agreement also envisioned a separate ceiling of 1,320 for those launchers adapted to deliver multiple, independently retargetable reentry vehicles, or MIRVs. An important provision contained in the aide-mémoire released at Vladisvostok stated that
missiles launched from aircraft with ranges exceeding 600 km, or 375 miles, would
be included in the overall ceiling for launcher vehicles.

V-2, the forerunner of modern ballistic missiles. Second, the relative success enjoyed by the Royal Air Force in detecting and intercepting the V-1 highlights the basic drawbacks of the cruise missile concept; their slow speed, compared to ballistic missiles, and their conventional, aircraft-like flight profiles make cruise missiles vulnerable to air defenses.

Despite these drawbacks, or more importantly, because of the technical challenges involved in perfecting ballistic missiles, cruise missiles were quickly developed and deployed in the early postwar period by the United States. A refined, nuclear-armed version of the V-1, the Matador, was deployed in Western Europe and the Far East in 1954, and by the end of the decade, submarine-launched cruise missiles were added to the growing American inventory, as was an intercontinental-range cruise missile which had been rapidly deployed in response to the new threat posed by long-range Soviet ballistic missiles. But the drawbacks that plagued the earlier generation of German weapons led to these missiles being replaced in the early 1960s by a more familiar class of systems, the land-based Minuteman ICBM and submarine-launched Polaris SLBM. Shorter-range cruise missiles, moreover, were replaced either by tactical ballistic missiles like the Pershing or by nuclear-capable aircraft possessing greater operational flexibility.

During the 1960s, however, the cruise missile did not disappear from the inventories of the superpowers. The Soviet Union's deployment of a new family of cruise missiles aboard naval vessels was a particularly significant development; for one, they gave Soviet submarines a capability to deliver nuclear strikes against the United States before the Navy was able to deploy a large force of ballistic missile submarines. For another, they provided the growing Soviet fleet with a substitute for a carrier-based aircraft, in the form of long-range anti-shipping missiles. Both the United States and the Soviet Union recognized another use for these systems: enhancing the firepower and the penetration capabilities of bombers. Thus, during the 1960s both Soviet and American bombers were armed with cruise missiles that enabled them to stand off from heavily defended targets and release their weapons. Despite these refinements, several of the traditional problems of cruise missiles remained. Whether directed toward their targets by inertial guidance or by radio signals, cruise missiles did not possess great accuracy and were vulnerable to jamming. The Soviet experience in antishipping missile deployment—which during the 1960s was to move to shorter, rather than longer-range, systems—revealed the problem that the Soviet navy had with cruise missile accuracy at long ranges. And even if accuracy problems could be solved, cruise missiles, like manned aircraft, had to face a new generation of more lethal air defense systems.

In the United States at least, recent developments on a wide range of technological fronts appear to have solved many of these problems. Four major advances can be singled out. First, the development of highly efficient turbofan, turbojet, and ramjet engines which burn high-energy fuels now enable relatively small vehicles (less than 20 feet in length) to attain ranges exceeding 2,000 miles. Second, precision-guidance techniques—seekers that home on the energy given off or reflected by targets, improved beacon-positioning devices, and terrain-matching systems—promise accuracies at these ranges below 100 feet CEP. Third, progress in the miniaturization of nuclear weapons and development of a new generation of conventional munitions give light-weight payloads increased destructive power. And fourth, low-altitude flight trajectories and airframe materials of extremely low radar reflectivity give cruise missiles an improved capability to penetrate air defenses.

Some of these technologies have already been exploited in the new class of anti-shipping missiles that are now undergoing deployment in the West, like the American Harpoon and the French Exocet. They are all being incorporated, however, in two programs now under way in the United States aimed at developing air-launched and sea-launched cruise missiles for deployment in the 1980s. These programs are still at an early state of development and it is wise to approach the claims made over their potential performance with healthy skepticism. But enough public information is available to conclude that these systems will qualitatively differ from earlier cruise missiles.

Compare, for instance, the projected capabilities of the U.S. Navy's sea-launched cruise missile (SLCM) with that of the SS-N-3 Shaddock, deployed over a decade ago on Soviet surface vessels and submarines. While less than half as long and a tenth as heavy as the Soviet missile, the American system, now designated the Tomahawk, could possess over five times the range. But this fails to adequately describe the performance potential of the new system. Unlike the Shaddock, the Tomahawk could be fired from the standard torpedo tube of a submerged submarine. The same missile could be launched from any number of surface vessels, and a prototype of the system has already been shown to be compatible with mobile, land-based missile launchers. Equipped with a 200-kt warhead—the same yield as a Minuteman III MIRV—the Tomahawk SLCM could be capable of striking targets deep in the Soviet Union from firing positions in the northern Atlantic or from the European mainland. If predictions concerning accuracy are borne out by testing, cruise missile warheads might be successfully used against a variety of targets, ranging from urban complexes, industrial and energy centers, military marshalling areas, and perhaps hardened military installations.

It is in the tactical sphere, however, that weapons such as the Tomahawk appear to offer the most intriguing and most important military options. In the European theater, longer-range cruise missiles may offer attractive alternatives to aircraft in the performance of some deep-strike interdiction missions. Armed with either nuclear or non-nuclear warheads, these systems—deployed on land or in European coastal waters—could provide an effective substitute to vulnerable, and, some argue, provocative, Quick Reaction Alert (QRA) aircraft now deployed in such countries as West Germany. Deployed on submerged platforms or on relatively simple mobile launchers on land, cruise missiles would be more invulnerable to preemptive attack than currently deployed aircraft, and they might be capable of attacking interdiction and other fixed targets in Eastern Europe, such as transport facilities, supply dumps, and air bases. If married to new hard-structure and earth-penetrator munitions, cruise missiles might also be used against sensitive and well defended high-value targets, such as hardened command bunkers. New families of low-level point air defense systems as well as "look down, shoot down" area defenses might prove successful counters to cruise missile penetration, but this would entail significant expense for the Soviet Union. The low costs of cruise missiles, moreover, would not rule out the use of saturation tactics against well-defended, high-value targets.

For maritime missions, SLCMs promise additional long-range firepower, which might be substituted for carrier-borne aircraft in the performance of antishipping roles and in the projection of sea-based air power ashore. In both Northern and Southern Europe, cruise missiles appear to offer interesting coastal defense possibilities. While deployed aboard aircraft, SLCMs would enable maritime reconnaissance aircraft to take on various sea control tasks. Equipped only with television cameras or other sensing devices, cruise missiles could be used effectively in reconnaissance and surveillance roles. In the performance of theater missions in and around Europe, then, the advantages of reducing vulnerability as well as costs appear to make the cruise missile a concept that merits full investigation.

It is somewhat ironic, therefore, that the new technologies encompassed by the cruise missile have been exploited by the United States, for it is in the US defense establishment that the concepts outlined above have traditionally met with most resistance. Although the Air Force and the Navy have their own cruise missile designs under development, both services are confronted with troubling questions over the possible impact of their deployment on existing roles and equipment. The Air Force has long placed the strategic bombing mission at the top of its list of preferred tasks, with manned penetrating bombers, like the B-52, as its chosen instrument for fulfilling this mission. Thus, in the 1960s, the Air Force argued that the penetrating bomber would remain the most cost-effective means of utilizing bombers, on grounds that a stand-off bomber equipped with long-range ballistic missiles could not strike accurately at well-defended military targets and would be enormously costly. The objection to ballistic missile-equipped bombers—essentially the Skybolt concept which was rejected fifteen years ago—perhaps remains valid, but developments in cruise missile technology raise real questions over the advisability of maintaining a capability to penetrate Soviet air space with bombers. The Air Force, then, while content to see the cruise missile as a complement to the B-52, or the new B-1, can be expected to resist a move that would replace these aircraft with a smaller fleet of stand-off bombers, made up of 747s or similar aircraft, equipped with 50 to 100 cruise missiles each. The Navy possesses a similar vested interest—the maintenance of large, multipurpose carriers with sophisticated attack aircraft. Here the threat is posed not by cruise missiles as strategic weapons, but by their possible use aboard other vessels in lieu of carrier-based air power. With the possibility of equipping smaller vessels or land-based aircraft with long-range cruise missiles to use in an antishipping role in the North Atlantic and other areas, the threat posed by cruise missiles to Navy interests appears even starker.

It is worth pointing out briefly three other ironies attached to cruise missile deployment: First, because of cruise missile technology's potential for lowering defense costs and reducing vulnerability, some of its most vigorous champions in the United States have been found in the arms control community (at least until it became a central obstacle to a new SALT agreement). Second, while the United States possesses the technology but is faced with bureaucratic impediments to the efficient exploitation of cruise missiles, it should be noted that the reverse is true for the Soviet Union. The Soviet armed forces have shown they are at home with the concept, but they will lack the technology for perhaps another decade. Third, Western European nations possess both the technology and the doctrinal framework to utilize it, but they will have little say in what constraints are placed on cruise missiles at SALT.

THE SALT EXPERIENCE

Cruise missiles—either deployed or under development—were not specifically singled out in the Vladivostock aide-mémoire. In commenting on the guidelines following the summit, Secretary of State Kissinger stated that the provision calling for air-launched missiles with ranges over 600 km to be included in the launcher ceiling only referred to air-launched *ballistic* missiles. This seems to be the genuine American interpretation, rather than a negotiating ploy, because only a few weeks prior to the summit, the US Air Force had dropped a Minuteman I missile out of the backside of a C-5A jumbo transport to test the feasibility of developing a modern Skybolt. The initial Soviet interpretation of the 600-km language is more difficult to unravel. In the light of the later Soviet insistence that cruise missiles be somehow controlled in a new SALT treaty, it is tempting to argue that in November 1974 the Soviets, like many in the West, did not fully recognize the potential of the new American cruise missiles. It is apparent, however, that by early 1975, the Soviet Union insisted on tight controls on cruise missiles in a proposal that reportedly said that if the United States were unwilling to include the longer-range missiles under the 2,400 ceiling, then strategic-capable cruise missiles had to be banned altogether.

For the United States, both alternatives were difficult to accept. A complete ban on long-range missiles would be almost impossible to enforce without placing heavy restrictions on missiles designed for tactical missions: with cruise missiles, range is highly sensitive to payload. A short-range "tactical" cruise missile might be banned on the grounds that, equipped with a lighter warhead, it could attain longer ranges and thus become a "strategic" missile. Similar problems would also plague an approach that included long-range systems in the 2,400 ceiling. To fully exploit the new systems for tactical roles, many hundreds, if not thousands, of the cruise missiles might be necessary. Yet this could hardly happen if cruise missiles had to be traded off against strategic systems the United States had already deployed. Regardless of what approach is finally successful in clearing the way for a new SALT agreement, a number of difficult problems will remain to be resolved, both within and outside the SALT context.

One of the most troubling aspects that analysts have confronted in contemplating a SALT accord that includes cruise missiles is the verification requirement. In part, this involves the sheer difficulty of reliably monitoring numbers of systems that can be easily hidden and deployed from literally thousands of different vehicles. But a more difficult problem concerns not counting, but *identification*—how can a means be found to distinguish between strategic and tactical versions of the new generation of cruise missiles? The answer is simply that there is no reliable way around this problem, because there need be no discernible difference between a tactical or strategic cruise missile. Thus, to understand this as a verification problem is to miss the essential aspect of the new technology—that it can be utilized in the service of numerous roles, including strategic and tactical missions. This does not mean that it is impossible with cruise missiles to distinguish between strategic and tactical roles, but instead that it may become increasingly difficult to single out exclusive categories of weaponry that perform these roles. This is not a new problem, and the versatility of aircraft has troubled negotiators in the past—as the FBS issue at SALT I and the Backfire at SALT II attest. But an important point should be emphasized here. The spectrum of capabilities of a single cruise missile is potentially wider than that of aircraft. A Soviet Backfire, for instance, might be considered a strategic or a theater nuclear delivery vehicle, but it is unlikely to be deployed as a tactical strike aircraft with conventional ordnance. And while it is possible to envision an F-4 Phantom jet carrying out tactical missions with conventional or nuclear armament, it is difficult to visualize the same fighter carrying out nuclear strikes against Soviet missile silos. But a cruise missile might be capable of carrying out such a variety of nuclear and nonnuclear roles, and, most important, with high efficiency. Thus, while it will remain possible to classify certain weapons by the missions they perform—"strategic" weapons or "tactical" weapons—it is likely that a growing class of weapons of increasing military importance still defy such a description. (One is reminded here of the ultimately futile effort of arms control efforts in the 1930s to single out mutually exclusive categories of "offensive" and "defensive" weapons.)

So a dilemma is confronted in a "functional" arms control forum, like SALT, that professes to control weaponry capable of performing strategic missions. Agreements can be constructed to cover only those systems that can clearly be identified and counted as strategic, or agreements can be extended to a wider category of "gray area" systems that can be exploited for tactical ends. In an era of cruise missiles, remotely piloted vehicles, and "smart" bombs, neither alternative is attractive. In the first, a growing category of strategic-capable weaponry would be excluded from controls; in the second, important theater options would be foreclosed by a decision taken from the perspective of superpower arms control.

The consequences of blurring the distinction between strategic and tactical weaponry must be placed in the context of the overall military balance in Europe. Here, the bilateralism of SALT raises difficult issues, for decisions taken at SALT could have important consequences for the NATO Alliance. This can be seen in two ways: first, decisions taken at SALT could affect the future military options open to the West for restructuring theater forces in Europe. An agreement that limits air-launched cruise missile deployment to a specific launcher like the B-1 would mean that these systems could not be exploited for tactical (nuclear or nonnuclear) missions in and around Europe. In addition, noncircumvention language that might accompany an agreement on cruise missiles could restrict the sale of cruise missiles or the transfer of cruise missile technology to the Europeans. This would have the effect of not only limiting future European strategic options, but of limiting tactical alternatives as well. The second implication of cruise missiles for the alliance is perhaps more interesting. While a US-Soviet agreement at SALT could act to restrict European options, the ultimate acquisition of these systems could undermine the very utility of a bilateral US-Soviet dialogue on arms control. There is little reason why, if it were thought appropriate, Europeans could not develop a cruise missile capability: most of the component technology is available. Nuclear cruise missiles might be viewed as a means of enhancing the survivability and destructive capability of either French or British sea-based deterrent forces. But even if the technology were only exploited for theater nuclear or conventional ends, the elasticity of cruise missile range would inevitably force the Soviet Union to view these systems as posing a strategic threat. This would also be the case for

other European powers, particularly those located close to Soviet territory, which might, with a new generation of conventional munitions,
see deterrent value in cruise missiles aimed at high-value targets on
the Soviet homeland—the so-called "strategic conventional" option.

From this perspective, cruise missiles can also be seen to raise important questions for the mutual and balanced force reduction (MBFR)
exercise under way in Vienna. Just as the multirole characteristic of
cruise missiles undermines an implicit organizing assumption of SALT
—that strategic weapons make up an exclusive class of weapons—the
multirange characteristic of cruise missiles further erodes an assumption underlying MBFR, that meaningful military outcomes can be
achieved by arms control efforts undertaken within the restricted area
of central Europe. The deployment of cruise missiles might be constrained within the MBFR guidelines area of central Europe, but cruise
missiles launched from aircraft or vessels operating outside this geographically defined area would make such an agreement essentially
meaningless. At the same time, an agreement that placed constraints
on cruise missile deployment within central Europe—either directly or
indirectly through noncircumvention language arising out of the agreements limiting other delivery vehicles such as aircraft—could act to
constrain future strategic options, conventional or nuclear, now open
to West Germany and other states within the region.

Finally, two points should be made concerning the relationship of
SALT and MBFR. First, the two forums are likely to become increasingly incompatible because of an overlapping of concerns. Decisions
taken in one arena, say SALT, over cruise missiles will act to prejudge
outcomes at MBFR and vice versa. Second, while the area of overlap
will raise increasing problems, so will the area not covered by SALT
or MBFR. Cruise missiles deployed outside Central Europe that can
target the Soviet Union will not be covered by an MBFR agreement, and like the British and French nuclear forces, these systems may
also escape inclusion in a SALT accord. The same is true for medium-
and intermediate-range ballistic missiles deployed in the western Soviet
Union that can target European cities. A growing number of weapons
that for one reason or another escape inclusion at SALT or MBFR will
not only increase the problems of reaching accord within these two
sets of negotiations, but, if agreements are obtained, they will be all
that less relevant for real arms control.

A VANISHING ERA?

What general points emerge from all of this? Three can be immediately discerned:

1. The era in which weaponry capable of long-range attacks against strategic targets consisted of a special class of clearly identifiable systems appears to be coming to an end. The concept of strategic weapons was based on the extraordinary differences that arose in the 1950s and 1960s between ballistic missiles and conventional military hardware. This gap is now narrowing. Weapons, like the submarine-launched Poseidon missile, which were formerly seen to possess only "strategic" qualities, are now being assigned theater-strike roles, while new weapons deployed for tactical roles are also well-suited to perform strategic missions. Perhaps a new approach to classifying weapons needs to be undertaken, but in the meantime, old labels should be abandoned in favor of more precise descriptions of weaponry that include their range, armament, and accuracy.

2. The blurring of strategic and tactical weaponry has made it increasingly difficult to conduct negotiations on a bilateral basis at SALT over a class of weapons that not only defies categorization, but has important implications for states not directly participating in the talks. It is becoming just as difficult to conduct multilateral negotiations on a regional basis at MBFR, when possible agreements there could have important consequences for the superpower strategic relationship. What technology seems to be doing, then, is forcing us to recognize two long-standing problems that hamper East-West arms control: first, the political independence of West Europeans which, if directed toward exploiting a new generation of missiles, could undermine the effectiveness of a strictly US-Soviet arms control dialogue; and second, the geographical character of the East-West relationship. On the one hand, this allows the Soviet Union to deploy weapons that are not treated at SALT but that can carry out strategic missions against European targets. And on the other, it allows NATO states to deploy weaponry in Europe ostensibly for theater roles, a possibility that, from the Soviet perspective, must be seen as posing a threat to the Soviet homeland. In this way, arms control efforts must recognize that the US-Soviet strategic relationship and the East-West military balance in Europe are becoming increasingly intertwined. If arms control is to retain its exist-

ing focus on controlling numbers of aircraft, missiles, and warheads, it thus seems necessary to integrate the SALT and MBFR processes in a multilateral framework that would better link the complicated set of relationships that are now emerging. If this is politically impossible or analytically too difficult, perhaps different approaches to East-West arms control might be more profitably explored over the remainder of the decade.

3. The cruise missile threatens not only tactical and strategic distinctions, but also the dividing line between nuclear and nonnuclear weaponry. Unlike the strategic-tactical problem, this is not a phenomenon that directly affects contemporary arms control efforts, but it does have important implications for prevailing conceptions of deterrence and defense. The increasing ability to use accurate, conventionally armed missiles in roles that were previously thought to require nuclear warheads is an important development, which could have the effect, if deterrence breaks down, of raising the threshold of nuclear use in Europe and elsewhere. But important questions must be addressed in assessing the implications of this development. In Europe, will a concerted US effort to raise the nuclear threshold with "smart" conventional missiles introduce new strains into the alliance by alarming those who maintain that the threat of nuclear escalation is essential for deterrence? Moreover, would a strategy based on raising the nuclear threshold, while making nuclear war less likely, be more likely to lower the overall threshold to conflict? Even more intriguing questions are raised by the possibility that, in a decade's time, conventionally armed systems might be capable of carrying out strategic strikes against the Soviet Union. Again, this might be justified in terms of raising the nuclear threshold as well as giving nonnuclear nations a conventional "deterrent." But such a strategy itself might have an unforeseen impact on escalation. Arms control bears indirectly on this problem. While moving in the direction of lessened dependence on nuclear weapons might, on the whole, be viewed as a positive development, arms control outcomes which constrained the modernization of forces necessary to bring this about would, ironically, serve to reinforce Western reliance on nuclear weapons.

For fifteen years, it has been a general tenet of American strategic thought that the best strategy is one that minimizes the role of nuclear weapons in the conduct of foreign policy. To achieve this aim, successive administrations have followed the dual approach of investigating possibilities for strategic arms control while attempting to bolster conventional capabilities. These two approaches may soon become incompatible. There are no easy answers to this dilemma, but the future choices open to decision-makers can be more clearly defined by arms control institutions better able to cope with new developments. The major problem with continuing to tread the path paved by SALT is conceptual: SALT essentially reflects the technological and political realities of a bipolar nuclear era that is fast disappearing. Learning to live with a more complex strategic environment will pose numerous challenges, but if these are discounted, the first casualty will be arms control.

CHAPTER 9

Limits of Budgetary Flexibility

David Greenwood

In a defense planner's ideal world, security objectives would be clearly laid down and the main parameters of strategic and tactical doctrine precisely specified. *Policy* would be a datum, and policy in turn would determine *posture* and would prescribe force structures and force levels, roles and missions, the equipment and deployment of arms and armed forces. For the requirements thus enumerated, *provision* would be made by allocation of the necessary resources of manpower, materiel, industrial capacity, technical ingenuity, and organizing ability. Budgetary allotments would represent the intended expenditures sufficient to secure these resources for defense.

But this "ideal" world conforms to no known circumstances. In all societies, security—or a sense of security—is only one objective among many. Provision for defense cannot therefore be settled by simple inference from expert calculation, based on "what the nation needs." Instead, it is just one outcome of the budgetary process, at the heart of which lies governmental adjudication of the competition for resources. Everything hinges on the political assessment of priority-in-value among competing goals. Choices about security policy and posture are accordingly constrained. Consistency or compatibility among doctrine, posture, and provision are no less important in this context. But, it is clear, they may be harder to achieve.

In fact, the presence of contradictions among these elements is commonplace, for reasons which are readily apparent. Economic and strategic circumstances change and so do national priorities. Resources and objectives are both variables, as are societal preferences about how much for what. But security organizations have no capacity for immediate and complete adjustment to such alterations; it would be most surprising if they had. Thus, postures are not adjusted instantaneously to accommodate shifts of doctrinal emphasis. Nor is the scale and pattern of provision modified at once, as the assumption of some novel posture may require. Indeed, since "steady states" are an exceptional condition, some inconsistency or incompatability in security arrangements is endemic.

What are the sources of inadequate capacity for adjustment? Why is the maintenance of coherence among policy, posture, and provision difficult? It is convenient to identify three main sources, each representing a different genus of "constraint" and thus a different problem when it comes to considering possible techniques of breach or circumvention. Expressed in cryptic form, they are the classic incapacitating factors: inability, inhibition, and inertia.

Put another way, appropriate adjustment to maintain coherence requires both willingness and ability to change. For analytical purposes, one can distinguish among situations where there is evidence of the first but not the second—straight *inability;* where this position is reversed and organizations are "able but unwilling"—because of *inhibition*; and where neither prerequisite is found—the case of clear *inertia.* Needless to say, these influences operate in any national establishment. Where alliance arrangements are at issue, the problems may be multiplied.

Such is the general setting in which budgetary choices on defense are made: not in direct response to policy development or postural change, but through the convolutions of an allocative competition embracing all collective goods. And not with convenient flexibility, but subject to the limits set by inability or unwillingness to change.

THE CASE FOR POSTURAL CHANGE

The purpose of this chapter is to elucidate the implications of the limits of budgetary flexibility arising from these sources for adjustment to NATO's policy and posture in the later 1970s and beyond. That such adjustment would be appropriate, indeed necessary—or even overdue—is taken for granted in what follows. Among those who pay attention to these matters a consensus has been built that this is so, and, even to the layman, the logic is compelling.

The threat of Soviet attack in Central Europe, with massive force in a conventional assault, remains a key contingency for which NATO must provide. But the conditions in which the calculus of advantage might favor such a course are hard to see, even for the most reckless and aggressive Moscow leadership. Among the confusions and contradictions of détente the more serious threats may be the latent, subtle, and oblique. The exploitation of convulsive change in Western states, implicit threats of Soviet intervention in areas of ambiguous alignment, and even operations in flank countries on some political pretext apparently tangential to central concerns—all these are possibilities which spring to mind.

Although formally encompassed by the doctrines of flexible response, these eventualities are not the kind for which NATO's forces are suitably configured and equipped. The alliance's capacity for "varying response with circumstance" in Europe is severely limited. Moreover, inadequacy in this respect degrades the credibility of the central strategy itself. For never have NATO's capabilities furnished the wherewithal for that refinement in the pacing and management of crises or hostilities which "controlled escalation" should ideally connote. Nor have options for limited, discriminate response been plentiful enough. Indeed, for many commentators the probability of paralysis of decision in the face of nuclear release means that the lack of provision for tough conventional ripostes, with weapons effects confined to military forces, has put the overall strategy in question.[1]

What makes this reasoning pertinent is the fact that new technologies, affording greater precision and discrimination in the use of weapons (conventional and nuclear), mean that reform of policy and posture is now feasible—if NATO has the will and the resources. The question is: what sort of provision may be required? And is there that margin for budgetary maneuver in alliance states to make it possible? Expressed another way, reflecting earlier remarks on the setting in which budgetary choice takes place, the issues are: (a) will allocations for security rate a high or low priority-in-value in the years that lie ahead? and (b) whatever the priority, how far might inability, or inhibition and inertia, set limits to the extent (and the pace) at which appropriate and feasible postural change can realistically take place? These questions are addressed in turn below.

THE BASIC CONSTRAINT: HOW MUCH FOR DEFENSE?

On defense's place in national priorities among the NATO powers, contemporary evidence is more than usually ambiguous. In the United States, clamorings for the "peace dividend" from disengagement in Southeast Asia have subsided. Pressures for troop withdrawals from Europe, too, appear to have abated. Indeed, a European reading of the current scene would note renewed concern about security and a climate less hostile to high and rising outlays for defense than hitherto. Skepticism about the SALT negotiations, awareness of the continuing growth of Soviet conventional forces, reactions to Angola, the presidential abrogation of the rhetoric of détente—all contribute to this impression. But firm evidence that this is more than transient is hard to find. When Defense Secretary Schlesinger revealed his last bid for funds in October 1975, he ran into heavy congressional cross fire, stuck to his guns (in every sense), but before long was replaced. In the early 1976 presidential campaigning, no candidate has thought it prudent to make priority for defense a major plank in his electoral platform. The inference must be that the "real program value" of the Pentagon's budget will continue to decline, as it has done since 1962.[2]

The position in Europe is no less confused. In West Germany, defense's share of GNP (at factor cost) rose steadily from 1970, throughout the period of Ostpolitik "successes" and commitment to détente. The 1975/76 Weissbuch sounds important warnings on the growth of Soviet power, but defense's share of output in 1976 is budgeted to fall.[3] For the United Kingdom, expenditure projections foreshadow constant outlays (in real terms) during the next decade, and hence a falling defense/GNP proportion. The benefits of whatever growth the British may enjoy are to accrue to the balance of payments and industrial investment, to personal consumption and civil public spending, but *not* to their defense. In France, too, where priority for defense is generally supposed to be assured, the expectation is that the *armées* will simply "ride" the growth rate as of late. That is, they will take slightly less than a proportionate share in realized growth so that the defense/GNP proportion edges downward over time. The Italian condition is, of course, a question mark. But, Signor Berlinguer's assurances notwithstanding, it is impossible to believe that the anticipated communist participation in government will lead to higher military expenditure. If rehabilitation of Italy's home economy is to be the first concern of future administrations, as one must realistically presume, the opposite is likely.

As for NATO's smaller powers, the Low Countries and the Nordic members, the indications are ambivalent. The Dutch and the Danes have given notice in the past of their unwillingness to forego civil benefits to sustain their own defense. Only in Norway—oil-rich and sensitive on that account—are there indications of factors which bolster defense provision against continuous erosion.

There are other straws in the wind to complicate this assessment, however. For instance, despite the high-flown phrases which accompanied the final act, few Europeans seem to feel that their security was enhanced by 1975's "Summer in Helsinki." Nor are they confident that Vienna holds more promise. Indeed, it is the steady growth of Soviet naval and military power which has commanded most attention lately, as have the writer Solzhenitsyn's forthright "warnings to the West." The détente euphoria of the 1970s has certainly evaporated. Thus one might argue that it may need only one instance of Soviet heavy-handedness—in Svalbard? Serbia? Salisbury?—to trigger demands for strengthened NATO dispositions.

Yet these are straws in the wind, and the Soviet leadership is unlikely to act ill-advisedly while the present Western mood of skepticism about détente prevails. Thus the balance of popular sentiment on "resources for defense or other things" may lie for some time firmly on the side of welfare and other social benefits. The familiar difficulty of sustaining support for postures based on deterrence and prudent provision for uncertain futures accounts for this in part. But other factors are becoming increasingly important. For one thing, as Daniel Bell has recently observed, the "revolution of rising *expectations*" vis-à-vis collective goods seems to have run its course. It has been superseded by chrematistic claims—from all groups in Western societies—for *entitlements*. A higher "baseline" has been established, upon which new societal demands are being framed.[4] In the second place, defense communities' staple arguments against reduced security provision, which are cast as a rule in terms of "critical levels," seem no longer to carry much conviction. Accumulated evidence of waste and duplication has seriously undermined them. Indeed, it is ironical that nothing has done more to discredit such reasoning than references to squandered military potential in recent campaigning for greater interoperability and standardization in the alliance.[5]

Thus a first, and most important, "limit of budgetary flexibility" can be established. Whatever resources are necessary to exploit the new technologies of information, precision, and discrimination required to validate desirable postural change in NATO will have to come from *within* existing allocations. No easy funding can be anticipated from within some unapportioned growth component of budgetary projections. On the contrary: choices and trade-offs within defense will be required, against the force of inescapable commitments and implicitly earmarked outlays, "suborganizational interests to maintain endowments," and bureaucratic inertia's own dead hand.

CONSTRAINTS ON DEFENSE BUDGET TRADE-OFFS

Identifying the problem as one of intradefense resource allocation (or reallocation) brings into focus the budgeting procedures which, almost without exception, alliance countries have adopted in the last decade or so. Most NATO defense ministries now operate planning, programming, and budgeting systems (PPBS) of one kind or another. Military plans are laid according to the precepts of existing doctrine. Envisaged future resource claims are embodied in "the program," which is scheduled, typically, to a horizon five to ten years hence. Budgetary projections define the counterpart financial outlays required to consummate these claims. In some cases, authority to incur future payments obligations is involved; under French "program laws," funds are implicitly committed up to five years ahead.

The purpose and merits of such arrangements have been debated in a now voluminous literature. Given the lead times of modern weapons and the military-industrial complexities of arms procurement generally, their introduction was seen as a contribution to more rational public choice. Furthermore, except where unrealistic expectations were engendered, this has been broadly true. At the same time, formalized PPBS procedures tend to encourage a form of blinkered incrementalism. To be sure, commitment to the program-in-being is at one level administratively functional, promoting stability and order in the allocation of resources; at another level, however, it may be dysfunctional, impeding flexibility.

The dilemma is inescapable, since organizations face the conflicting requirements of continuity and change. But clearly, in the present context, these formal processes represent a further basic source of *potential* budgetary rigidity. All NATO countries have their defense "programs-in-being" to the early or mid-1980s. Major adjustment to military dispositions may be more difficult—another hint of irony—than when earlier practices, based on strictly annual allocations, were in vogue.

It has not yet been established, of course, that it is *major* adjustment (in financial terms) which is at issue here. What is the scale of budgetary provision that effective investment in new technologies requires? How substantial are the program trade-offs which might be necessary to accommodate it?

It is impossible to answer questions such as these directly, for two reasons. First, there is insufficient data in the open literature to support definitive costings. Requests for development funding for specific systems provide some indication of the magnitudes involved; and estimates of unit costs appear occasionally. But, since it is *new* technologies which are involved, both pure uncertainty and natural official secrecy preclude precision in these matters. Secondly, proponents of postural change are prone to imprecision when it comes to prescribing who should be equipped with what, and in what numbers. Broad assertions that new systems offer relatively cheap capacities, even cost-saving opportunities, are commonplace. But "cheap" to whom? And "cost-saving" on what assumptions about such things as weapons inventories, systems for target identification, acquisition, and designation, communications, command, and control facilities, and on and on?

However, even though general quantification is impossible, some points are clear. Whatever the American position, equipping European forces with the wherewithal for "discrete and accurate tailoring of attacks with conventional and nuclear munitions" (Holst's formulation) would be, *for European states themselves*, expensive. These things are relative, but nothing is more certain than that individual European countries cannot explore technology's options as the United States so clearly can and does. To illustrate the point: the Pentagon's request for funds to keep the air-launched and sea-launched cruise missile programs in advanced development in the financial year to June 1976 (FY 1976) totalled $153 million; that is more than the United Kingdom's *total* allocation for guided weapons research and development in the comparable period (1975-76: £74 million).[6] Similarly, broad-brush "per round" estimates for precision-guided munitions come out around $10,000 apiece; if these are right, the sums explicitly allotted in recent British estimates for ammunition and explosives would buy some 12,000 to 15,000 "rounds" (a dubious calculation, but none the less indicative).[7]

Regarding the surveillance, communications, command, and control facilities without which exploiting improvements in weapons accuracy and precision is impossible, the position is the same. Presumably "appropriate provision" in this context would include not only a $3 billion NATO AWACS program (and associated ground equipment costs) but also such items as several satellite ground terminals compatible with the US AFSATCOM (and related systems) plus, ideally, whatever the GAMO project on tactical communications may prescribe.[8] A further matter for consideration here is how far "varying response with circumstance" presupposes both freeing alliance members from the unanimity requirement *and* allowing that devolution of authority which, in theory, emphasis on more discriminate weapons should make acceptable. The point is: would autonomous, national command facilities—for some, or several, NATO countries—then be necessary?

No further elaboration is required. On any reasonable reckoning, significant budgetary recasting *is* involved. Effective investment in new technologies would not be possible simply by making marginal adjustments to existing allocations. What is "cheap" is in reality quite expensive. Trimming and paring would hardly be enough. What then are the limits of flexibility in NATO program budgets for the later 1970s and beyond?

LIMITS OF FLEXIBILITY: COMMITTED FUNDS

It goes without saying that, in a discussion of this kind, no useful purpose would be served by detailed, country-by-country scrutiny of the budgets of all the NATO nations in an effort to establish for each one what margin for maneuver may exist. The approach must be discursive and eclectic, identifying the various species of "constraint" encountered and citing illustrative examples. The distinctions made among inability, inhibition, and inertia provide a useful frame of reference.

Inability to make program adjustments is, in the strictest sense, a rare phenomenon. Comparatively few resource commitments are irrevocable: projects can be abandoned and existing systems scrapped. Similarly, of the scarcities and bottlenecks which apparently preclude quick innovation, few are absolute; in principle and at a price, resources can be diverted to breach or circumvent them. But in financial terms and in the shorter run, the position is somewhat different. Attempting rapid change in the procurement field may soon bring one to areas where "savings" will be offset by nugatory expenditure on current projects and contract cancellation charges. With personnel, similar conditions hold because of severance payments, pension rights, compensation for premature redundancy, and the like.

In the United Kingdom, for example, officials have asserted that "some 80 percent of equipment expenditure is effectively committed up to four years ahead," including funds allotted for "projects in development, on which large sums have already been spent" and "for production, maintenance, and support of existing weapon systems."[9] Striking such funding from the program would not, it is implied, realize commensurate savings by any means. In the very short run, counted in months (or even years in certain contexts), flexibility is further diminished by the "simple" problem of how to give administrative effect to highest level choice. On this matter, a Pentagon official recently gave striking testimony:[10]

> If the Congress in its judgment elected to stop all strategic research and development on the MX and D5 ballistic missiles, if you stopped our cruise missile programs, if you eliminated our antiballistic missile research programs, and if you stretched our Trident buy, if you canceled our B-1, if you canceled our AWACS, if you canceled our SAM-D, if you canceled our XM-1 tank development, *altogether you could not save $1 billion in fiscal year 1976 outlays in that year. . . .* if you decide to try to save $1 billion through reductions in Defense personnel. . . . if we started on the first day of the fiscal year and eliminated all military accessions for the fiscal year 1976, *we would not quite save that $1 billion.*

The $1-billion figure used for this illustration represented approximately 1 percent of the Department of Defense's requests for fiscal year 1976 (total obligational authority sought: $105 billion, outlays: $93 billion). The official quoted went on record, in fact, to the effect that:

> less than $20 billion of fiscal year 1976 outlays are "controllable"— and *a $5 billion reduction would cripple us completely.*

It is interesting that the same approximately 20 percent measure of the upper limit of annual "discretion" is cited here, as in the British illustration earlier.

It might be argued that in this discussion the boundary has been and the effects of inhibition, born of an instinct to avoid disruptive crossed between what is strictly inability (in terms of our formulation) change. It may be true. But for present purposes it is beside the point. After all, if, in the process of postural change, the defense establishments of NATO states were to be "crippled"—albeit temporarily—the exercise would be manifestly self-defeating.

LIMITS OF FLEXIBILITY: PRIORITIES AND INTERESTS

The way in which inhibition must enter this analysis is rather different. At the heart of the debate about policy is the thesis that NATO should strive to generate a wider range of military responses, stressing in particular restraint, discrimination, and—as far as possible—conventional options. Rowen and Wohlstetter have suggested certain mission categories which especially commend themselves for limited contingencies:[11] (a) *blocking* action, within the territory of the country attacked (or at sea); (b) *shallow* cross-border responses, *restricted* to the bases and lines of communication of attacking forces; and (c) cross-border responses countrywide, but still *confined* to facilities related to support of the focal battle. Clearly, any shift of doctrinal emphasis in this direction, which one would wish to signify in posture and —perhaps later—in declaratory policy, would have far-reaching implications for mission priorities.[12] The clues are in the words italicized above. The importance and thus the status of force components geared to offensive roles and to deep penetration—particularly for general reprisal—would be diminished. Accordingly, their constituencies would resist.

In one sense, of course, this is not a matter of "budgetary flexibility" at all. In another, however, it obviously is. Certainly it is germane to this analysis to pose the following questions: (1) Within that margin for adjustment available without "crippling" military establishments, how much intended equipment spending is attributable to projects falling within "lower priority" categories (on this reasoning)? (2) For which of these might one anticipate support sufficient to frustrate change, defense organizations being for practical purposes "able but unwilling" to summon the administrative courage of their intellectual convictions?

For three countries, Italy, the United Kingdom, and West Germany, these questions are particularly pertinent, because of a single dominating project. These countries are completing development, and on the threshold of scale production, of their Multi-Role Combat Aircraft (MRCA). In each state's procurement budget, this item looms unusually large, especially for the next few years. Yet there would clearly be a case for assigning the project to the "lower priority" heading implied by the Rowen/Wohlstetter analysis. "Multi-role" or not, what differentiates this aircraft from others in the planned inventories of European air forces is its capacity for offensive operations. It is designed for deep-strike interdiction, first and foremost, with the requisite—and costly—performance characteristics necessary for this mission: high speed, large payload, and long-range, elaborate penetration avionics. Naturally, it does have the capability for shallow, or battlefield, interdiction. But it provides the wherewithal to engage appropriate targets in this context at a higher price than other means available, that is, alternative aircraft, missile, and artillery systems. Nor is the price in question here exclusively financial; there is also a political cost, because of the absence of unambiguous defensive emphasis.

Yet the interests engaged in the MRCA program are such as make it difficult to imagine some trade-off for investment in cheaper aircraft, remotely piloted vehicles, precision guidance for air-delivered or cannon-launched munitions, and the like. Industrial considerations feature prominently, not least because the project is a symbol of successful European collaboration. That the three participants are all Community members gives added weight to this. Even more important, the *status* of air power in European forces is at issue. Without MRCAs, three major services would be in the position, by the 1980s, of lacking effective means to undertake the full spectrum of tactical air missions, including the most demanding—and prestigious. Indeed, limitation of response exclusively to targets related to attacking forces implicitly calls into question the truly independent application of air power and thus, again implicitly, the independence of air forces themselves.

In more muted form, the same mission priority dilemmas present themselves in relation to field force formations, especially armored units. The modern tank is a "multirole armored fighting vehicle," relevant, among other things, to antitank defense. Nevertheless its raison d'être resides in the offensive power for armored thrust or counterattack which it embodies. If new technologies can confer on gunners and infantrymen the means to block opponents' attacks, and if thereafter "limited response" is all that is required, then the main battle tank (MBT) presumably becomes a lower priority item too.

Yet funding for new MBTs is another substantial element in the program budgets of all the continental European alliance members. Moreover, because standardization appears possible with the next generation of MBTs, the procurement issue itself is invested with great political significance. The intra-European aspect is important. With the Federal Republic's Leopard development admitted to competition for the US operational requirement, the Atlantic dimension is even more so. Here too, therefore, the possibility of trade-off for investment in new technology cannot be rated high.

Hazardous though it is to generalize from instances such as these, the outlines of a conclusion do emerge from this analysis. Substantial elements of planned equipment spending relate to missions of marginal priority in terms of the modification of posture sought. But clearly they constitute hard demands. Doubtless, there is some budgetary scope in softer spots—although, admittedly, no evidence for this has been adduced. What seems altogether more plausible is that the effective limit resides in modest incremental funding where systems embodying capabilities for greater precision and discrimination already have their place in program budgets. That may be all.

RIGIDITIES AND SENSITIVITIES

What, finally, of inertia? Or is that what the foregoing argument has really been about: not defense organizations, "able but unwilling," but rather bureaucracies stuck in their procedural ruts? Perhaps a bit of both. Be that as it may, some remaining sources of budgetary inflexibility await their mention. And they are considerations which, more than anything else, reflect inherent rigidities or sensitivies in allies' and alliance decision-making processes which make them refractory to change.

First, there is the matter—mentioned earlier—of institutional arrangements for defense resource allocation, especially the almost universal PPBS approach. Programs exist. So do the associated budgetary projections. They represent an investment, both intellectual and administrative, which will not be lightly set aside. Quite apart from the interests vested in particular program elements, advocates of change have therefore to contend with the organizational self-interest of the budgeteers themselves.

Secondly, the adjustments to defense provision which postural change requires call for heavy commitment to technologies and systems in the production of which it is the United States that holds the decisive comparative advantage. Accordingly, to concede the logic of the strategic analysis may be tantamount to perpetuating that American technical domination of alliance affairs which has been moderated only relatively recently. There is always a constituency to be mustered in Europe for opposing *that*. Moreover, this will continue to be the case until traffic is seen to flow on Atlantic "two-way streets" with some measure of reciprocity in both scale and sophistication.

Thirdly, and related to this last, the pedigree of the strategic analysis itself is not self-evidently respectable, that is, for Europeans, predominantly "official" and expressly "European." Irrational though it may be, when advocacy of shifts of doctrinal emphasis in the alliance emanates from Washington in certain quarters, antibodies start to form at once.

In sum, it would appear that the limits of budgetary flexibility are tightly drawn. The boundaries are not, of course, both rigid and immutable. But tact and ingenuity may be required to breach or circumvent constraints impeding change, perhaps as much as elaborating the need for change itself involves. Generals are frequently accused of "preparing for the last war" and acting as though today were yesterday. What may be more significant, however, is that most of our tomorrows were indeed shaped the day before.

NOTES

1. See the contributions to this volume by Holst (Chapter 14), Nerlich (Chapter 1), and Rowen and Wohlstetter (Chapter 11).
2. *Hearings on Military Posture and HR 3689 Before the Committee on Armed Services*, House of Representatives, 94th Congress, First Session, Washington, D.C. (U.S. Government Printing Office, 1975—cited hereafter as HASC 94-8), part 1, p. 1820.
3. *White Paper 1975/1976: The Security of the Federal Republic of Germany and the Development of the Federal Armed Forces* (Bonn: Press and Information Office of the Federal Republic, 1976), especially p. 215.
4. D. Bell, *The Cultural Contradictions of Capitalism* (London: Heinemann, 1976), ch. 6, "The Public Household," esp. pp. 232-36.
5. See, for example, G. L. Tucker, "Standardization and the Joint Defense," *NATO Review*, January 1975.
6. Secretary of Defense James R. Schlesinger, *Annual Defense Department Report FY 1976 and FY 1977*, February 5, 1975, pp. 11-40.
7. See Chapter 5 in this volume, by Hudson and Haas, and *Supply Estimates 1975-76*, House of Commons Paper 198, 1974-1975, pp. 1-28.
8. HASC 94-8, part 1, pp. 347, 350, 371-72 and passim; also part 4, pp. 4321 ff. (on AWACS).
9. Second Report from the Expenditure Committee, Session 1974-75, *The Defence Review Proposals*, House of Commons Paper 259, 1974-75, evidence p. 58.
10. HASC 94-8, part 1, p. 1839 (Statement of Leonard Sullivan, Assistant Secretary of Defense, Program Analysis and Evaluation).
11. See Chapter 11.
12. See Chapter 14.

CHAPTER 10

Precision Guidance for NATO: Justification and Constraints

Graham T. Allison and Frederic A. Morris

From 1965 until the bombing halt of 1968, the bridge complex at Thanh Hoa in Vietnam withstood 600 American sorties (a sortie being a single attack by a single aircraft). This effort cost the United States twelve aircraft (replacement price: $60 million) and over $5 million in operating expenses.[1] On resumption of the bombing in 1972, eight aircraft carrying laser-guided bombs knocked out the bridge in a single mission. As Air Force Secretary Robert Seamans put it, "One tactical fighter can now accomplish what twenty-five might have done in the past."

The history of warfare is marked by watersheds in which new technology dramatically alters the way in which wars are fought. Precision-guided weapons may constitute such a watershed. The wide variety of terminally guided, high-accuracy weapons now under development or actually being deployed are outlined in Chapter 7 of this book by James Digby. As Director of Defense Research and Engineering Malcolm R. Currie has put it, "A tactical series of technical breakthroughs has brought us to the threshold of what I believe will become a true revolution in conventional warfare."[2]

The question arises: how likely is such a revolution? Most of the current debate on this issue focuses on the complicated issues of technology, economics, and strategy. Yet however those issues are resolved, the inescapable fact remains: PGMs will be developed, deployed, and used by large, cumbersome institutions, the Western defense establishments. Inevitably, organizations and politics will play a big role in determining whether and how PGMs are used. This chapter explores those organizational and political factors.

This discussion is presented in three parts. Section I offers some historical perspective on the adoption of new weapons. We argue that the availability of an attractive new technology does not ensure its adoption, much less its effective utilization. Section II examines that proposition in somewhat greater detail, with reference to the introduction of "smart" bombs in Southeast Asia. Section III draws implications from these sketches for the integration of precision-guided weapons into the NATO arsenal.

I

The term "revolution in warfare" carries more meaning than most casually selected metaphors. As Elting Morison has observed, "It is possible . . . to look upon invention as a hostile act—a dislocation of existing schemes, a way of disturbing the comfortable bourgeois routines and calculations, a means of discharging the restlessness with arrangements and standards that arbitrarily limit."[3] In the usual case, a new weapon has long "simmered on the back burner," ignored or denounced, before it reaches the battlefield. Often, only the pressures of combat and the revolutionary zeal of iconoclastic sponsors overcome official skepticism and hostility so as to give the weapon a chance. Typically, too, the weapon is misused. Again to quote Morison, "men tend to continue the patterns of behavior developed in earlier conditions into the new, often quite different conditions set forth by the introduction of different mechanisms."[4] A reexamination of some of the "watershed weapons" mentioned in the introduction should serve to highlight these tendencies.

At Crécy in 1346, English archers turned the tide of battle against the far larger French army. Yet the longbow had not just emerged from a carefully contrived English effort to develop a counter to its enemy's superior numbers. In fact, the longbow had been available to the English for nearly 250 years before Crécy. In the twelfth century, a historian had reported on Welsh success with the longbow in border wars with the English and recommended that Anglo-Norman armies use the weapon on the Continent. The advice was not taken. In the thirteenth century, Edward I employed the longbow to good effect in border skirmishes against the Welsh and the Scots, culminating in a smashing victory at the Battle of Falkirk in 1298. Still the weapon did not become a standard part of the army. Indeed, it was not even credited with the victory. Chroniclers of the battle "forgot that the archers prepared the way, and only remembered the victorious charge of the knights at the end of the day." Ignored by the English themselves, the lesson was learned instead by the Scottish enemy. Only through decades of fighting with his northern neighbors did Edward III come to appreciate the longbow's potential. Crécy was the result.[5]

Of equal interest is the longbow's successor, small arms. Well into the nineteenth century the standard weapon was the muzzle-loading smoothbore musket, difficult to reload and hopelessly inaccurate beyond a few yards. Despite the musket's obvious firepower, infantry tractics remained remarkably similar to those of the Roman era.[6] In the American Revolution, the attacking British infantry would march close-ranked —until they could "see the whites of their eyes"—fire a volley in the general direction of the enemy, and finish the job with their bayonets. Accuracy was so poor that aiming at a specific target was considered a waste of time. Standard infantry tactics held the bayonet, a vestige of the ancient spear, the decisive weapon. The British continued to fight in this fashion despite the successes of the inadequately indoctrinated American militiamen, whom Washington had taught to pick their targets and to aim, never mind the inaccuracy of the weapons. As Bruce Catton has put it, an infantry charge in the smoothbore era "was just the old Macedonian phalanx in modern dress—a compact mass of men projecting steel points ahead of them, striving to get to close quarters where they could either impale their opponents or force them to run away."[7]

Americans and British alike could have chosen a more accurate alternative, the rifled-bore musket. The Americans did make some limited use of the weapon, with telling effect. Still the rifle did not gain broad acceptance until after the Napoleonic wars. When it was adopted, military thinking again lagged behind technological potential. In logic, the rifle's vastly greater accuracy made standard tactics murderously obsolete. In practice, commanders still ordered their soldiers to attack in the old style. The carnage at Fredericksburg, Gettysburg, and Cold Harbor testifies to their persistence.[8]

Meanwhile, technical innovations beyond rifling (and addition of the percussion lock) met firm resistance.[9] In 1842 the War Department's colonel of ordnance was approached with a proposal to buy a breechloading carbine. The colonel was skeptical, and not only on his own account. As he explained, "a prejudice against all arms loading at the breech is prevalent among officers, and especially the Dragoons." Nonetheless, the colonel allowed tests to proceed. The carbine fired more than 14,000 rounds before breaking down in proving trials. Still the colonel was not convinced; he predicted that such weapons "will ultimately all pass into oblivion." Meanwhile he recommended the military not be "ensnared again by the projects of inventors."

With the colonel's departure and the growing possibility of civil war in the 1850s, the breech-loader fared somewhat better. The War Department promised to adopt the weapon on "convincing proof" of its superiority. But by 1861 the current colonel of ordnance still maintained that the Army's old muzzle-loader was "unsurpassed for military purposes." Should the front-rank men be issued repeating arms, he feared, they would be "more in dread of those behind than of the enemy." The possibility that repeaters would obviate the need for multiple ranks to attack in close order appears to have escaped him. One of the colonel's subordinates captured the prevailing spirit: he proposed that the Ordnance Department simply refuse all requisitions for novel weapons.

By 1864 the heat of combat and the presence of new men in the Ordnance Department began to soften the resistance to innovation. A few breech-loaders and repeating arms were sent to federal troops for field testing. By 1865 the few soldiers who used the new weapons attested to their superiority. Still, neither breech-loaders nor repeaters ever found wide use in the Civil War. According to Liddell Hart, the few that were used achieved "decisive influence" out of all proportion to their numbers. A Confederate general asserted that the war might have ended within a year if the federal infantry had been equipped from the outset with even crude repeating arms.

The story of the tank evokes parallels.[10] At the outset of World War I the basic technology for the tank lay on the shelf. Indeed, paper studies in several countries had advocated tanks, but these suggestions were rebuffed. After the outbreak of the War, British Lt. Col. Ernest Swinton, royal engineer and military historian, proposed developing an armored, armed, tracked vehicle to break through the evolving German trench barrier in Belgium. GHQ swiftly vetoed the idea, but it caught the ear—and the fancy—of First Lord of the Admiralty Winston Churchill. Churchill obtained government money for the project. First results in battle were mixed. Then on November 20, 1917, the British launched the first massed tank raid, committing all 476 vehicles of the newly formed British Tank Corps to the battle at Cambrai. The result was an outstanding success. Supported by artillery, infantry, and cavalry, the British tanks took 10,000 Germans at a cost of 4,000 British soldiers.

Cambrai sparked wide interest in the tank. The US Army, for example, formed its own Tank Corps in January 1918. But armistice was achieved too soon to test a truly major commitment to the weapon. The tank would mature in a peacetime environment.

In the United States, this environment was harsh. The Army established tactical and technical schools for the tank at Fort Meade, Maryland. There a young infantry officer named Dwight D. Eisenhower and cavalryman George Patton studied the tank in detail. They learned that during the war the tank's role was to precede and accompany the infantry. As Eisenhower recalls,[11]

> George and I and a group of young officers thought this was wrong. Tanks could have a more valuable and more spectacular role. We believed that they should be speedy, that they should attack by surprise and in mass. By making good use of the terrain in advance, they could break into the enemy's defensive positions, cause confusion, and by taking the enemy front line in reverse, make possible not only an advance by infantry, but envelopments of, or actual breakthroughs in, whole defensive positions.

Patton and Eisenhower spent a year in the field testing and refining their ideas. Soon they decided to give their theories wider circulation. Patton wrote articles on the tank in the Cavalry journals, Eisenhower in those of the Infantry. The Army responded decisively. Eisenhower was called before the Chief of Infantry. As he recalls the episode,[12]

> I was told that my ideas were not only wrong but dangerous and that henceforth I would keep them to myself. Particularly, I was not to publish anything incompatible with solid infantry doctrine. If I did, I would be hauled before a court-martial.

Shortly thereafter Congress abolished the Tank Corps, placing tanks under the control of the Infantry. Patton sought reassignment to the Cavalry and Eisenhower joined the US Army in Panama.

In Germany, the tank fared better. Colonel Hans von Guderian, given protection by von Seeckt and Hitler from a skeptical German army and government, steered German doctrine in the direction advocated by Eisenhower and Patton: strategic penetration by independent armored forces. The results are well known. Leading a smaller and less powerful tank force than that of his opponents, Guderian crushed Allied defenses in Belgium and reached the English Channel in a single week of May 1940. Within weeks, France fell and Britain was isolated. As Liddell Hart has put it,[13]

> The Battle of France is one of history's most striking examples of the decisive effect of a new idea, carried out by a dynamic executant . . . as decisive as other new ideas had been in earlier history—the use of the horse, the long spear, the phalanx, the flexible legion, the "oblique order," the horse-archer, the longbow, the musket, the gun, the organization of armies in separate and maneuverable divisions.

This "new idea"—the technology and the tactics—had been available to the Allies as well, for nearly two decades. Yet even so active an observer as Winston Churchill was caught unawares. As he recalls in his memoirs,[14]

> Not having had access to official information for so many years, I did not comprehend the violence of the revolution effected since the last war by the incursion of fast-moving heavy armor. I knew about it, but it had not altered my inward convictions as it should have done.

New weapons are ignored, resisted, misunderstood, misused. The reasons are not hard to discover. To perform the complicated task of fighting wars, armed forces are necessarily divided into suborganizations, each with its own missions, procedures, doctrines. New weapons rarely fit neatly into the old patterns, so they are made to fit, like the odd-shaped piece in a child's puzzle, or they simply fall between the cracks. To seize the implications of a new weapon, to create the new missions, procedures, and doctrines through which the weapon can realize its full potential, requires extraordinary vision and determination. As the examples illustrate, that vision and determination all too often come very late in the day.

II

From this perspective, the development and deployment of laser-guided bombs—the first generation of precision-guided weapons—becomes comprehensible.

The United States first developed "smart bombs" during World War

II, when American aircraft successfully employed them in the Mediterranean and China-Burma-India theaters. They were used also in the Korean conflict.[15] During the era of "massive retaliation" the problem of conventional bombing accuracy slipped from the development agenda. Then about 1964, the fighting in Vietnam began to exert pressures on the weapons acquisition process. Partly because military hardware had not caught up with Robert McNamara's "conventional response" doctrine and partly because the conflict in Vietnam diverged sharply from the sort of European war for which the United States had planned, American weapons often poorly suited operations in Southeast Asia. In response, the Department of Defense (DOD) created various ad hoc mechanisms to generate new technology for use in Vietnam.

Among the new agencies sprouted was "Detachment 5," stationed at Elgin Air Force Base.[16] Detachment 5's commander, Colonel Joseph Davis, hit on the idea for laser-guided bombs in consultation with Army engineers whose funds for exploring laser-guided antitank weapons had recently dried up. Davis shepherded the concept through a reluctant Air Force bureaucracy. The development succeeded. In early 1968, production began at the rate of about 100 guidance kits per month.

Recommendations that the Air Force commit itself more strongly to the use of "smart bombs" fell largely on deaf ears. Staff analyses used operational test data to demonstrate that the laser-guided bomb was more cost-effective than unguided ordnance (in targets destroyed per dollar) and required fewer sorties for 23 out of 25 target categories. In 1967, General John Lavelle, head of DOD's Defense Communications Planning Group (DCPG), tried to sell the Air Force on an extensive "smart bombs" program, on the order of 3,000 weapons per month. The Air Force rejected the suggestion out of hand.[17]

Soon the complexion of the air war in Vietnam changed. President Lyndon Johnson ordered the halt to bombing of the North above the 20th parallel in March 1968, and a halt to all bombing of the North in November 1968. While the force of the air war scarcely diminished, its focus shifted.[18] Bombing efforts now concentrated on the interdiction of supply trails running through Laos and Cambodia into South Vietnam—and on interdiction, close support, and harassment missions in the South itself. Although smart bombs were now available, they were not used extensively in the interdiction effort. According to Alexander Flax, "pilots found during late 1969 and early 1970 that the new smart bombs were superbly adept at hitting trucks and small targets" along the trails of Laos and Cambodia.[19] Yet the manufacturer (Texas Instruments) was not ordered to speed up its production of laser guidance kits beyond the leisurely rate of about 100 per month. On a trip to Southeast Asia in 1968, Air Force Secretary Harold Brown offered to "sell the Secretary of Defense" on increasing production to 600 units per month—this at a time when the United States was flying nearly 20,000 fighter-bomber sorties per month. The Seventh Air Force Commander, General George Brown, politely declined. Indeed, through 1971, General Brown and his successor, General Lucius Clay, made no request for the increased production of smart bombs. Few were used. Reportedly, the Seventh Air Force held the attitude, "Let's see how we do with 100 bombs per month," and asserted that the lack of high-value point targets outside North Vietnam made smart bombs cost-ineffective.[20]

Their logic was bizarre. The standard argument held that it was wasteful to expend a $3,000 bomb to destroy a $1,000 truck. This analysis ignored the obvious point that spending ten $1,000 bombs on the same target was even worse—and the only slightly subtler proposition that the dollar replacement cost of a target bears no necessary relation to the value of destroying it.

In addition, the scarcity and vulnerability of designator aircraft impeded even the limited effort. Only four to six converted gunships (slow and piston-powered) were available as designator aircraft in all of Vietnam. Until 1971/72, all operations with smart bombs depended on these and such designators as could be held by hand in the rear of F-4s.

The skepticism of Tactical Air Command (TAC) and Seventh Air Force commanders should not surprise us. Early in the Vietnam conflict, a great deal of gimmicky weaponry had found its way to the theater, where much of it proved ineffective.[21] Smart bombs could be seen to fit this pattern. Field commanders did not immediately grasp the fallacy of the $3,000 bomb versus $1,000 truck argument. It took time for them to be convinced that the aircraft designating the target, which had to loiter until the bomb reached its prey, could do so above the range of antiaircraft fire. And Air Force officials feared that smart bombs would adversely affect force structure. If Secretary Seamans' assertion that one aircraft using smart bombs could do the work of twenty-five armed with standard ordnance were shown to be correct, the conclusion that TAC could get by with fewer airplanes might not be far behind.

Perhaps only a change of personnel would overcome this resistance. In 1971, General Lavelle left the DCPG to assume command of the Seventh Air Force. Retaining his conviction that smart bombs were cost-effective on a variety of targets, he requested greater production. Acting through General Clay (now Commander in Chief, Pacific Air Forces) and the Deputy Chief of Staff, Air Force Logistics; he obtained production of 300 to 400 guidance kits per month. Lavelle personally experimented with the weapons against various interdiction targets. In his view, bad weather, the ability to travel at night, and camouflage made supply trucks less vulnerable to smart bombs than he had previously believed. But under appropriate circumstances, he found the weapons remarkably effective. In particular, bridges, road cuts, caves, and exposed trucks all fell to Lavelle's pilots using smart bombs. In the spring of 1972, as the air war against the North resumed, the Air Force used the weapons even more extensively, and with dramatic success. Operation Linebacker knocked out bridges and other targets that had eluded the Rolling Thunder campaign of 1965/68.[22]

III

It took a hot war in Southeast Asia, determined entrepreneurship, and a lapse of several years for the US Air Force to adopt smart bombs. Following their widely heralded success, however, the US services embraced precision guidance. Indeed, PGMs fit neatly into the American military's "doctrine of quality," according to which the United States counters the quantitative superiority of its potential adversaries with costlier but presumably far more unit-effective weapons. The United States' NATO allies have not yet caught up. Although numerous "smart weapons" developments are under way in Europe, procurement lags. No NATO members, other than the United States and Turkey, are acquiring smart bombs or Maverick missiles for their air forces. Nor do any of these countries *plan* to buy such weapons: none is included in any NATO ally's five-year defense plan.[23] Surface-launched antitank weapons have fared somewhat better. But while the United States has placed Dragon antitank missiles in every European rifle squad and is deploying TOW antitank missiles at a rapid rate, no other NATO army has such an ambitious program.[24]

Analytic uncertainty and long lead times, as well as tight budgets and the absence of a decisive combat experience, may substantially explain the leisurely pace of the allies' smart weapons programs. Reasonable people can differ as to the appropriate resolution of the many complicated technical, economic, and strategic issues posed by precision guidance. For both the United States and its allies, however, such considerations are at least partially beside the point. Our look at previous innovations, including American experience with PGMs to date, underscores the point: analytic considerations rarely pace the application of new technology, any more than analysis determines force posture generally. NATO's failure to make changes far less ambiguous on the merits than adoption of PGMs lends further support to this conclusion.

NATO's current inadequacies are widely appreciated:

1. *The design and structure of NATO forces do not match the Soviet threat.* Whereas the Soviets plan a short, quick armored thrust, NATO force planning implies a long war of attrition across a broad front.[25]
2. *The equipment and supplies of the various NATO allies cannot be used interchangeably.* Some examples: The various national armies stationed in West Germany have no common communication system with which they can talk to each other over a secure line.[26] If five destroyers from as many NATO countries embarked on a joint mission, not one would be able to refuel any other at sea because all hoses and fuel inlets differ.[27] In the Northern sector, each national army uses a different size artillery shell, meaning each must depend on its own supply.[28] There are twenty-seven different types of ship-borne radars in the NATO navy.[29] Lack of standardization costs NATO an estimated $6 to $10 billion per year.[30]
3. *Each NATO division requires far more "tail" than a Soviet division with equal teeth.* For example, *adjusted* (equal front-line strength) peacetime division slices (the division plus its share of nondivision support) total about 42,000 for US forces in West Germany, but only 18,500 for Soviet forces.[31] With manpower absorbing a major (40 percent) and growing share of the annual US defense budget, the implications should be obvious.

The obstacles to redressing these critical deficiences have been largely political and organizational. In most NATO countries, defense policy is high politics. And the political english on most issues does not cut in the direction of reform. Take, for example, redesigning forces and restructuring divisions to match the Soviet threat in conventional war-fighting capability. Although Canby, Komer, and others have argued persuasively that redesign can take place within current budgets, this proposition does not correspond to the broad political perception that NATO cannot afford to match the Warsaw Pact in conventional capabilities. Consequently, proposals for movement in this direction have generally encountered hostility or skepticism. In addition, European publics and politicians tend to believe that conventional defense is not "real," that the US nuclear umbrella provides the actual deterrent, and that attempts to make conventional war-fighting a live option strengthen rather than weaken deterrence. Reinforcing this perspective are powerful memories of World War II and the inference that a major conventional war in Europe will inevitably result in devastating civilian damage.

Standardization also faces political obstacles. The imperative of "buying domestic" commands broad support from European business and labor communities. Developing major hardware items indigenously often becomes politically necessary even when the economic and coordination costs point in the other direction. Cooperative ventures (such as MRCA and Jaguar) and arrangements whereby the user nation manufactures weapons or components designed elsewhere (such as the Lightweight Fighter) provide only a partial solution. Experience with such programs suggests that domestic pressures for each venturer to exercise "design leadership" often make cooperation difficult: national pride either impedes analytic trade-offs or kills the deal off altogether.

The organizational obstacles to reform are even more severe. Most stem from the key fact that NATO consists of fourteen separate national defense establishments, most comprising three services. Each service has a large stake in preserving existing priorities. Any major adjustment poses a potential threat to budget, hardware, men, and responsibility. In support of the status quo, each service has an established set of doctrines: the procedures and hardware built into the incentive and belief structures of the service's professional cores. Proposals running counter to existing doctrines are resisted.

Restructuring to counter Soviet blitzkrieg strategy provides an illuminating example. Essentially, most of NATO's national defense establishments have modeled their capabilities on the American example. Prevailing doctrine calls for the capability to fight extended conflicts and to meet global (non-NATO) contingencies. In support of these objectives, NATO's services have bought expensive, all-purpose forces, including navies to keep open the sea lanes, airborne units that have little application against armored attack, air forces oriented toward air superiority, supply interdiction, and deep interdiction missions, and antisubmarine warfare forces. One observer has estimated that in all, less than 30 percent of the NATO nations' annual defense pays for warfighting capabilities in the central NATO region.[32] Whether doctrines drive forces or forces determine doctrines is a question best left to metaphysics. The important point remains: doctrines and forces powerfully reinforce each other in resistance to change.

The same organizational factors impede standardization. Each national defense establishment, and each service, claims its logistics as its own responsibility. Each reserves the right to arrange for its supplies, from lubricants to stretchers to petroleum to tire pumps to ammunition. The ability to rely on other sources, the goal of standardization, would mean a cession of control incompatible with maintaining the organization's autonomy. The difficulties escalate by an order of magnitude when the issue moves from fuel hoses to major pieces of hardware, such as tactical aircraft. In such instances, not only is each national air force wedded to elaborate doctrines as to the relative importance of various missions and performance requirements in its front-line weapons, but the service also deploys an elaborate, hierarchical requirements generation process. Officials at successive levels must sign off on countless details of design before a new weapon can be approved. Reconciling differences within a service is difficult enough; between services and across national boundaries the problem becomes immense, and can place taxing burdens on the design or doom the project entirely. At best, each buyer typically orders a distinct version of the weapon, undercutting the scale economies and interchangeability that standardization is supposed to provide.

Organizations and politics impede reform. The introduction of new hardware, such as PGMs, is a predictably slow process. Perhaps more important, organizations *channel* reform. When innovative hardware is not resisted, it is accommodated to fit existing doctrines, missions, and procedures. In fact, in some cases the incrementalism may be appropriate. Our review of such examples as the tank and the musket, however, demonstrates that some innovations call for nonincremental adoption if they are to achieve their full potential. Canby and others have argued forcefully that PGMs are of this character, requiring creation and destruction of long-standing missions and tactics.[33] Short of the drastic experiment of a hot war, this conclusion will remain controversial. Meanwhile, organizational inertia seems likely to systematically bias the adoption of PGMs in the direction of incrementalism. At least, the evidence to date is consistent with this hypothesis.

Consider, for example, the close support mission. To be sure, there are analytic difficulties with PGMs in this role. The effectiveness of Maverick and similar weapons is severely constrained by European weather conditions. The worst winter months restrict the use to about 20 percent of daylight hours.[34] Moreover, the use of precision weapons against ground forces is costly: the requisite high-resolution sensors and environmental preparation ECM/defense suppression capabilities absorb a lot of resources. Thus the European air forces can point to a number of reasons for continuing to rely on area weapons. Indeed, the US Air Force may be returning to a similar view. As retiring AAFCE Commander in Chief John Vogt recently put it, "You could not have smart bombs and nothing else. In spite of USAF trials in Europe designed to prove the contrary, if the weather was bad there were problems.[35]

Yet whatever the merits of precision guidance for close support, the environment for innovation is not fertile. Effective performance of the close air support mission is peripheral to the central ambitions of the professional cores of the European air forces. Air superiority remains their dominant concern: witness the NATO consortium's dominant preoccupation with air-to-air performance in choosing a follow-on to the F-104.[36] While the US Air Force has little more real attachment to close support, the threat of losing the mission to Army helicopters (equipped with PGMs such as Hellfire) triggers at least some sustained attention. In the absence of this incentive, the Europeans seem likely to continue to ignore the problem.

The outcome for surface-launched antitank weapons is less clear. The Europeans have not bought many American-made antitank PGMs, in part apparently, because "made in USA" makes a politically unattractive selling point. Indigenous developments are in progress, but procurement in numbers remains in doubt. Several organizational considerations point away from buying in quantity. First, antitank PGMs are not essential to the professional cores of the European armies. In fact, in an era of stable or declining budgets, they compete with weapons central to the armies' essence, namely, tanks. Second, Europeans armies have traditionally not purchased much ordnance at all; given the current budgeting squeeze, *additional* outlays seem unlikely. Third, the high unit cost of PGMs implies low numbers, creating the fear that the armies will "run out" by the "second day of the war." Traditionally, the military likes to save something for the whole war.

As mentioned above, American commanders are generally more enthusiastic about PGMs than their European counterparts. Thus far, however, the US services have essentially adopted the new technology within the constraints of current doctrines, missions, and procedures. Consider, for example, one of the latest generation PGMs, the cannon-launched guided projectile (CLGP). The Development Concept Paper for that weapon includes the revealing directive:[37]

> To the maximum extent, the projectile will be employed within the framework of current tactics, organization, and equipment of field artillery units.

As a result, such standard artillery procedures as placing observers on forward slopes and restricting the number of observers greatly limits fulfillment of CLGP's potential.[38] And if changing procedures by which existing missions are performed is hard, departures that eliminate or downgrade entire missions will likely prove impossible. A strong though far from conclusive case can be made that land-based precision-guided missiles and artillery ought to replace tactical air in most air-to-ground missions—in the process, removing the justification for the air superiority mission. That the Air Force would acquiesce in such a departure appears unlikely in the extreme.

In short, political and organization considerations cast doubt on the proposition that NATO will adopt PGMs other than incrementally. Gradual assimilation and extended failure to exploit the weapons' full potential—even if the technical and cost problems are solved—appears the likely prognosis. This pessimistic assessment recalls the view of Eisenhower when he was Allied commander a quarter of a century ago. According to Drew Middleton, Eisenhower "told visitors that if the Alliance was able to reach high qualitative standards, Europe would be able to defend itself and the Americans could go home."[39] Those standards seem no closer now than when Eisenhower spoke.

NOTES

1. Based on an average cost of $8,500/fighter-bomber sortie. Raphael Littauer and Norman Uphoff, eds., *Air War in Indochina* (Boston: Beacon Press, 1972), p. 235.
2. Quoted in Phil Stanford, "The Automated Battlefield," *New York Times Magazine*, Feb. 23, 1975.
3. Elting E. Morison, *Men, Machines, and Modern Times* (Cambridge, Mass.: The M.I.T. Press, 1966), p. 9.
4. Ibid., p. 10.
5. This account of the longbow is based on I. B. Holley, Jr., *Ideas and Weapons* (New Haven, Conn.: Yale University Press, 1953), pp. 3-5.
6. See Bernard and Fawn M. Brodie, *From Crossbow to H-Bomb* (Bloomington, Ind., and London: Indiana University Press, 1973), pp. 103-6.
7. Bruce M. Catton, *Mr. Lincoln's Army* (Garden City, N.Y.: Doubleday & Company, 1954), p. 192.
8. Ibid., passim.
9. This account relies on Holley, op. cit., pp. 6-10.
10. This sketch of the tank is based on Kenneth Macksey, *Tank* (New York: The Two Continents Publishing Group, 1974), pp. 24-107.
11. Dwight D. Eisenhower, *At Ease: Stories I Tell Friends* (Garden City, N.Y.: Doubleday & Company, 1967), p. 170.
12. Ibid., p. 173.
13. B. H. Liddell Hart, *History of the Second World War* (New York: G. P. Putnam's Sons, 1971), p. 66.
14. Winston S. Churchill, *The Second World War*, vol. II: *Their Finest Hour* (London: Cassell, 1967), p. 39.
15. For an account of Azon and Razon in World War II, see James Phinney Baxter, III, *Scientists Against Time* (Boston: Little, Brown, and Company, 1946), pp. 193-200. For the story of Razon and Tarzon in Korea, see Robert Frank Futrell, *The United States Air Force in Korea 1950-1953* (New York: Duell, Sloan and Pearce, 1961), pp. 292-97; see also James T. Stewart, ed., *Airpower/The Decisive Force in Korea* (Princeton, N.J.: D. Van Nostrand Company, 1961), p. 81.
16. Except for specific citations to the contrary, the development history of the laser-guided bomb relies on Peter de Leon, *The Laser-guided Bomb: Case History of a Development* (Santa Monica, Calif.: The Rand Corporation, R-1312-1-PR, June, 1974).
17. Interview with a participant.
18. See Littauer and Uphoff, op. cit., p. 281.
19. Quoted in *The Washington Star*, June 18, 1972.
20. Interview with a participant.
21. Interviews with participants.

22. Ibid.
23. *Armed Forces Journal International,* June 5, 1975, p. 5.
24. Ibid.
25. See, for example, Steven Canby, *NATO Military Policy: Obtaining Conventional Comparability with the Warsaw Pact* (Santa Monica, Calif.: The Rand Corporation, R-1088-ARPA, June, 1973); Steven Canby, "NATO Muscle: More Shadow than Substance," *Foreign Policy,* no. 8 (Fall 1972); and R. W. Komer, "Treating NATO's Self-Inflicted Wound," *Foreign Policy,* no. 13 (Winter 1973-74). Recent Soviet expansion of support capabilities and the like may give the Soviets alternatives to complete reliance on a blitzkrieg strategy. See U.S. Congress, Senate, Committee on the Armed Services, *Military Appropriations for Fiscal Year 1976,* Hearings, Manpower, 94th Congress, 1st Session, 1975, part 5, p. 2279.
26. Paul Kemezis, "NATO Forces Are Seeking to Standardize Equipment," *The New York Times,*
27. Drew Middleton, "Doubts and Anxiety for NATO Officials," *The New York Times,* January 1, 1976.
28. Kemezis, op. cit.
29. Thomas A. Callaghan, Jr., *U.S./European Economic Cooperation in Military and Civil Technology* (Arlington, Va.: Ex-Im Tech, Inc., 1974).
30. Kemezis, op. cit., and Middleton, op. cit.
31. Canby, "NATO Muscle," pp. 39-40.
32. Ibid., p. 44.
33. Steven Canby, *The Alliance and Europe: Part IV: Military Doctrine and Technology,* Adelphi Paper No. 109 (London: The International Institute for Strategic Studies, Winter/1974/75).
34. Steven Canby, *Terminal Guidance on the Battlefield: Obtaining Its Potential Payoff* (Santa Monica, Calif.: Technology Service Corporation, May 2, 1975), p. 11.
35. *Flight International,* October 16, 1975.
36. See Bill Gunston, "Fighters and a European Mission," *Flight International,* December 12, 1974.
37. Quoted in Canby, *Terminal Guidance,* p. 2.
38. Ibid., pp. 25, 34-35.
39. Middleton, op. cit.

V

DEVELOPING THE ABILITY TO RESPOND SELECTIVELY

CHAPTER 11

Varying Response with Circumstance

Henry S. Rowen and Albert Wohlstetter

The members of the Western Alliance have long focused their attention and resources on preventing a massive Soviet attack against Western Europe, especially one directed at the Center. Despite this focus on massive threats, the allies have for just as long recognized many potential challenges to their interests that are less massive, but of enormous importance, and less risky for the challengers. The likelihood of direct military challenge to the Center has been kept small up to now, in good part because of the efforts made to counter it. Such efforts need to continue and improve, to match the steady and formidable improvement in Soviet capability. However, it is clear that a wider variety of threats that strike less directly at the heart of Europe is growing in importance. One is painfully evident: the threat to Europe's energy supplies in the Middle East. Such indirect threats, and some more direct but still less than an attack on the center, could erode the security and shape the politics and economics of all of Western Europe and surrounding areas.

These more limited Soviet challenges include military support, short of military intervention, where governmental changes favoring the Soviet Union have occurred in a Western country or in a country important to the West; military intervention in an area neighboring NATO territory; or military attack on the NATO flanks. Any of these challenges by the Soviets or one of its allies might bring about undesired changes or accommodation in the West.

SOVIET FORCE AND ITS RISKS

The Russians, it is familiar, take force very seriously. They like to have it "in the bank" to draw on. But they are not daredevils or adventurists. They naturally prefer the pursuit of political objectives, using military force only as a background factor. The shadow of an apparently overwhelming force can, however, be very effective, and using the shadow is safer than sending in tanks. They may express this preference for limiting risks by sending arms and advisors and by letting their allies do the fighting. Only when the risks have seemed low, or the situation too dangerous to let stand, have the Soviets initiated the use of force. Then they have used it massively for limited ends—and even then without using all of the available types of weapons. Examples can be found in the Winter War in Finland of 1939-40, in Hungary in 1956, and in Czechoslovakia in 1968.

Western analysts, who are keenly aware that the Soviet Union is quite cautious, nevertheless sometimes assume implicitly that if it should use force today against the West, it would abandon both restraint and hope of survival. This assumes that the only choices open to it are doing nothing or assuming unlimited risks. This assumption is a comforting one for us. For if any Soviet military action against us would be extreme, then we need only prepare for the worst; but if their only possible moves amount to being suicidal ones, the Soviets will not, we reason, act at all. Therefore, we do not need military capabilities for the lesser contingencies and we shall not have to use our capabilities for the grand contingency. The Soviet Union will not engage us at any level. Unfortunately for this theory, there are a good many things in between doing nothing and committing suicide. And there is little in the record of Soviet behavior to suggest a taste for either suicide or total quiescence.

Soviet declarations, of course, may suggest that there is nothing between accommodation and suicide for the West in a conflict. It obviously serves their purpose to have NATO believe that any response it makes, no matter how limited, is going to lead to an unlimited disaster. However, the evolution of Soviet discussion of the possibility of limiting conflict to the nonnuclear level is instructive. Russian commentators once scoffed at the idea that there could be a substantial conflict in the NATO area that would not immediately become nuclear. After much invective on the subject, they eventually admitted the need to plan for nonnuclear engagements. For good reason, we might witness the same phenomenon with respect to other forms of limitation, for example, within nuclear conflict. Now a great deal of Soviet rhetoric flows about the absurdity of the notion of limiting the use of nuclear weapons; on the other hand. there is no real evidence that the Soviets would abandon all caution in a nuclear or any other conflict.

The Soviet preference for pursuit of a political strategy with force in the background fits the opportunities now presented. There are many manifestations of Western weakness and vulnerability: a marked reduction in Western cohesion; a reduced willingness to spend money on military forces; political instability in several Southern European countries; strengthened isolationist sentiments and a reduced capacity for administrative action within the United States; vulnerability to Arab use of the oil weapon; and a continuing improvement in the quality and quantity of Soviet military forces. The central problem posed in the near term by Western weakness is not so much a direct Soviet military move against the West, but Soviet exploitation of the forces of fragmentation and instability.

Given these prospects, should we worry at all about direct attacks? One reason for being concerned is the effect capabilities for conflict at a higher level can have on contests at a lower level. Many of the contests between East and West take place in third areas, places of importance to us, if not always of the most central interest. In such contests, outside powers provide support to countries in the contested area, may threaten to intervene, try to prevent others from intervening, and occasionally send troops. A threat to intervene in such contingencies is more plausible if one is prepared against counterintervention. Moreover, these matters are uncertain. A large conflict growing out of a local one, although far from certain or even likely, is by no means impossible.

INCREASING SOVIET POWER AND ITS POSSIBLE USES

We should expect the Soviets to continue to try to increase their power compared to that of the NATO countries, to do this both by acquiring new weapons and by discouraging our acquisition of new strength. Four new types of ICBMs, two new types of SLBMs, naval deployments in the North Atlantic, the Mediterranean, and the Indian Ocean area, new equipment for ground and tactical air forces in Central Europe, new MIRVed mobile IRBMs, higher-performance dual-capable fighters and fighter-bombers, improved theaterwide command, control, and communication—all are products of a continuing program of increasing Soviet military spending. These efforts have not, for some time, been matched by the West. The Soviets also may work to improve their relative power by reducing that of the West—encouraging denial of bases to the West such as the Azores, fostering neutralist tendencies in Western countries, and trying to establish closer ties themselves, possibly even getting some use of bases, for example, in Portugal.

Having power has its uses. For one thing, it helps affect the choices made within other governments. Situations of uncertainty and ambiguity exist in several countries. Compromises among factions, some friendly to the East, can be encouraged. Cooperation on matters of European or NATO concern become more costly in terms of domestic politics. In this environment, the mere presence of a powerful Soviet Union can coerce; arrangements are more likely to be made which are acceptable to this powerful neighbor. Such adjustments took place in Eastern Europe and in Finland; they are not beyond happening elsewhere. Furthermore, overt interventions might be made to try to make permanent what otherwise might be a transient period of communist party influence or control in government.

Soviet actions could extend to actual military intervention in countries just outside the NATO area, for example, in Yugoslavia, Finland, or Iran. Such interventions in the past have taken place in areas occupied by Soviet troops in World War II; we should not forget that these three countries also have had the Red Army on their territory.

Under circumstances of low Western cohesion and a high likelihood of keeping the conflict isolated, an attack might occur against some part of Western Europe. Clearly the flanks are most exposed: North Norway, Greece, Turkey. For the near term, such attacks seem risky; but given current political trends, in the future they might be much less so.

Finally, there is the possibility of large-scale attack on the West. If it were to occur, it would most likely happen through spreading of a local conflict at a time when there were sharp divisions within the alliance.

PROGRESSIVE TECHNICAL CHANGE AND CONTINUITY IN NATO DOCTRINE

NATO doctrine has undergone much change over the years. It is broad enough to cover politically sensible responses in concept. Technology is now catching up with doctrine and making it easier to implement. What is needed is the gradual introduction of weapons and plans for their use that are better adapted politically to the purposes that have been recognized in NATO doctrine.

First, we need forces that a political man might agree to use when they are needed. They should be designed for military effectiveness, not simply for demonstration effects. Sometimes a supposed "demonstration of resolve" merely shows a reluctance to do anything effective. Democratic governments, although they sometimes try, find it hard to be convincingly reckless or unpredictable on matters of security. And as with Wellington's troops, such policies may or may not frighten the enemy but they certainly frighten us.

Second, our forces should be able to conduct a wide range of nonnuclear operations. Moreover, at any level of the use of force, they should produce low collateral damage. This is a requirement wherever we use weapons, on our own territory, in Eastern Europe or other third countries, or in the Soviet Union. The need to be both effective and restrained implies that we adopt a *dual criterion* in using force, one which takes account both of effectiveness in destroying targets and of the preservation of things we want to avoid destroying.

Third, although the possibility of coordinating NATO response is its greatest strength, we should not insist on unanimity as a condition for any action. If we did, then it might paralyze us. In fact, it is unrealistic to expect unified NATO action in responding to all contingencies. Therefore, there should be planning and cooperation among those European countries most likely to be directly affected by limited contingencies, together with the North American countries, on how to forestall and to meet them. The ability of the European countries to act effectively in limited contingencies is important because their interests are most directly involved, because their ability to act effectively and in a controlled way (e.g., without having to initiate use of nuclear weapons in limited contingencies) would have an especially discouraging effect on Soviet initiatives, and because this would help assure US support.

Fourth, our responses should be designed to help arrive at mutual limitations and reduce the likelihood of a wider conflict.

Fifth, the forces bought have to fit the budgetary realities. Given this constraint, we need to see where effective and cost-saving new technology could be introduced. These technologies are principally the technologies of information and improved munitions.

THE TECHNOLOGIES OF PRECISION
AND DISCRIMINATION

There are extensive discussions of these and other technologies else-where in this book. Here we discuss only the most significant developments.

Accuracy.   Among these the most significant is improved accuracy for both aerodynamic and ballistic vehicles from very short ranges up to ranges of thousands of miles. The high accuracy of precision-guided munitions at short ranges is well known. But impressive improvements in accuracy are also taking place at long range. For example, the accuracy of inertially guided intercontinental missile systems has improved by an order of magnitude in roughly a decade. With ballistic or aerodynamic vehicles, another order of magnitude improvement may be expected without terminal guidance, or even more with it. It is clear from public information that the area of the median circle of error for strategic rockets has long been measured in tenths of a square mile; it appears that it will soon be measured in hundredths and in the long run in thousandths of a square mile or less. The contrast with the accuracy of the original V-2 technology is dramatic. V-2 guidance technology, if it had been extended to intercontinental distances, would have had a median circle of error measured in the tens of thousands of square miles.

With sufficient accuracy, efficient attack using nonnuclear ordnance can be carried out against many types of targets; the quantities delivered would be very much less than in past conflicts. For nuclear weapons, the attainable precision will be good enough to permit us to substitute nuclear weapons of about 1-kt to 10-kt yield for higher-yield weapons for most targets. This would greatly reduce collateral damage from the levels produced by today's nuclear weapons with today's accuracies. Moreover, if accuracy improves enough, we will be able to substitute nonnuclear weapons for nuclear ones for many targets.

Munitions.   In sum, these include new weapons that distribute and focus energy more effectively over critical parts of the target and, where possible, limit the spillover of energy that causes unwanted collateral damage. Nonnuclear types of weapons include fuel-air explosives, improved cluster munitions for area targets, and hard-structure munitions. In addition, fundamental work on nonnuclear explosives may produce a significant increase in their yield-to-weight ratios. In the past, it has been assumed that nonnuclear unit warhead costs had to be quite low because combat consumption totals would be very high. This discouraged R&D because higher-yield chemical explosives are much more costly per pound. But with accurate weapons, used for selected purposes, high unit costs per warhead can be more than offset by even higher unit effectiveness.

For nuclear weapons, the use of earth-penetrating warheads and low fission yields can reduce collateral damage—but with some chance of radioactive fallout and rainout, depending on weather conditions.

Vehicles. Many types of delivery vehicles, short- and long-range, ballistic and aerodynamic, manned (with the pilot in the vehicle or in a remote location connected to the vehicle with a data link) and unmanned, could play a role in these contingencies. Of particular interest are cruise vehicles, guided both manually and automatically. These are efficient at carrying payload, should be able to penetrate successfully to most targets, and should be able to achieve high accuracy. But ballistic missiles of varying ranges will also be experiencing impressive improvements in accuracy and could be needed for certain missions, especially nuclear, but possibly including nonnuclear.

For these vehicles, various types of basing methods are possible: land mobile, air mobile, surface ship, submarine. Improved accuracy on both sides makes fixed points more vulnerable and mobility more important. Moreover, new guidance technologies are especially compatible with mobile basing modes. Basing methods which have low cost or low vulnerability, or preferably both, are needed. Land and submarine mobility may be especially interesting prospects for European countries.

SURVEILLANCE AND COMMAND AND CONTROL

Fully exploiting improved accuracy depends critically on the surveillance function: to locate targets, to measure their characteristics, to determine post-attack damage. Major advances in sensors, communications, and information-processing are taking place. In addition to automatic systems, having a man in the loop is useful for real-time surveillance and for target acquisition.

A strategy of flexibility and discrimination to deal with small contingencies plainly puts greater demands on command and control than a strategy that is deliberately and carelessly indiscriminate. The ability to implement the dual criterion of destroying targets and preserving nontargets from destruction depends crucially on the attacker's ability to control his forces. This need for precise control applies at all levels of the military command chain and at the level of government control as well. For individual weapons, having positive control suggests having a man in the loop; for example, weapons missing the target could be aborted by him. For higher levels, arriving at appropriate rules of engagement and monitoring them are vitally important for contingencies of this kind. With weapons that are more focused and limited in their effects, once rules of engagement have been decided, there are much greater possibilities of devolution of authority to lower levels than with indiscriminate weapons.

Similar issues arise concerning the process of reaching decisions among governments. The possibility of freeing member countries from a requirement for unanimity depends on how much less than suicidal the action is. The more focused and specific, the easier will be the acceptance of decentralized action and the more rapidly decisions can be taken.

EXAMPLES OF DISCRIMINATE RESPONSES

Political interests will dictate that where force is used, it be used in a focused way. A variety of types of targets might be appropriate, depending on the contingency. We do not pretend to be able to anticipate the particular types of targets that might be selected in any given contingency. However, we can illustrate the effects of the technologies of precision on different types of targets.

A historical example is provided by the Cuban missile crisis in 1962. An attack on the Soviet IRBMs and MRBMs in Cuba was seriously considered by President Kennedy. He believed it important for such an attack to be sharply focused on the missiles, for the attack to be highly effective and to kill as few people as possible. But the weapons available did not permit effective, discriminate attacks. With today's precision-guided nonnuclear weapons, the number required to achieve high target damage in that 1962 situation is less by a factor of over 100 and unwanted fatalities could also be considerably reduced.

For the unlikely contingency of a nuclear strike against a large target system consisting of military bases, logistics facilities, and government controls, the substitution of 10-kt weapons for 1-mt ones, the careful selection of targets, and the avoidance of those most highly colocated with population would reduce collateral damage greatly. In one case, the combined fatalities and casualties would be reduced by about 96 percent.

A third example is provided by the case of discriminate attacks on selected industries, such as electric power, steel, petroleum refining, or primary aluminum production. These targets constituted the bulk of our strategic target list up to the mid-1950s, and are likely to come under attack even in wars in "third" areas. For nuclear attacks on such targets, future yield-accuracy combinations give an estimated reduction in civilian fatalities of 500 to 1,000 times from the level with high-yield, less accurate weapons. Moreover, a detailed examination of critical facilities shows that many types of plants are vulnerable to precise nonnuclear attack. With accurate delivery, delivered munitions payloads per plant would be reduced by several orders of magnitude by comparison with World War II, in order to do significant damage to important components within these plants. Damage to civilians living outside of the plants would be quite small. With high accuracy, the total number of delivered weapons needed to put out of commission a large proportion of certain key industries for a significant period of time would not be enormous.

In sum, greater accuracy improves effectiveness in destroying targets, because more bombs hit the target, and reduces collateral damage, because fewer bombs miss the target and hit civilians and fewer and smaller bombs can be used. Within given political constraints, this greatly increases mission effectiveness; it is likely to increase the speed and even the likelihood of a decision to release weapons for use, especially if it is a question of using nonnuclear weapons. The reduced requirements for delivered weapons also means reduced losses to defenses, reduced numbers of aircraft or missiles that need to be assigned to these tasks, and reduced logistics needs.

FINDING WHAT MISSIONS MIGHT BE APPROPRIATE

There is a good deal to be done between estimating some of the targeting implications of certain technological trends and designing or choosing missions for these weapons in particular contingencies.

Developing responses that are appropriate to Soviet limited attacks seems to require the further development of some missions that we have considered in the past. However, such familiar mission categories as "strategic" and "tactical" impede thought more than they help it. The word "strategic" may refer to (1) attack by US or Soviet forces on opposing homelands; (2) attack on population (and/or industry) as distinct from military targets; (3) attack on missiles in silos and other long-range forces versus attack on general-purpose forces; (4) attack on "deep" targets; (5) nuclear as opposed to nonnuclear attacks; (6) attacks using long-range vehicles against any targets; or (7) any attack launched from outside the theater.

The word "tactical" may mean (1) avoiding superpower homelands, fighting in allied territory only; (2) attack only on military targets; (3) attack only on general-purpose forces; (4) nonnuclear attack or perhaps nuclear attack only on the battlefield; or (5) attack using short-range vehicles.

The range of responses that seem to be best suited for limited contingencies cuts across these familiar categories. We suggest for discussion the following types of responses.

Blocking action within the territory of the country attacked or at sea. This is the most natural and immediate response: to stop the invasion. Almost certainly it would be the first decided upon. The advances in technology discussed in this book significantly improve the effectiveness of blocking forces in many contingencies: the use of improved sensors to detect and localize invading forces; land and sea mines to slow, attrite, and channelize them; the use of highly accurate weapons to destroy concentrations of military value—ships, tanks, and aircraft. In addition to locally based short-range vehicles, remotely based long-range ones might be used. Although there would presumably be a strong preference for blocking action against a nonnuclear attack to be conducted without the use of nuclear weapons, there are some sorts of incursions where this would not be possible. In such a case, there might be use of nuclear weapons to destroy Soviet forces within allied territory. The object of blocking actions is to buy time, to require a larger—and therefore less likely—commitment of forces by the Soviets, and to increase the likelihood of unambiguous warning of attack by forcing the use of larger enemy forces.

Shallow, cross-border responses. These might be in the territory of Soviet allies or into an adjoining region of the Soviet Union which is the source of the attacking forces. Such attacks would be a natural response to an invasion. This response might be limited to a shallow region but also limited to the bases and lines of communication of the attacking forces. This would help the blocking forces in allied territory. Responses might be nonnuclear or nuclear; however, as we have observed earlier, the ability to use advanced technology to conduct effective cross-border responses with only nonnuclear weapons could ease the problem of getting early decision.

Within the regions subject to attack, there would also be military forces and industrial facilities less immediately related to the conduct of the invasion but important for Soviet military strength: large radars, naval forces, airfields, electric power stations, petroleum refineries, and other war-related industries. Attack on these facilities within the area which was the source of the invasion is another possible response. Their destruction would serve as an offset to gains the attacker might seek. The Kola Peninsula area provides a case in point: if northern Norway were attacked, Kola would be the principal base area for the invasion. A response against the bases and lines of communication in the area, and only in this area, would be a natural response. Kola also contains a large concentration of military force as well as important industrial facilities. If the Soviets were to launch an attack from this area, the radar, naval, electric power, and other installations in the region might be appropriate targets of a response. With high accuracy, the forces needed to have significant effect, with little collateral damage, would not be large; they could be well within the capacity of the European countries most directly affected.

There are, of course, many important questions to be asked about such cross-border responses. One that arises naturally in an alliance context is by what process such missions might be decided upon and how they might be controlled. Another concerns the risks. Each possible regionally limited cross-border response against the source of attack has different sorts of risks. But the issue is one of relative risk, for example, compared with such alternatives as:

1. the use of nuclear weapons to destroy Soviet forces within allied territory in reply to a nonnuclear incursion;
2. limiting oneself to a nonnuclear response within the territory involved and, where this is unfeasible,
3. simply accepting defeat;
4. attacking a remote geographically unconnected but geographically limited area, say, in the territory of a Soviet ally (an area which is not naturally connected to the source of the attack); or

5. a deep retaliatory response that surrenders the possibility of exploiting natural geographical boundaries as a means of limiting the conflict.

A nonnuclear counterstrike at the source of attack just across the border in the Soviet Union, to take one example, has its dangers. Are such dangers greater than those brought on by attempting the nuclear destruction of Soviet forces within the country they have invaded?

Cross-border responses countrywide. The adversaries would have a powerful incentive to limit the scope of a conflict. Nevertheless, responses over a wider geographic area are possible to imagine. As with shallow responses, these might be limited to the military bases, logistic facilities, or industrial plants closely related to support of the battle. Responses might also be directed against other military facilities or industries related to Soviet overall war potential. At no stage would it make sense for there to be indiscriminate attack on populations.

How might the Soviets react to such responses? The most important point is that blocking, shallow, and other selective and natural responses are not wildly implausible responses to a Soviet attack, especially if these capabilities are in the hands of the countries threatened. But if an attack were to occur nonetheless, would mutual constraints be arrived at and maintained? No one can be entirely confident on this matter. We would only repeat the observation that (1) the Soviets are more likely to be impressed by usable Western capabilities than by suicidal ones; (2) they have exhibited a pattern of prudent behavior in crises; (3) they would have a powerful interest to arrive at mutual constraints were conflict to occur.

Will the Soviet Union develop comparable technologies and an improved capability for discriminate operations? These are broad families of technologies and the Soviet Union will surely be pursuing them to some degree. If it makes such an effort, it could gain an important advantage; it would surely do so if we ourselves do not pursue them vigorously. If the Soviets do not match the capacity of the West in this area, then they may be faced in a crisis with the alternatives of engaging in indiscriminate operations or backing off. This would be bad for them, but not necessarily good for us. We might be better off encouraging them to shift away from indiscriminate weapons to more discriminate ones. Our example should provide that encouragement.

SOME OTHER ISSUES AND QUESTIONS FOR DISCUSSION

Various governments will perceive threats, their interests, and the costs and benefits of alternative possible courses of action differently. We need to think through in advance the set of possible contingencies and possible responses to these contingencies. For this we need an appropriate planning mechanism. How might this best be accomplished?

A good deal of work needs to be done to examine what kinds of capabilities might best suit the needs and resources of different European countries. How might vehicles best be based? What restructuring of forces and logistics are suggested by these trends? What specific missions might be planned for?

Will these technologies of precision intensify the qualitative competition in arms between East and West? It is widely assumed that any new weapon intensifies the qualitative race and is bad because it increases spending, destructiveness, and instability. Historically, this assumption has no basis in fact. The effects of particular innovations have varied. But in long-range delivery systems since the mid-1950s, new technology, on balance, has permitted sharply decreased US strategic budgets, a reduction in the indiscriminate destructiveness of strategic forces, and a more stable, less vulnerable, and more easily controlled force. Although more work is needed before we can be confident on this matter, we see little reason to be concerned that the further development of the technologies of precision will have adverse effects. There is good reason to believe they can greatly improve our situation. As for effects on budgets, for equal effectiveness they should save costs by replacing many ineffective, inaccurate weapons with fewer precise, effective ones.

In any case, these developments are not at all likely to be stopped. The technologies of information-processing are pervasive in industrial societies; many of these developments are being fostered by applications in the civil sector, and they will diffuse among advanced industrial states.

We have said little about countermeasures to these technologies. Countermeasures and counter-countermeasures will be developed, as always. But these technological trends are fundamental ones and there is no doubt—whatever the outcome on any specific measure-countermeasure contest—that they will have a very large political-military effect.

More work is also needed on targeting studies, for example, on implications for deep interdiction attack against military targets and selected industries. The level of precision attainable in the future raises questions, especially for industrial attacks, which have rarely been examined in past bombing campaigns and not at all for over twenty years. The invention of the H-bomb effectively ended detailed examination of the vulnerability of many types of targets, and, much more important, discouraged fundamental thinking about targeting selection and the purposes of target destruction. It is high time to rethink this problem.

There are some related issues: Will the offense benefit more than the defense? That is not the best way to phrase the issues of interest, since both sides use offensive and defensive weapons in attack or counterattack. More precisely, one might ask, will the new technologies benefit an invader or the country invaded? Under specific conditions of terrain, climate, and opposing forces, what will be the effect of introducing various new individual weapons now in development or in the early stage of research? For some specific contingencies we have examined, the invaded country can greatly benefit from the new technology. Will this increase or decrease the advantage to the side that strikes first? Is the military posture and industrial structure of Western Europe more or less vulnerable to these technologies than those of the Soviet Union? Is NATO capable of exploiting the opportunities they offer for effective discriminateness and control more or less successfully? These and other questions require much thought, and much will depend on the answers.

CHAPTER 12

Limited Options, Escalation, and the Central Region

Peter Stratmann and René Hermann

NEW TECHNOLOGIES: THE POLICY FRAMEWORK FOR ASSESSMENTS

The extent to which new weapons technologies (NWT) can be used for the strengthening of NATO's defense posture depends upon the perception of political urgency by governments and parliaments. The optimal integration of NWT will necessitate thorough changing of traditional tactical and organizational concepts. These changes can be imposed only through top-level political decision. At the beginning of the NWT debate in the United States, expectations were put forward which resurrected old European fears. For example, some said NWT could contribute to the "raising of the nuclear threshold," to "manpower reductions," or to a geographically constrained "limited nuclear defense option." Suggestions of this sort explain the hitherto less than enthusiastic reaction of Europeans to NWT.

In order to overcome skepticism, the first priority is to clarify the politico-military aims for which the conventional and nuclear potential of NWT should be used. This clarification would be a starting point for progressing from the verbal consensus of current NATO doctrine, which only bridges continuing dissent, to a common strategy in the proper sense of the word. This, in turn, would contribute to NATO's political cohesion vis-à-vis the growing regional and global strength of the Soviet Union (SU).

Without question, NATO has a basic interest in enhancing the flexibility of its conventional and nuclear defense options as well as its coercive bargaining options. Possible gains in flexibility, however, are limited by the basic factors which determine the context of NATO defense. These factors are influenced only marginally by technological change.

NATO's defensive concept gives the opponent the advantage of the initiative, that is, the determination of time, location, and scope of the attack. For this reason, the land battle will take place on NATO territory. The depth of the defense area available to NATO is small. Those forces deployed for initial defense, that is, with a very high degree of readiness, are expensive. Traditional resource allocation patterns make scarcely any funds available for the buildup of reserve forces. Futhermore, the densely populated and highly industrialized Western European countries do not allow for any form of intense, extensive, and sustained warfare because of its evident suicidal implications.

If the Warsaw Pact should start a major conventional aggression, or an intensive theater nuclear campaign in order to win militarily irrespective of costs, the probable outcome would be the destruction and/or occupation of the Federal Republic of Germany and its neighbors. NATO would face the unpalatable choice between retaliation and capitulation. The behavior of the WP would determine whether the conventional and nuclear defense options of NATO is "stable" or whether they could only be limited "intermediate" options in the context of an escalation strategy.

NATO's "flexibility in response" concept is obviously a strategy of *limited* flexibility. It is not designed to cope with a ruthless Soviet will to win at any cost. Implicitly it is oriented toward types of aggression such as inadvertant war or war resulting from a relatively low-risk perception by Moscow. Only in these cases can NATO hope to change the Soviet cost-benefit calculus and to achieve war termination.

The most important task of NATO after a breakdown of prewar deterrence is to analyze the specific risk assessment which led to the aggression, especially the aggressor's assumptions about the politico-military reactions by NATO. NATO has to deal with these assumptions. That is, NATO has to change the aggressor's calculus instead of confirming it. Consequently, NATO's strategic flexibility must consist of adequate strategies for each type of challenge; any hope to deal with all challenges by a uniform strategy is quite unrealistic.

There are three basic principles, however, which seem to be valid under any circumstance:

1. Without a resolute conventional and, if necessary, nuclear forward defense, no strategic flexibility is possible. It must exclude the hope for a quick and easy victory. Forward defense has to maintain the territorial status quo ante as long and as extensively as possible. It thus serves to limit damage and keeps intact an essential precondition for early war termination. Moreover, it buys time for a strategy of coercive bargaining.
2. Survivability is another essential precondition for flexibility in the conventional as well as the nuclear area. It contributes to the stability of forward defense, discourages preemptive disarming attacks, and makes escalation control easier.
3. NATO should not overreact, and should not give rise to a WP perception that NATO can do nothing but overreact. In such a case, the WP might drive warfare to a level of risk which does not correspond to its original political intentions and which is unacceptable for both sides, and the possibility of terminating the war under circumstances which still make sense for Western Europe could be forfeited.

Interest in restraint should not, however, lead to excessively rigid consequences, such as keeping the nuclear threshold under any circumstances as high as possible or making it a principle to refrain from attacking Soviet territory as long as possible. Such an inflexible posture would be dangerous in cases where the Soviet decision to move is based on the expectation that NATO is politically unable to decide upon an adequate use of tactical nuclear weapons, or cases where the Soviet side considers an extension of fighting to the strategic level to be highly unlikely. In the case of Soviet major aggression, these notions would severely curtail NATO's option of controlled escalation as a means of coercive bargaining.

Thus, readiness for local defense as well as readiness for controlled escalation by selective nuclear employment options on all levels is a necessary condition for an effective policy of strategic flexibility. We will now suggest a basic outline of how to assess possible contributions of conventional and nuclear NWT toward improvement of NATO's military options.

In current NWT debates, areas have often been selected that look promising from a technological "systems" point of view in terms of cost-effectiveness, avoidance of collateral damage, and so on. However, the overriding consideration should not be to isolate various types of responses, but rather to recognize their functional interdependence.

Since certain options are promising only if certain other options are available, the range of responses has to be seen in a comprehensive manner.

Obviously a comprehensive approach is more likely than a mission-related or system-by-system approach to be susceptible to criticism both in terms of insufficient data and in terms of analytical deficiencies. Some of the major difficulties and uncertainties are the effectiveness and, indeed, the availability of many systems under discussion, the capacity of new systems to become integrated in terms of organization and doctrine, the costs in terms of budgets, manpower, and procurement choices, and, above all, the impact of potential Soviet countermeasures and of the acquisition of similar equipment by WP forces.

On the other hand, the need for a comprehensive approach also means we must strive, in early policy formation, to get beyond mere incrementalism, which probably would not make any important difference in the present security context. And without major changes, neither conventional defense nor deliberate nuclear escalation seem to offer appropriate options should deterrence fail.

NATO'S CONVENTIONAL DEFENSE AND NEW TECHNOLOGIES: SOME STRUCTURAL REQUIREMENTS FOR IMPROVEMENT

There are three aspects of conventional defense where new technologies may have some impact: forward defense, conventional interdiction, and long-range conventional systems for demonstrative or coercive bargaining purposes.

Forward defense is considered an indispensable element of NATO's overall posture, but under present conditions it hardly provides viable options in case of surprise attack or major sustained aggression. New technologies may not be a panacea, but there is every reason to study their proper applicability.

While conventional shallow interdiction and long-range options may be even less feasible with presently deployed weapons systems, their importance may not be as crucial either. Yet if new technologies offer new or improved options, this would undoubtably enhance NATO's chances to make the outcome of WP operations less calculable and aggression less likely.

Conventional Forward Defense

Superiority in tanks is a decisive factor in Soviet planning for offensive warfare in Central Europe. Hence, advanced antitank defense is of crucial importance. Modern antitank missiles permit an effective defense against armored vehicles even at long distances. They are reliable and easy to handle. They can be fired and controlled from concealed positions, and compared to the presently prevailing antitank system, namely another tank, they are relatively inexpensive and could be procured in great quantities. They are easy to transport and can be fired from various types of vehicles or from helicopters.

Modern antitank guided missiles are supplemented by a variety of medium- and short-range antitank weapons, as well as scatterable mines which are deliverable by artillery or aircraft. It is also feasible to use cannon-launched precision-guided munitions against tanks, the target being illuminated by laser, either from forward designators or from remotely piloted vehicles (RPVs). RPVs may also be used separately as precision-guided weapons. It will thus become possible to engage tanks effectively beyond the line of sight of front-line platoons. Varying concentrations of precise indirect fire may back up direct local antitank defense.

These developments are likely to enhance the role of infantry considerably. Units would fight dismounted and would not need armored personnel carriers (APCs) of the present quality. Light and relatively inexpensive armored vehicles with cross-country mobility would suffice to protect them from small arms fire and fragments, to give them mobility, and to serve as a weapon platform for portable antitank guided missiles, for a light antitank gun, or for a heavy machine gun. These units could operate in small combat teams and be largely independent. They could make the most of advantages of the territory for the defender—camouflage, protection, natural and artificial obstacles.

Armed forces of this light infantry type could—as forward area defense forces—take over current functions of the armored and mechanized units, which are more dependent on heavy material and hence are much more expensive. In addition to the relatively low procurement and maintenance costs, light infantry troops could promise an essential manpower advantage: they could be based on cadres to a higher degree. Their weapons and equipment are relatively easy to handle. Therefore, tactics would be simpler and so would training. A much greater reliance could be placed on reserve troops without impairing the combat strength decisively. Because of the low functional differentiation, a large pool of trained reservists could be held available. It would be possible to call up reservists close to their planned deployment areas as a precondition of a rapid mobilization of cadre units. This mobilization should be backed up in legal as well as administrative terms by a kind of "enhanced reserve readiness." This way, reservists could rapidly and significantly reinforce forces for direct defense. The WP could thus lose some of its relative advantages in being able to mobilize additional forces quickly. This would be important not only for defense, but also for crisis management.

Obviously a comprehensive adjustment of the present force structure would be indispensable. The entire forward defense system would have to consist of several layers of forces. The first layer should consist of covering, delaying, and attriting forces. These would have to be deployed close to the border and be permanently kept in a high state of combat readiness. They would serve to slow down the movement of the attacking forces, kill as many as possible, and identify the main avenues of attempted penetration. They would have to provide the time necessary to build up the main defense lying behind the delaying zone.

These first-line units should be capable of fighting independently. They should consist primarily of tank and armored infantry units, in order to allow highly flexible fighting, and should have their own self-propelled artillery units and mobile air defense components. These units would be so organized as to make optimum use of the whole panoply of NWT means. Above all, they should have the combat electronics required to achieve high first-shot kill probability for tank cannons, antitank guided missiles (ATGMs), and precision-guided tube and rocket artillery.

On the average there should be about six small combat battalions of delaying forces (equivalent to one brigade) in front of every defense division, with divisional frontages varying according to the terrain and probability of massive attack. These battalions could fight with the heavy equipment made available by shifting the main defense to light infantry units.

Since the covering forces would have to absorb the first shock of attack, attrition could be substantial. Once their mission was fulfilled, they could fall back to the rear area of the main defense layer and regroup as armored and divisional reserves. They would then serve as counterattack formations in the main defense, backed up by mobilized tank battalions of the reserve. This component would be crucial because infantry units can hold terrain and attrite hostile forces, but cannot attack and regain lost terrain. If the main defense setup is to effect a stable defense in tactical depth and not be restricted to a delaying and attrition function—which would also mean unredeemable loss of territory—the light infantry units of the forward-area defense forces must be supplemented by armored and mechanized units.

The stability of the main defense could provide sufficient time to significantly reinforce the available armed forces through the mobilization of reserves and reinforcements. Rapid replenishment of strong antitank defense infantry units would also offer advantages. Besides, the good transportability of these lightly armored forces could be utilized in order to move them rapidly to those main defense sectors where a critical development could be anticipated in time. That would also apply to noncommitted defense forces in the forward defense layers in less endangered sectors.

The limiting factor for this kind of rapid reinforcement would be the availability of air transport capacity. If the light infantry units had to be carried and employed without their vehicles, with greatly restricted ground mobility, lacking armor protection, and with limited staying power, their combat mission would be restricted to a temporary blocking function.

The bulk of the operational reserves should therefore best be organized as a third layer behind the main defense zone. It would consist of NATO reinforcement troops transported by air, rail, and road and of favorably deployed cadre units of the West German home defense brigade variety. These territorial defense and security forces could also be earmarked as operational reserves for the field army. They would have an artillery and a tank battalion (with heavy equipment phased out in the delaying forces) which could be employed separately, and a high proportion of light mobile infantry. Compared to the forward area defense forces, they would have more time to get mobilized, and they could perhaps do without enhanced reserve readiness for most units.

This is a possible structure of a conventional NATO defense posture for ground forces in Central Europe that fully utilizes new technologies. It tries to match those operational factors which would guide Soviet military operations in Central Europe: the surprise element, the fast gain of terrain, and the utilization of a superiority in initial mobilization and reinforcement capabilities. A comprehensive force-on-force calculation is required to gain additional insight into whether such efforts are apt to be successful. New technologies could possibly offer important advantages for the WP forces too. It is conceivable that new technologies can enhance significantly the effectiveness of the surprise element of a preemptive disarming attack and of efforts to rapidly disorganize NATO's defense system during its mobilization phase. Moreover, the element of quantitative WP superiority is likely to bear more strongly on the military outcome if very high attrition rates are to be expected. Therefore, it must be all the more important to make optimal use of new technologies for defense. Forward defense is quite precarious under present conditions. The suggested conventional posture could make a considerable difference.

Conventional Interdiction

The chances for interdiction are improved if forward defense prevents a rapid WP penetration. If WP forces become involved in a sustained battle with high rates of fire and attrition, then logistics would become increasingly important and interdiction could influence the conduct of combat in an important way.

Interdiction is impaired by a variety of factors. The lines of communication in Central and Eastern Europe form a very dense network. This redundancy requires the destruction of a great number of targets—even repeated destruction for certain targets, because of the limited effect of conventional weapons—before interdiction could have significant impact. NATO would have to employ large quantities of delivery means which must be sure to reach their targets. Because of the weight and volume of conventional ordnance, aircraft would be about the only means of delivery beyond artillery range. For fixed targets, cruise missiles and remotely piloted aircraft could be employed in the future, provided they have the extreme target accuracy necessary in order to successfully kill hard targets such as bridge piers with conventional explosives. It is still uncertain whether RPVs with all-weather capability will become available. Remote control poses the difficulty of secured data links. Moreover, post-attack assessment and reconnaissance as well as acquisition of mobile targets still offer problems.

The effectiveness of manned aircraft, as a main delivery means for conventional interdiction in the foreseeable future, will be mainly determined by the duel between air defense and air defense suppression. The outcome is uncertain because it involves the interaction of weapons systems with highly complex electronic technology. In view of the density and increasing sophistication of the WP anti-air defense system, NATO's air attack forces will probably experience a high initial rate of attrition. Their interdiction capacity will then depend on how long their airfields can be held intact and how many external reinforcements can be flown in and be readied for employment. Finally, the strength of WP air defense aircraft plays an essential part.

conventional interdiction. Even if forces were to be engaged in a highly concentrated way in space and time, the way would have to be paved for significant impacts. Thus the specific qualities of precision-guided munitions (PGMs) will become effective only to the extent that air defense suppression is successful. However, the complexity of interacting technologies and the decisive improvements in performance and effect of a number of weapons components increase the overall incalculability. This will enhance the deterrent effect of conventional interdiction weapons in very much the same way new antitank defense means do.

Long-Range Conventional Options

The long-range use of conventional weapons would probably have only marginal immediate impact on the battlefield campaign. In particular, overall damage would be rather limited. It could, however, signal resolve and increase political-economic and even military costs to the WP. It would thus enable coercive bargaining below the nuclear threshold.

If these options are implemented by nonnuclear weapons with clearly limited effects, they would not jeopardize the political value of escalation control. There would not be a special weapons release problem. Hence, these options offer a high degree of flexibility. First, they could be considered as an immediate NATO response in case of any major limited or major conventional WP aggression, functioning as a "collateral measure" for NATO's conventional forward defense. Second, as elements of a declaratory policy, they could add effectively to the deterrent value of NATO's conventional defense with regard to limited WP aggressions. Third, they could be applied in case of a major aggression to restore deterrence at a very early point. They could immediately signal NATO's determination not to exempt Soviet territory from military response, but rather to go after a broad spectrum of military and industrial targets of high value regardless of where they might be located.

Long-range conventional options should not be presented as a means for independent European retaliation, but as part of an integrated concept, demonstrating the firmness of the coupling of US and European defense regarding the full spectrum of possible escalatory action in an early state of war. They have to be regarded as a precursor to pre-planned selective nuclear options in the framework of an overall escalatory concept. This effect would be enhanced by utilizing delivery means and guidance systems which could also be employed in a nuclear mode and by relying upon "strategic" reconnaissance and communications facilities. The selection of targets could be directed to the same objective by including WP military objects of conspicuous functional importance with regard to conceivable follow-on nuclear exchanges (such as large radars or air defense command and control centers).

In order to generate that option, two preconditions have to be met, one political, the other technological. First, the availability of this option would require considerable cohesiveness of the US-West European common defense posture. By the same token, however, any policy tending toward that option may well turn out to produce divisive issues. In any case, one has to assume a considerable degree of common political resolve under crisis conditions. On the other hand, considering the paralyzing effects of the emerging nuclear parity in the past, the technological potential for implementing a policy of conventional long-range options may well help to improve the prospects for joint escalatory action in future conflict situations.

Second, a technological solution has yet to be found in order to sufficiently minimize the weight of conventional warheads. Cruise missiles are the most promising means of delivery. But further improvements of high accuracy are required, as are further advances in warhead technology. If that could be achieved, functionally vital components could be attacked and eliminated by means of microtargeting within major target systems, in order to paralyze the entire target system for at least a certain period of time.

NATO'S NUCLEAR POSTURE AND NEW TECHNOLOGIES: THE SCOPE FOR CHANGE

Modernizing NATO's nuclear posture has to be seen in terms of war-fighting capabilities rather than deterrence only. For NATO, the only military purpose of using nuclear weapons is to stabilize the alliance's nonnuclear defense as long as its continuance is politically and militarily meaningful. Presently deployed nuclear weapons in Central Europe do not favor this integration of conventional and nuclear defense. Hence doctrinal positions in NATO capitals either focus on a strictly nuclear deterrence posture or else consider war-fighting capabilities in terms of nuclear emphasis or conventional-only postures. Neither of these postures would buy security if a major conflict should emerge. Modernizing NATO's nuclear posture presupposes improved conventional capabilities. New technologies may or may not offer these improved capabilities, depending on whether they are introduced along with structural changes. But without nuclear options for stabilizing conventional defenses, if necessary, NATO cannot hope to resist a major Soviet military campaign.

Nor can it hope to maintain the preconditions for meaningful coercive bargaining on the higher levels of escalation. While NATO's present nuclear posture has only a marginal capacity for discriminate limited employment options, new technologies may offer some chances for a more flexible nuclear capabiilty.

The Survivability of NATO's Nuclear Capabilities

Survivability of NATO's nuclear potential is a prerequisite for selective and discriminate nuclear options. In view of conceivable Soviet progress in NWT development, NATO's potential could become vulnerable even to conventional attacks. Its increasing vulnerability to discriminate nuclear attacks may increase Soviet incentives for massive or selective preemptive nuclear disarming strikes. Such strikes would probably defeat any chance for a controlled escalation through a selective and discriminate use of nuclear weapons by NATO, at least in the battlefield and theater area. In order to deny these options to the Soviets, improved survivability appears indispensable.

In addition to such measures as the sheltering of nuclear aircraft, nuclear ammunition sites, command/control/communications (CCC) components, or assignment of additional relatively invulnerable Poseidon submarines to NATO, a variety of technological improvements could enhance survivability. Advances in electronics could be used in order to reduce the vulnerability of communication links and to increase the redundancy within CCC systems as well as the effective range and flexibility of reconnaissance systems. Improved safeguards against unauthorized use could allow for a better dispersion and mobility of nuclear munitions. Warheads with variable yields as well as shorter reaction times and improved firing sequences for surface-to-surface systems would have the same effect. In addition, a new weapons generation of dual-capable standoff weapons and cruise missiles is in the offing. They could be fired from most of the presently available weapons platforms, which would make disarming attacks much more difficult. In this area, new technologies look promising.

NATO's Nuclear Battlefield Option

It has been very difficult to design suitable tactics for the battlefield employment of nuclear weapons. Battlefield employment early in the war would have to be confined to NATO territory in order not to provoke Soviet retaliation. But any use on NATO territory would be caught between two conflicting requirements, military efficiency and the avoidance of suicidal outcomes. The high vulnerability of the Central Region is the dominant consideration. If the purpose of battlefield employment of nuclear weapons is to back up NATO's nonnuclear defenses, it has to be governed effectively by a policy of constraints. Moreover, the timely release of nuclear weapons in order to stabilize NATO's defense is conceivable only within a framework of constraints. Presently deployed nuclear capabilities rule out the implementation of such a policy of constraints. Hence the dilemma of deterrence versus war-fighting capabilities seems inescapable under present conditions. New technologies could conceivably make a difference here. The important requirement, however, is to find nuclear weapons whose use would be both nonsuicidal and effective in actually stabilizing NATO's conventional defenses.

Enhanced radiation weapons, for example, have the same effect against protected tank crews, but permit a reduction of yield (as well as of the heat and blast effect) by an order of magnitude compared to normal fission weapons, and produce only minor sustained radiation. They seem to be indispensable, therefore, if NATO does not want to renounce any plausible nuclear battlefield option. Nuclear earth penetrators also play an important role in this context. Since their collateral damage is comparatively low, they could be used instead of atomic demolition munitions (ADM) to block fast approach routes and bottlenecks by means of cratering. Since they would require no prepositioning, they would not have the familiar political and psychological implications of

ADM. They could therefore be employed flexibly, and would not bear critically on the issue of political control of nuclear employment.

The weapons system most suitable for a first-use option—in addition to earth penetrators employed for delaying functions—would be nuclear artillery using shells with high accuracy and reaction speed. They are mobile and dispersed, therefore relatively hard to detect and kill. Their integration into the reconnaissance and CCC system of conventional artillery makes them particularly suitable for the discriminate engagement of hostile forces in the immediate vicinity of friendly units. Their clearly limited range is a constraint obvious to the other side. The target points would probably be located exclusively on NATO territory at the time of release. The initial renunciation of aircraft and surface-to-surface missiles as nuclear means of employment would not only demonstrate this range limitation, but would permit the conventional use of aircraft and rockets in extended areas with reduced risks of preemptive instabilities. Moreover, it could be conducive to restrained Soviet behavior to confine the first use conspicuously to those sectors of forward defense where an imminent breakthrough had to be reckoned with, and to make sure that the effect of this strike were not utilized for counterattack operations of NATO forces. The objective would simply be to enforce a temporary local pause upon the attacking forces.

Whether it is realistic to hope that the WP command would accept the offer implicit in this kind of employment is hard to determine. This will depend on the specific character of its risk calculus. The possibility cannot be ruled out. But the WP leaders could also react by a selective blanketing fire with higher-yield weapons against NATO's forward defense system, in order to achieve fast penetration, with or without parallel disarming attacks against NATO's nuclear potential. The acceptability of the first-use option thus will also be determined by the ability of NATO to cope with such a response in kind. This tactic could lead to a quick military decision. Local defense forces and operational reserves of NATO would then possibly be almost completely destroyed. The same is true for surveillance, target acquisition, and CCC components, as well as for the organic nuclear means, which at present determine the ability for effective discriminate battlefield nuclear operations. In this situation, NATO would possibly be left only with the option to fall back on an extensive indiscriminate use of high-yield weapons and to suffer corresponding collateral damage in order to stop—under time pressure—the enemy forces which might advance in a rapid and highly dispersed manner. Such a tactic would have suicidal consequences for the FRG and perhaps for others as well.

Therefore, it becomes desirable to use the new technologies, if possible, to develop an overregional surveillance, reconnaissance, and target-acquisition system in connection with precision-guided long-range attack means. This may help to achieve a sufficiently survivable discriminate nulear capability for blunting the exploitation of terrain-blanketing tactics.

Nuclear Interdiction

There are certain kinds of targets, such as underground command centers or runways, which cannot be effectively destroyed by conventional means. Discriminate nuclear capabilities would offer the obvious advantage of reduced collateral damage, compared to current nuclear means. Earth penetrators could be used effectively against runways or underground centers. Similarly enhanced radiation weapons would be more suitable than presently available nuclear weapons for locally limited attacks. They could impede a WP breakthrough attempt by engaging enemy forces in the rear, with prior nuclear blanketing fire.

The crucial issue of any nuclear interdiction remains, however, whether strong nuclear WP reactions against NATO territory have to be reckoned with. It is difficult to see that reduced collateral damage is going to make a vital difference in the WP decision on appropriate reactions. In any case, discriminate nuclear capabilities will become important for interdiction purposes only with regard to special targets. Thus, their role will be somewhat limited.

Nuclear Coercive Bargaining

NATO attempts to prevent further WP escalation by nuclear coercive bargaining on a higher level, and to move toward a deescalation and termination of military operations, would probably take place under conditions of great time pressure. Coercive bargaining would have to be initiated before the situation on the battlefield turns critical if the decision is not sought in a highly dramatic, and therefore hardly controllable, nuclear action on the strategic level from the very beginning. Isolated "symbolic" nuclear strikes will hardly suffice. Thus, it is crucial to have selective follow-on options for theater and strategic use with substantial damage effects which nevertheless obey perceptible constraints.

Discriminateness is one way to elucidate these constraints, although here, too, the essential limitations might have to be of another quality. The number of weapons, the character of targets, and the timing of attacks would be more important criteria. The main advantage of a discriminate nuclear capability may not be the actual expansion of the effective scope of action usable for limited nuclear options within the framework of selected exchanges, but rather its influence on the subjective expectation of NATO leaders concerning the provocation of a catastrophic counterblow by the Soviet Union. This expectation, once materialized in respective hardware and contingency plans of NATO, would certainly influence the calculation of risk by WP leaders. An obvious linkage of demonstrative employments with more substantial follow-on options, and the presumed willingness of NATO to actually apply them in an emergency, could reduce the ambivalency of demonstrative nuclear strikes and increase their strategic significance.

The above considerations suggest that by utilizing NWT in a systematic manner, some of NATO's most vexing strategic problems could be alleviated. Even if the intentions and character of a Soviet attack continue to determine the extent of NATO's flexibility, and even if against certain types of aggression no sensible defense options are available, the deterrence and defense capabilities of NATO's posture still can be substantially improved by NWT.

A conventional forward defense option as outlined earlier would deter any type of low-scale military probing attack. Thus, it would continue to reduce the danger of a war by miscalculation.

Such an option would also have a substantial deterrent effect in relation to major aggression. Since high rates of attrition can be expected, WP prospects for rapid attainment of operational goals would be uncertain. Thus, outcomes are difficult to calculate and the decision to attack becomes harder.

WP planners will have to proceed from the assumption that NATO's nonnuclear defense could hold close to the border for at least as much time as is needed for request and release of the initial use of nuclear weapons. Thus NATO would have flexibility with regard to the initiation of nuclear defense, without having to abandon the principle of strict political control of nuclear weapons use.

At the same time, NATO's conventional forward area defense facilitates surveillance of the battlefield situation, as well as maintaining a cohesive zone of defense. This is a precondition for nuclear battlefield use which is both restricted and tactically rewarding.

This capability is enhanced by the discrete and discriminate employment options offered by NWT. It opens the vista for integrating selective nuclear employment options with a concept of combined forward defense, thus providing an escape from the horns of an old dilemma. In the past, the use of the existing nuclear systems in an effective military fashion would have been quite destructive and thus quite escalatory; therefore, the release of nuclear weapons in time—as part of forward defense—would have been quite doubtful. On the other hand, a very limited demonstrative use would not have resulted in a stabilization of the military situation. In the future, the limited and selective first use as well as the follow-on use could be linked to nonnuclear forward defense in a fashion which enhances the credibility of both. WP planners would hardly find a calculable chance to penetrate NATO's forward defense below the nuclear threshold.

An improvement of NATO's coercive bargaining options on the theater and strategic level by NWT is made possible by the option of stressing other than geographical constraints; at the same time, these constraints do not have to be traded off against military and political effectiveness. Deemphasizing geographical constraints has two advantages: the risk assessment which determines the occurrence and the scope of a WP aggression can be influenced directly. This improves the chances for war termination under conditions which are acceptable for NATO. Furthermore, it eliminates the prospect of a nuclear war limited geographically to Western and Central Europe and excluding the territory of the attacker. Such a "limited" war, which would destroy the territory of the FRG and its neighbors, would be militarily hopeless for NATO.

Rules of engagement could be developed as a consequence of increased flexibility of NATO's selective follow-on use options by the combination of an appropriate constraints policy with new military effectiveness. This step in the direction of a common NATO strategy would not altogether eliminate the most divisive issues in the Atlantic Alliance's strategic debate, but it could contribute to their substantial alleviation.

This indirect contribution of NWT to political alliance cohesion can hardly be exaggerated if the political threat of using force, rather than actual use, is perceived as the main danger in Central Europe.

CHAPTER 13

Flexibility in Tactical Nuclear Response

Laurence Martin

Tactical nuclear weapons within the NATO armory, for long the subject of only a rather esoteric debate, have in recent years become the center of a much more widely attended discussion. The SALT and MFR negotiations and the downward pressures on conventional force levels, particularly the questions raised about the continued US presence in Europe, have all contributed to this new flurry of interest. Nothing has done more, however, to reinvigorate the debate, with the sense that something might at last be achieved, than recent technological advances. Developments in nuclear design and in guidance and control systems offer real possibilities of shifting the margins between the nuclear and the conventional responses.

Any new departures will be conditioned by the now quite long history of tactical nuclear weapons in NATO. They were originally introduced in the early fifties as a supplement to conventional firepower. At that time, the Soviet Union had very few nuclear weapons, even for strategic purposes, and it was in any case not imagined that war in Europe could be divorced from a strategic exchange which would overwhelmingly favor the West. The problem of controlling escalation and collateral damage consequently did not seem important. When growing Soviet strength made the problem inescapable, tactical nuclear weapons became for some the answer to escalation, the limited response for the weaker, conventional side, fearful of all-out "strategic" war. By the sixties, in the Kennedy era, even the tactical nuclear weapon came to appear unacceptable, because of the dangers of escalation and because of the damage tactical weapons alone might do in Europe. The nuclear-conventional firebreak was marked out in NATO doctrine and the present flexible response resulted. This did not stop the continued deployment of large numbers of tactical nuclear weapons to both US and European forces.

In this way the alliance struck a posture of ambiguous deterrence. Depending on emphasis, tactical nuclear weapons are both a trigger for strategic action and a reinforcement of NATO's local war-fighting ability. Tactical nuclear weapons are intended to deter Soviet nuclear action in the theater, to match it if it occurs, and to plug gaps in the NATO line by first use if the conventional resistance should fail. Recourse to the nuclear weapons in this way is supposed to help NATO forces win on the battlefield and to promote a satisfactory negotiated ceasefire, both by frightening the enemy with the danger of escalation and by gaining time for opposing leaders to draw the appropriate conclusions.

It is not surprising that a strategic posture, arrived at historically in such a way for such a variety of purposes, has attracted a variety of strong criticisms. To many critics, the essential ambiguity of the doctrine is a major failing in a deterrent, when what is required is a clear, credible, and unmistakable threat. A degree of ambiguity is inescapable in a deterrent strategy for a coalition of only partially congruent interests. But ambiguity is not synonymous with confusion, and there is considerable suspicion that the disarray in NATO thinking about tactical nuclear weapons is not only excessive, but could easily inhibit effective action in crises. The disarray would be all the more serious if it conveyed such timidity about nuclear weapons as to deprive the tactical deterrent of all credibility.

Other criticisms assail the flexible response as a doctrine for actually using tactical nuclear weapons as a defense. Perhaps the most thoroughgoing objection is the assertion that the Soviet Union itself will inevitably use nuclear weapons from the start, that it will certainly not concede NATO the privilege of deciding the moment of escalation, and that therefore any effort to fight conventionally, however brief, is suicidal. A major source of disaster would be the dual deployment imposed by the doctrine, compounded by the uneven distribution of conventional and nuclear capability across the allied front. Flexible response also entails the peculiar dangers of transition from one mode of resistance to the other; in particular the inadvertent revelation of intentions by signal traffic and by the actual redeployment of forces, a process that would itself involve a period of weakness for either mode of combat.

These dangers all arise from the fact that any flexible response combining both nuclear and conventional weapons must result in impure tactics, less than optimally designed for either type of warfare. Many difficulties inevitably arise from a doctrine that for reason of alliance politics or higher strategy, such as fear of escalation, compels delaying military measures that would be most effective if taken promptly. Consequently, most radical prescriptions for improving NATO doctrine envisage the early and, often, indeed, the immediate, use of tactical nuclear weapons upon the onset of hostilities.

Some of the cruder—or, as their protagonists would claim, more realistic—alternatives look no further than a settled determination to use tactical nuclear weapons on a grand scale, possibly removing all capacity for conventional defense to make the intention unmistakable. Such a strategy is thus a trip wire either for the strategic forces or, if the advocates prefer not to face this, for the devastation caused simply by the tactical nuclear weapons themselves. In either case, the deterrent arises from the threat of widespread damage.

The weakness of such prescriptions is that they offer the Soviet Union little incentive to curb its retaliation within the European theater so long as the major Western strategic arsenal is in American hands. For if the American deterrent remains linked to Europe, the strategy reverts to the massive retaliation from which the retention of the tactical leg of the NATO Triad is intended to afford an escape.

For this reason, more interest has been aroused by proposals to employ new nuclear technology in strategies of denial and defense rather than "punishment." Tailored warheads, improved accuracy, better target acquisition, and better command and control are said to facilitate more discriminatory use of nuclear weapons within limits that can enhance military effectiveness, constrain collateral damage, and reduce the incentives for Soviet escalation. A few, particularly French, strategists envisage a narrow continuous "radiation belt" through which no enemy penetrations would be possible. More commonly, the details of application are left less defined; however, discriminate, primarily battlefield use restricted as to yield, target, and, particularly, range are almost universal features of the proposals popularly, if misleadingly, characterized as "mininuke" strategies. Whether explicitly or by implication, these proposals involve the reduction of the conventional defense, either as a deliberate signal of nuclear determination or as the inevitable consequence of budgetary pressures, once primary reliance is openly placed on the nuclear arm.

A central purpose of most of the mininuke strategies is to permit the decoupling of the US strategic arsenal from European defense, or to recognize what some regard as existing de facto decoupling in the age of parity, mutual assured destruction, and SALT. This decoupling is regarded as the price paid for continued US participation in a European defense, especially one with a nuclear component. The obvious and long-recognized objection to such an arrangement is the Soviet ability to trump any local nuclear balance with its unmatched capacity for destroying the Western European homelands, many of them within the framework of a generously defined battlefield engagement. Solving this problem by reengaging the American strategic force to deter Soviet escalation negates the whole purpose of the mininuke exercise for some of its advocates; while relying on the European strategic forces for this deterrence, though far more plausible and to a degree inevitable, raises serious questions about the technical adequacy of those forces, the practicability of decoupling them from the US strategic force, and the peculiar difficulties of the Federal Republic of Germany. Reliance on the greater desperation of the countries invaded to give their deterrent threats plausibility, as is implicit in classic Gaullist strategy, is a doubtful option for an alliance, as the Gaullists were first to recognize. Relying on "local retaliation," that is, the use of Eastern European targets outside the Soviet Union as hostage, depends upon a questionable evaluation of Soviet concern for its allies. Finally, faith in Soviet reluctance to destroy the areas they are about to conquer—the "asset value" argument—rests on the belief that the Soviet decision to go to war, or to take lesser military action, will be made in cold, mercantilist, cost-effective terms, whereas it may in fact be taken as the least inexpedient way of handling a crisis in which preventing losses rather than achieving gains may be the aim. Such desperate circumstances indeed seem much more plausible as the occasion for the momentous outbreak of war in Europe than some ambitious gambit.

More serious perhaps, and probably less speculative, are doubts about the defensive merits claimed for a strategy involving the early, controlled use of tactical nuclear weapons. No one, of course, has any experience on which to draw; indeed, there is no experience even of conventional war with modern weapons waged on the scale conceivable in Europe. It seems highly improbable, however, that the hope of denying all penetrations and thereby achieving a barrier defense would be vindicated. In that case, nuclear action could not be contained to a narrow strip of devastation and the problem of restoring the front and recovering lost territory would not be solved. More fundamentally, there can be no assurance that the introduction of tactical nuclear weapons would assure a successful stand on any line. There is not space here to rehearse the well-known case for believing that Soviet forces might profit at least as much as NATO. It is not necessary to prove that the Soviet Union would win, but merely to believe it cannot be proved it would fail, to deprive the strategy of deterrence by the prospect of nuclear "denial" of its extreme claims to success. Thus the consequences of actually implementing a tactical nuclear defense cannot be dismissed, but must be carefully weighed, a process that has always had, and will continue to have, profound political implications within the alliance.

Other objections can be brought against the strategy of immediate tactical nuclear response. The strategy is wholly dependent on early nuclear release, possibly on predelegation. While advocates argue that political objections to this should be overcome by the military, and hence deterrent, merits of the strategy, it remains improbable that this would be done to the degree at which no residual discretion would remain. The consequences of last-minute political hesitation would then be fatal. While it may perhaps be secretly believed that even nominal adoption of the strategy would remove any residual doubt that the Soviet Union would go nuclear from the start, and thereby solve the problem of allied indecision, such a prospect suggests a less than ideal beginning to the war, and is far from likely to disarm the objections of political leaders who perceive the possibilities clearly.

The implications of primarily tactical nuclear strategies for the conventional forces of the alliance also have serious political aspects. Conventional efforts would be almost sure to decline more rapidly than otherwise. If they did not, all suggestions that the tactical nuclear strategy is cheaper or an answer to security in reduced military circumstances would be falsified. There are parts of the alliance, however, where the absence of a conventional response would raise special problems. On the Northern flank, there is a traditional reluctance to accept nuclear weapons and something of an established diplomatic convention with the Soviet Union not to do so. In the South, there are numerous possibilities of ambiguous events that might fall far short of overt aggression yet require military response. On both flanks, the immediate issues at stake could appear of less than ultimate significance to the major powers of the Center. Even the Central Front powers are very conscious that at present most of the tactical nuclear weapons and the bulk of the overshadowing strategic nuclear power are subject to US veto. Consequently, a shift to nuclear defense is a shift to increased dependence on the United States. Without a substantial conventional response, the Europeans cannot even begin to defend themselves. Moreover, the US conventional presence, on which faith in the American guarantee depends, would be increasingly hard to justify to the taxpayer.

Such considerations suggest that the strategies of immediate use of tactical weapons offer full assurance neither of effective deterrence nor of successful defense and denial. Insofar as the danger of catastrophic escalation is eliminated by decoupling, the Soviet Union would enjoy a guarantee of limited liability rather like that sought in the Soviet concept of forward-based systems (FBS). If, however, coupling continues and the threat of escalation remains, the strategies fail to solve the American dilemma.

It can be argued that it is beyond American power to decouple absolutely; given US links to Europe, particularly if an apparatus for American participation in European local defense remained, and in view of the independence of strategic weapons from basing in the areas of conflict, the possibility of US strategic action and therefore the Soviet incentive to preempt could never be wholly eliminated. Coupled strategies of instant tactical nuclear action would therefore leave the United States worse off than at present, when at least there is some hope that nuclear action might be avoided altogether.

Supposed Soviet doctrines and Soviet military dispositions lead many observers to conclude that the Soviet Union believes war in Europe must be nuclear and will act accordingly. But so long as American strategic forces are coupled to Europe, such a doctrine, if held, must be a powerful influence for self-deterrence on the Soviet Union. If war nevertheless were to break out, it is by no means clear that the Soviet Union would be eager to see its gloomy prediction fulfilled, and it might therefore at least attempt to confine hostilities to conventional means. Western strategies of instant use would remove this chance of impoverished moderation, while presumably adding little to the self-inhibiting effects of the Soviet Union's own gloomy expectations.

An optimistic advocate of instant-use strategies may argue that there is not necessarily a greater likelihood of further escalation once the original nuclear threshold is crossed. A pessimistic observer of the present balance might assert that the flexible response would lead to precisely the same nuclear exchanges, but with the advantages of timing conceded to the Warsaw Pact. But even if the difference were small militarily, there is all the difference in the world politically. The ambiguity in the present strategy, and the at least specious possibility of confining defense to conventional arms, plays a major part in making the US guarantee to Europe politically tolerable to American opinion. Nor, for all the misleadingly oversimplified talk of European preferences for deterrence rather than defense—a distortion of undoubtedly real divergences of interest between allies concerning rules of engagement— is it likely that the majority of Europeans would welcome a more blatant emphasis on the nuclear option. By their adherence to the flexible response, they have testified to this, if not always wholeheartedly. Even French doctrine is moving toward blurring the nuclear line as the French nuclear arsenal becomes more diversified. Rejecting a wholly conventional defense is not the same as accepting one that is entirely nuclear.

From all of this we may conclude that the early employment of tactical nuclear weapons provides no guarantee of success on the battlefield, that the United States must concede some coupling of its strategic deterrent if it intends to play a continued part in European security, that tactical nuclear weapons are an essential link in the deterrent and defensive chain, but that, as decades of debate have now made clear, it is politically tolerable neither in Europe nor in the United States to surrender discretion over the final decision to go nuclear in even the most limited ways. Only a complete assurance that the lower end of the nuclear spectrum would not lead to the catastrophic destruction possible at the higher end could remove this inhibition. Even if it were possible, however, it is far from clear that it would be wise to do this and to deprive the nuclear weapon of its special deterrent characteristics.

On the other hand, the mininuke advocates have undoubtedly seized on an important truth—which, ironically, they share with those advocates of flexible response who try to provide a conventional defense rather than excuse its absence—in stressing the advantages of a capacity for denial and defense rather than a mere threat of strategic retaliation. Strategies of denial are appealing not merely because they may be all that we dare do, but also because they enhance our ability to deal with a wide range of contingencies that mere retaliatory threats could never deter. In this category would fall the onset of war arising from crisis and miscalculation, rather than from planned aggression, and incidents too limited to justify extreme responses. Thus, capacity to respond in kind to limited outbreaks is an appropriate recognition of the great flexibility in response to emergencies with which its array of military power endows the Soviet Union. Not to have some flexibility of response might indeed increase the range of contingencies for which the Soviet Union might consider its military force appropriate. Limited "grabs," for instance, or, more probably, the threat of them, might become more plausible as a way to connect Soviet military predominance with the otherwise shadowy concept of "Finlandization."

The flexibility ideally sought in flexible response is thus highly desirable. New technology may be able to enhance and enrich this flexibility and, in so doing, combine nuclear and conventional weapons in ways more subtly graduated than the mere sequence of conventional first and nuclear afterward.

It seems likely that recourse to conventional weapons would almost always precede nuclear action, both because of the initial military effect required and because of the ineradicable apprehension of the consequences of using nuclear weapons. New technology can, as many of the chapters in this volume indicate, do much to bolster the effectiveness of the conventional defense. The favorable cost-effectiveness of some new defensive systems, as compared to such offensive weapons as armor and strike aircraft, have been widely remarked. Much more impressive advantages could be secured, however, if really accurate indirect fire could be widely achieved, so as to compensate much more decisively for NATO's unfavorable ratio of force to space. Such improvements might also help reduce the problems of transition by more nearly equating conventional and nuclear deployment.

New technology might diversify as well as strengthen conventional options by making long-range action by conventional means effective, so that "strategic" or long-range action was no longer wholly associated with nuclear weapons. Some caution may be advisable in seizing on the idea that this would necessarily permit much less inhibited use of long-range strikes, particularly on superpower territory. The previous identity between nuclear and strategic action may have led us to underestimate the intrinsic significance of the "strategic" category in itself. Certainly the decision to undertake even conventional strategic strikes will be approached in a different frame of mind from battlefield action. Undeniably, however, the technical possibility of separating the nuclear and the strategic is an important departure, and the Europeans will reflect with interest on the fact that breach of the Soviet sanctuary need no longer inevitably entail crossing the nuclear threshold. If the pos-

sibility that some conventional actions may be strategic compels us
to approach them with caution, the threat of such actions should gain
equally enhanced importance as a prospective deterrent.

Although strategic uses of conventional weapons will constitute a
distinct category of action, there seems no reason to doubt that conventional action will be relatively more susceptible to military initiative
and discretion than nuclear. This characteristic will be enhanced by
the tendency of improved technology to facilitate control of the considerable collateral damage that even conventional weapons can cause.
The dual consequences should be to permit the dispersed control that
seems desirable to enable full exploitation of new battlefield capabilities and, at the same time, to allow the centralized command of those
capabilities, particularly nuclear weapons, the use of which entails
special risks and opportunities and should therefore be decided on
wider considerations than local tactical necessity.

The application of new technology to tactical nuclear weapons opens
up many possibilities for using them in more discriminate ways. While
this prospect does not justify the full confidence of the mininuke enthusiasts that nuclear weapons could be "destigmatized" or "conven-
tionalized" and used freely, it does make it possible to consider orches-
trating them in more complex ways with conventional warfare. If the
combined operation of nuclear and conventional weapons can be made
technically possible and compatible with the maintenance of control
and order on the battlefield, it will be no longer inevitable that the start
of the nuclear phase would mean the abandonment of efforts to maintain resistance by conventional forces. Technology can also contribute
to control of escalation by making NATO weapons less vulnerable to
counterforce strikes by Soviet theater forces and thus retaining the
capacity to retaliate in kind for Soviet increases in the scope and intensity of nuclear action. Moreover, by providing means to redress
the effects of surprise and to support counterattacks if WP penetrations
are disastrously successful, a tactical nuclear reserve or covering force
may permit putting more of NATO's conventional strength in the
first lines of defense, thereby fulfilling some of the requirements of forward defense and of the "counterblitzkrieg" advocates of force restructuring. Used in this way, the tactical nuclear forces, rather than
eliminating the conventional phase of defense, could strengthen it with
all the attendant advantage for political cohesion, morale, and flexibility
of maneuver in crisis that that implies.

Attempts to control the consequences of using tactical nuclear weapons cannot wholly eliminate the risk of further escalation, and they should therefore retain most of the deterrent aura they enjoy within the present strategy. Thus, the decision to employ nuclear weapons would still constitute an ominous warning signal to the enemy. Maintenance of a variegated arsenal of nuclear weapons would also permit their early use on a large scale if NATO were so taken by surprise as to make that necessary. Indeed, a centrally controlled nuclear force of discriminate weapons would be better suited to rapid response than the present system, which, being based on requests from hard-pressed commanders, would encourage piecemeal use. To enjoy these options it is not necessary, however, to deprive the alliance of all discretion when the occasion arises. Catastrophe may ensue, but there is no need to make it inevitable by refusing to provide the capacity to proceed by less than catastrophic means.

The nuclear threshold is conspicuous and awe-inspiring, but it is not the only formidable line that an aggressor must breach. Western inhibitions about using nuclear weapons too early may enable the attacker to postpone the moment of nuclear confrontation, but so long as there is a reasonably stalwart framework of conventional defense, he must still take the initial step of launching war in Europe. Given the history of the past few decades and a reasonable appearance of cohesion in the Western alliance, such a step must entail daunting risks.

Proponents of full-fledged nuclear strategy are quick to point out that by enabling the aggressor to contemplate the first steps in conventional terms, the ultimate nuclear risks are somewhat blurred. But for several reasons, the nuclear threshold cannot be simply substituted for the conventional line of resistance. Hardly any practical statesman would be willing to abandon all conventional capability, depriving himself of the means to deal with even the smallest incidents in a moderate way. Thus it is already a question of to what degree the nuclear threshold should be overlaid with conventional forces, and not one of absolute distinctions. More important, however, the decision to go to war will only remain truly formidable in the present state of Western Europe's own strength and unity if the United States is unmistakably involved. This, in turn, precludes wholly nuclear strategies, not merely because the United States has repeatedly demonstrated its unwillingness to accept the risks of a trip wire, but also because only a conventional strategy requires the presence of American forces in such numbers as to ensure American participation in European confrontations from the beginning.

Thus, both the logic and the history of the alliance make it clear that a strategy satisfactory in both military and political respects must combine deterrence with a credible capacity for defense if deterrence fails. The compromises in weapons, forces, and tactics demanded by a flexible response run counter to the clear definition of lines and consequences so beloved by theorists of deterrence. But the richer variety of options afforded by the exploitation of the full range of modern technology greatly reduces the danger of paralysis in crisis, and increases the probability of at least some decisive action when the occasion arises. The plausible prospect of at least some effective military resistance ought to be a better deterrent, and certainly a sounder basis for Western confidence and cooperation, than bold threats of immediate nuclear action that are likely to be neither proclaimed with conviction nor executed without hesitation.

CHAPTER 14

Flexible Options in Alliance Strategy

Johan Jørgen Holst

STRATEGIC DOCTRINE AND THE FRAMEWORK FOR POLICY-MAKING

Alliance strategy constitutes inter alia a framework for perceptional alignment as well as for the allocation of roles and missions. It is not only or even primarily a blueprint for how to deal with adversaries. The inevitable and inescapable test is how it permits allies to work together for a common purpose in recognition of the diversity of concerns and interests which structure the outlooks of the individual members of the alliance. Such alignment and coordination of outlooks constitutes a formidable task in an alliance which includes member states with very different resources, strategic locations, and traditions. The least common denominator may easily become so vague and diffuse as to entail innumerable problems for the transition from conception to operational implementation. A major problem in this context is associated with the propensity to conduct doctrinal discussion in a fairly abstract conceptual mode. Arguments about logical consistency and conceptual neatness become the currency for intra-alliance bargaining in a manner which may exacerbate disagreement and transform differences in emphasis to a dispute about theological absolutes. Fears abound that doctrinal positions have been thrown up as camouflage for disengagement, decoupling, or centralization of control. Thus NATO has at times been absorbed in great debates of strategy in a manner which has generated tensions of an order that the Russians have been hard to put to emulate.

Most of the initiatives for doctrinal change in NATO have come from the United States. For a variety of institutional and political reasons, European member states have not been in the forefront with reforms. Most often, some of them have become defenders of established orthodoxy. Such orthodoxy has tended to reflect least common denominators, and it has provided rationales for British and French independent policies as well. The institutional inflexibility of the alliance and the complex bargaining process which precedes decisions in Washington have conspired to make proposals for doctrinal reform synonymous with American unilateral initiatives. Such initiatives have seemed erratic and insensitive to political continuities from the West European perspective. Washington played a heavy role in persuading NATO to accept West German rearmament in the early fifties in order to produce the conventional force posture which otherwise would be unattainable, only to turn around in the mid-fifties to push through a decision to nuclearize NATO forces as a substitute for a conventional equilibrium, thus changing the original rationale for German rearmament. The Republican administration which brought the alliance to support the "new look" priorities was succeeded in 1960 by a Democratic one which turned around once more in arguing for flexible response and a greater conventional effort. As that policy became adopted as alliance doctrine, there arose in Washington an increasing congressional pressure for American force withdrawals from Europe, and the nuclear enthusiasts were again proposing another technological panacea with the euphemistic name of "mininukes." Europeans have become used to viewing doctrinal discussions as the normal currency in which Washington seeks to structure the political roles and missions within the alliance. There is a built-in resistance to change. Incrementalism has become the established mode of reform—clearly an inadequate approach for coping with present challenges.

It is necessary, therefore, to view with caution and prudence the process of doctrinal and strategic adjustment within the alliance to novel political, military, and technological circumstances. Management of the process is as important as the substantive content of the adjustments. An important perspective in this context is to adopt the view of a continuous process of strategic adjustment rather than periodic major overhauls. Because of the difficulties involved in arriving at doctrinal consensus, the latter will, when finally arrived at, quickly become enshrined in a manner which makes alterations extremely costly in terms of alliance cohesion. Doctrinal "labeling" contributes to making transitions dramatic and salient. There is an understandable propensity in the American political system to mark new departures and to make a personal imprint on the way that strategy is presented. But terminological oscillations and constant doctrinal reformulation have an unsettling impact on the alliance, which reacts to the receipt of new formulations with a certain reserve and hesitation. More often than not, the formulations are sufficiently ambiguous to lend themselves to interpretations that confirm existing fears and suspicions.

It seems clear now that the NATO force posture as well as the strategy associated with that structure should undergo substantial changes over the next few years. But it is not at all clear that the changes which may be undertaken will necessitate a formal repeal of *MC 14/3* and the negotiation of a successor doctrine for embodiment in *MC 14/4*. The formalization of doctrinal consensus could presumably be accommodated within the existing framework for flexible response. There should be considerable emphasis on doctrinal continuity for purposes of preserving cohesion and flexible adaptability. Adjustments should flow from the solution of concrete problems and operational tasks rather than from the resolution of conceptual inconsistencies. There is a case for undramatic continuous updating of plans and doctrine without an attendant reconfiguration of the overall strategic framework. The alliance has been able to survive and function in spite of salient doctrinal inconsistencies. The process of updating and adjusting both doctrine and posture will inevitably produce a mosaic, the structure of which may not conform to idealized notions of aesthetics.

Technological developments providing options for an increased range of accurately tailored, discrete attacks with conventional as well as nuclear munitions are bound to motivate doctrinal and operational adjustments in NATO strategy. Such adjustments may accumulate to a major change in strategy, but need not be approached with the immediate aim of negotiating such a change. It would seem preferable to approach the process with the aim of creating specific options rather than structuring an overall design.

The primary reasons for a serious consideration of the options provided by the new military technologies are not rooted in any notion of technological determinism. There is very little determinate about the way in which technological possibilities are translated into specific decisions with respect to force postures and strategy. The need for a specific set of options must be assessed first of all with reference to the policy environment in which the options would apply. In the years ahead the most serious threat to the security of Western Europe is unlikely to remain a major Soviet attack in Central Europe. Security challenges are more likely to be rooted in the sociopolitical instabilities within the polities of Europe—particularly in Mediterranean Europe—which may provide occasions and incentives for external intervention. There is no suggestion here, of course, that military technologies will provide "solutions" to the governability problems of European societies. It would be dangerous indeed to assume that because the big military threat no longer seems very credible, military ways should be found for handling minor political crises. But military technologies may provide plausible options of response which will reduce the risk of external exploitation of the instabilities by the use of force or the threat to use force.

Since we should expect the need to assess the implications of the new technologies to be a long-term one, ways must be found to anchor the process of alliance consensus-building within a permanent institutional framework which can provide continuity and coherence to the adjustments to be made. The Nuclear Planning Group (NPG) provides a useful framework precisely, and paradoxically, because much of the technology is not primarily relevant to nuclear weapons. Thus an examination of the opportunities and options associated with the new weapons technologies has been initiated within the NPG. A military implications team (MIT) has been assigned the task of assessing the technological options, including substitutions between conventional and nuclear munitions, inherent in the emerging technology of warfare, while a political implications team (PIT) will assess the policy implications for the alliance.

It is a fact that nuclear weapons in the alliance have assumed a certain symbolic, talismanic quality. They have become the primary carriers of the message about American commitment and protection, and are usually perceived as the critical links in the chain of deterrence. A major focus of attention in the work of the NPG has been the role of tactical nuclear weapons (TNWs) in the defense of the alliance. Guidelines have been laid down for the initial use of TNWs, but most of the operational problems have been transferred to decision-making concerning follow-on use. Functionally, precision-guided conventional munitions and area-effect weapons should in principle be able to substitute for TNWs in several roles, and hence contribute to raising the nuclear threshold and improving deterrence by providing credible and effective options for defense and denial. However, in the event that precision-guided munitions (PGMs) were to be discussed separately and in isolation from TNW options, the danger would arise that they be perceived as symbols of an American withdrawal of the nuclear umbrella. There is the compounding danger that the new technology may be viewed as another American gimmick, an ostensible panacea, to justify American manpower reductions and TNW removals, or as a palliative from the US executive in response to congressional pressure for cuts in Europe. From such a perspective, the selling of PGMs could come to sound like the overture to an American policy for the "Euro-peanization" of the defense of Europe.

The dangers are depicted here more starkly than is perhaps warranted by a realistic assessment of the current state of the trans-Atlantic dialogue. However, the rather sharp contours have been drawn for purposes of emphasizing the political need for a framework of management. That framework should provide for an overall assessment of the defense options available to the alliance, conventional and nuclear. The complexities of deterrence and defense should be considered in an integrated fashion, allowing for a broad consideration of substitutability, overlap, and complementarity between nuclear and conventional munitions. It is also very important to assess the options provided by the new technologies in connection with the current interest in restructuring the NATO force posture in Europe, for there is a serious danger of suboptimal outcomes here.

The NPG however, has, to some extent become the repository of orthodox positions as well, particularly as concerns the role of nuclear weapons. Should the policy assessments be confined to the somewhat cumbersome procedures of the NPG, strong propensities would be operating in favor of concluding that the changes are at best marginal, natural extensions of existing capabilities, and that the effects of bilateral acquisitions would tend to cancel out. The NPG could then proceed to largely ignore the problem. Fears of American "industrial imperialism," of course, would remain, as would the natural resistance to change which threatens to render obsolete over time much of what has been acquired both in terms of organization and doctrine. Hence, in order to transcend the forces of incrementalism, ways have to be found to stimulate the NPG process through feedbacks from more flexible and innovative mechanisms. Furthermore, it is important that studies and planning for new contingencies and the employment of novel means be integrated into the work of the NATO commands. Studies of the implications of new weapons technologies can be incorporated into the flexibility studies which are currently under way in the staffs of SACEUR and SACLANT, as well as in the Military Committee. These studies have to take into account the significant accretions to Soviet military capabilities in Europe, including a two and a half times increase in the number of helicopters and a move away from emphasis on air defense to frontal aviation aircraft on the central front. The number of attack aircraft has risen by 800 to over 4,000 units, while the number of air-defense aircraft has decreased to some 2,600.

With respect to the institutional flexibility that may be required, one may envisage a system of shifting and multiple *task forces* of alliance states studying possible options. The Berlin task force constitutes a pilot example. The work in such task forces would not, of course, commit the alliance to particular actions or decisions. But the very process of joint examination of options and potential interests could serve to identify the area of potential consensus, and hence reduce the chances of disruptive and unilateral actions on behalf of the stronger allies in particular crisis situations. There is, of course, always the problem that some states may be suspicious of deliberations from which they are excluded, and may seek access for purposes of blocking undesirable conclusions. Ways should be found to consult and inform, while preserving the flexibility to pursue specific matters on an exploratory basis among those most immediately concerned. Thus the United States, Germany, and France might explore potential contingencies in the Mediterranean area, while the United States, Britain, Canada, and Norway might explore potential Arctic situations and problems. There are no absolute ways of avoiding the dilemmas posed by the need for both flexibility and cohesion. A distinction should be drawn between planning and execution. But prior examination and contingency studies will enhance the possibilities for rational and effective execution.

The approach to novel problems should focus on concrete problem-solving rather than raising matters of principle and proposals for structural reform. A system of *multi-bilateral study groups*, whose reports would be channeled into national bureaucracies, would seem to constitute the most promising approach to the problem of nontraditional crises and the introduction of new weapon technologies. Decision-making in an actual contingency would remain a national responsibility.

What is needed is a flexible mechanism for injecting the perspectives and interests of allies into the process of policy planning and decision-making in each of the member states of NATO. The study groups could focus in part on specifically bilateral issues, but they should deal also with the broader parameters of political and technological change. The United States would be a key node in any system of multiple bilateral study groups. What is envisaged is a broader and more focused ex-ploration of future issues than is presently encompassed by the Euro-pean bilateral staff talks. Such a mechanism could force governments to cope with difficult choices and help them to transcend the confines of incrementalism. The aim would be a crystallization of consensus based on new facts and novel challenges.

For Europeans, it is of particular importance to be able to provide inputs into the process of American decision-making prior to the harden-ing of American positions, which are particularly hard to unscramble once they have been bargained out and the compromises have been ordained. Entering the process while the outcome is still open consti-tutes a sine qua non for obtaining genuine influence; delegation to ob-server status or to the position of being on the receiving end of hardened positions, on the other hand, produces a psychology of latent resentment and resistance to change.

FLEXIBLE OPTIONS AND ALLIANCE CONSENSUS

The concept of flexible response which emerged in American strategic doctrine in the early sixties, to be officially promulgated as NATO strategy several years later, encompassed the notions of graduated and limited response to aggression. However, in the context of fighting off pressures for the procurement and deployment of active defenses against missile attacks, flexibility on the strategic level came to be pre-empted by the notion of deterrence through assured destruction. Strat-egy became curiously divorced from both politics and ethics, and thus conformed to the generally emerging estrangement between the state and society. The existing condition of mutual vulnerability to enormous damage infliction became confused with a normative prescription, rais-ing this condition to the level of a desirable objective per se. Flexibility in terms of selective and discriminate targeting and firing was ruled out by many people on doctrinal grounds. A curious policy of inflexible response became enunciated doctrine as the Russians established a condition of numerical parity and proceeded to build beyond it. In this context, it appeared to many Europeans that the coattails of deterrence were getting shorter. American arguments about the need for a conventional option in the European theater tended, under the circumstances, to confirm suspicions that Washington was trying to get the American cities off the Soviet nuclear hook. Europe had no such options: Soviet intermediate-range capabilities had established an asymmetrical hostage relationship between the states of Western Europe and the Soviet Union.

The American emphasis on an "assured destruction" posture only reinforced European propensities to maximize deterrence at the expense of war-fighting capabilities. As long as the external danger to the alliance was perceived in terms of a major Soviet attack in Central Europe, a strategy of rather inflexible options served the purpose of preserving the internal cohesion of the alliance. However, the potential conflicts of the seventies and eighties are not dominated by the massive invasion scenario. Instead, they include *intervention* in NATO countries in the wake of sociopolitical turmoil and succession crises, into "gray areas" such as Yugoslavia, or in conflict between NATO countries, as well as possible *spillovers* from Soviet "police actions" in Eastern Europe or from conflicts in the Middle East and Africa. Thus NATO is in need of military capabilities which provide options for dealing with the political processes which will dominate the agenda in the years ahead. Plausible military response options in relation to these political processes are likely to constitute an important precondition for alliance cohesion. In the absence of such capabilities, political fission is likely to follow from the differential risk assessments to which the political processes will give rise.

Meanwhile the increasing tension between state and society in Southern Europe may exert strains on the alliance, creating a need for flexible adjustment to novel domestic alignments without abandoning established structures. Indeed, the absence of a viable international framework in Eastern Europe, which leaves the burden of preserving the status quo to the Red army, as well as the relative absence of instrumentalities for channeling social and economic change, constitutes a major source of instability for all of Europe.

It will be necessary in the years ahead to broaden the range of contingencies for which the alliance must generate potential response options. The paradigm for defense planning will include at least eight types of scenarios:

1. Central war (limited and general)
2. Major aggression across the Central Front in Europe
3. Limited attacks for territorial aggrandizement
4. Soviet suppression of East European countries
5. Soviet involvement in intra-Western disputes
6. Soviet exploitation of sociopolitical turmoil in Western Europe
7. Soviet intervention in extra-European conflicts of vital importance to the West
8. Demonstrations of force (implicit or explicit) for purposes of inducing adaptive behavior

Obviously, it is possible to envisage combinations and progressions across the spectrum of potential contingencies. The policy planning problem is one of generating relevant *options*, rather than constructing alliance consensus about the design *contingencies*. Many conceivable contingencies of a limited nature would affect the various members of the alliance in different ways. The states in the alliance would be reluctant to lock themselves in by precommitment to a certain response in a given set of less than extreme circumstances. The issues have instead to be approached parametrically, that is, based on an examination of things that may happen, alternate ways of dealing with them, and the consequences of dealing or not dealing with them in certain ways. The purpose is to identify, to the extent possible, generic capabilities for action that are not tied to specific contingencies.

The differential impact of various contingencies on the members of the alliance may, of course, strengthen interest in the option of quitting at a time and place of one's own choosing. But the extent of this danger is probably largely inversely correlated with the availability of less than suicidal responses to aggression. Too many options may, of course, increase collective indecision. Deterrence considerations would seem to require that the members of the alliance that are most directly affected by a given challenge have available options of effective response. Increased capability to act on their own may increase the probability that the smaller allies will be on their own in the event of limited challenges to the integrity of the alliance structure. Hence, it is equally important that the options are such as to establish boundaries to the conflict without deterring other members of the alliance from lending their support. In other words, the options must provide for flexibility in the availability and orchestration of individual and collective responses.

In the current phase of increased tension between state and society in industrial countries, which has brought into question the legitimacy of established institutions and the governability of polities, the need for plausible responses to external dangers may become an important prerequisite of credible government. This may be particularly true in the context of the reduced acceptability of force as an instrument of policy in Western democracies. Reliance on an application of force that is clearly incommensurate with the challenge at hand might also cause alliance cohesion to disintegrate, as the alliance comes to be viewed as irrelevant, or even as a threat to national security during emergencies in Europe.

Generally speaking, it is desirable from the point of view of alliance cohesion to focus on options for direct defense rather than on promises of punishment. The former are less vulnerable to surprise and to a failure of collective willpower in ambiguous circumstances. Hence, the military effectiveness of the alliance's strategy is of crucial importance. The problem is to deprive the aggressor of the certainty of success rather than to assure the certainty of NATO success. The heavy initial-phase casualties which must be expected in the presence of new weapon technologies could produce an important deterrent to an attack. That effect may be reinforced by the improved ability to destroy interdiction targets and thus to interrupt the supply chain and delay the arrival of reserves. The availability of systems which may give the commanders up-to-date and detailed knowledge of the deployment of enemy forces up to a depth of around 100 km, without physical penetration of enemy territory, could be of major political importance during times of tension. Precision-guided munitions might reduce the tension between the political propensity to delay the decision to use nuclear weapons on the one hand and the fact that their early employment would produce maximum effectiveness on the other.

Flexibility of response could, of course, amount to a flexibility of commitment, and fears may arise in Europe that the United States will adopt a French policy at opting out. Conversely, European fears may also develop that an expanded range of military options will provide member states with the propensities for adventurism, or for a particular state to commit the rest of the alliance through a process of deliberate provocation and/or escalation. Such dilemmas have no final solution, and will presumably affect intra-alliance discussion of strategic doctrine and force posture for years to come. The dilemma will be weakened only to the extent that the expanded options are designed and chosen with explicit reference to their potential for providing measured and tailored response which will permit the establishment of reasonable boundaries to armed conflicts.

It is also important that the options provided by the new weapons technologies be examined from the point of view of cost-effectiveness. Fewer but more costly units for a given mission may produce a higher degree of effectiveness for a given cost than more and less costly units. But there is, particularly for the smaller countries, a quantity-quality calculus to be kept in mind. Certain threshold numbers have to be achieved in order to perform the mission in question at all and to permit a "graceful degradation" in war. Here the issue of absolute costs is essential. The issues may look different to different allies and hence become a matter of contention and dispute. Typically, the alliance has never been able to establish criteria by which to judge the priority of requirements for improving the defense posture in Europe. How, for example, should $5 billion be spent so as to produce the maximum improvement in the total posture? Such studies are not available. The pattern is rather for some, most often expensive, capability to become available and the subject of sales efforts. AWACS, the American airborne warning and control system, is a case in point. This very impressive system bears a NATO price tag of some $3 to $4 billion, depending on the size and configuration of the force. Should the alliance decide to procure this system, the funds available for equipping European forces with PGMs, RPVs, FAEs, etc., would be seriously curtailed. There are always competing claims on scarce resources.

EXTENDED DETERRENCE

Reliance on nuclear deterrence, together with the implicit threat of rapid escalation, has been a central element in the NATO posture. It reflected an outlook which made a major Soviet assault on Western Europe the design contingency in NATO force planning. It has worked, in the sense that Soviet military power has not been used against Western Europe. Still we cannot establish causation here, only correlation. We do not know what would have happened if NATO had pursued different policies, or had not come into being at all. History is not in the habit of revealing its alternatives. Futhermore, NATO has also worked in the sense of providing a framework of assumptions and a definition of the common goal which made it possible for the members of the alliance to commit themselves to a multilateral response. As we have already observed, the political realities of the 1970s and 1980s are going to require the alliance to design against a much more complex and differentiated set of contingencies. It will in no way be easy to design force posture to implement multilateral responses to bizarre crises and limited challenges.

Alliance consensus, as indicated above, will have to concentrate on the provision of options for response, rather than on the implementation of a limited number of detailed war plans. NATO may be confronted with a flexible Soviet injection of military force—directly or indirectly—into complex contingencies, particularly contingencies which may open up differences in interest, assessment, and willingness to assume risks in the alliance. Heavy reliance on large-scale nuclear response will not only imply inflexibility, which could lead to catastrophic escalation or *self-deterrence* (preemptive surrender) in the event of war; it seems likely to produce a considerable degree of *self-paralysis* and internal conflict in serious crises as well. There is also the important objective of designing a military posture for NATO which is consistent with East-West reconstruction and the amelioration of structural instabilities in the military infrastructure of the European political order. A failure to align the military dimension of the alliance with its political objectives and operations will not only generate institutional tensions within it; it is likely also to have an erosive impact on the support for the alliance in the domestic politics of the member states.

Tactical nuclear weapons (TNWs) are often viewed as a critical link in the chain of deterrence, making it more likely, and hence more credible, that US strategic forces would be employed in the defense of Europe, and remain a key element in prewar as well as intrawar deterrence. However, the establishment of a condition of essential equivalence and mutual second-strike capability in the central balance could, in the view of some observers, produce reduced coupling. In this context, it would seem that the design of options for limited and flexible strategic response would strengthen the web of extended deterrence, particularly to the extent that such options include counterforce, low collateral damage strikes. However, the results would be different if flexibility in the application of force were to be limited to central war campaigns. Stark asymmetries between the rules of engagement prevailing with respect to Central and European war scenarios could produce fears of decoupling and rapid disengagement. Continuity of deterrence presumes a continuity of options across the spectrum of potential conflict.

Discussions of strategic doctrine have often been marred by differences between Americans and Europeans with respect to the relative importance to be given to deterrence and defense in the defense planning of the alliance. This dispute has tended to establish a false contradiction between the infrastructure and the superstructure in the posture for deterrence. A particular configuration has been endowed with the quality of constituting the symbolic expression of US commitments and guarantees. Improvements in the operational efficiencies at the non-nuclear level may thus under certain conditions be accompanied by a perceived degradation of political credibility. The NPG has served in important ways to narrow the differences of outlook with respect to the deterrence-defense calculus. Hence it is right that the discussion of PGM options should take place inter alia in the body that has been able in concrete terms to cut through some of the symbolic conflicts.

Early and automatic use of TNWs is an inappropriate policy premise under conditions of essential equivalence, quite apart from being inconsistent with the requirements for crisis response in the years ahead. The very concept of using TNWs as a means of increasing the shared risk of continued conflict, the shot-across-the-bow analogy, may reflect the condition of minimal alliance consensus. However, the critical issues are merely postponed; the question of follow-on use is inevitable in the event that the warning is not heeded. To the extent that TNWs are used for purposes of affecting the military situation on the ground directly, it has to be done at a time when NATO would still have forces capable of exploiting the results. But early use is likely to maximize intra-alliance conflict. It would seem desirable to provide for a panoply of options which does not make a particular employment of TNWs into a strategic sine qua non. Hence, new conventional and nuclear weapons are likely to be necessary for purposes of providing the alliance with the flexibility necessary to cope with crises growing out of dynamics different from the East-West confrontation per se. Such contingencies are also likely to pose novel requirements for escalation management, intra-war deterrence, and war termination.

The residual uncertainty about the nuclear genie will be a primary factor in any European conflict. Ambiguity is consistent with the maintenance of deterrence, and there is really no politically acceptable way in which it could be reduced to zero. Any conflict in Europe will be nu-

clear in the sense of having nuclear eruption as a shadow hanging over
it. PGMs of a conventional variety will not alter this fundamental fact.
NATO will have to structure a posture that retains ambiguity, in the
sense of not being preconditioned on any definitive, inflexible resort
to nuclear weapons. It will use nuclear weapons if necessary, but not
necessarily nuclear weapons. PGMs will be an important element in a
posture of expanded options. They are important in terms of structuring
a broader set of options than those that flow from the saliency of the
nuclear firebreak. Flexibility in the choice of strategy will also necessitate a reconfiguration of the TNW posture in the direction of reducing
its vulnerability to first-strike attacks and sabotage and improving the
communications, command, and control (C^3) system, the battlefield
surveillance and target acquisition capability, and the options for selective and carefully controlled employment.

The introduction of low-yield theater nuclear weapons which would
lend themselves to discriminate and controlled use would make the
tactical-strategic threshold rather salient, and potentially divisive, if it
should be coupled with a strategy for massive and uncontrolled nuclear
strikes against the Soviet homeland. Discontinuity in the mode of response could cause expectations about discontinuities of deterrence, or
a decoupling of the strategic nuclear umbrella. TNW would obviously
constitute an important element in a broad range of flexible options.
Some significant reconfiguration of the TNW forces and reassessment
of the roles to be performed by such forces is likely to take place. NATO
is unlikely to adopt a posture which is dependent on the use of TNWs
to fight a campaign. They will be used to deny the enemy certain key
military objectives, to speed up a termination of the conflict, and to
signal shared risks and boundaries to the enemy. There will presumably
be a heavy emphasis on weapons with low collateral damage and high
precision. The number of battlefield weapons and weapons for shallow
interdiction would presumably be considerably smaller than the current
arsenal in Europe.

The de facto division of labor within the alliance will to a considerable extent determine the distribution of control over the choice
of options. Hence, the near US monopoly over strategic forces in the
context of the alliance constitutes a structural inequality in regard
to access and control of the implementation of alliance strategy in a
crisis. From the point of view of Western Europe, credibility becomes
a function of US decisions. Direct attacks on the Soviet Union in re-

sponse to aggression in Europe would be basically the result of American decisions. Traditionally, attacks over such long range have implied a crossing of the nuclear threshold. Hence, the willingness to cross that particular threshold has assumed a salient role in the calculus of deterrence.

It is quite possible that in the future, precision-guided munitions will permit long-range strategic attacks against targets in the Soviet Union with conventional munitions, launched by Europeans from European territory. The option of direct attack on Soviet targets may be a particularly dramatic expansion of flexibility from the point of view of alliance countries bordering Warsaw Pact countries, and which may be capable of implementing shallow retaliatory strikes against targets of direct relevance to the Soviet ability to persist in a military campaign against them. A separation of the nuclear threshold from the superpower sanctuary threshold could have a substantial impact on the pattern of intra-alliance as well as interstate relations and bargaining. A limited conflict in Europe may not necessarily imply a territorial confinement of the conflict to the territories of the attacked powers. Deterrence could conceivably become more equal. It could, so to speak, be parcelled out in credible increments, and need not be based on allied acquisition of a catalytic trigger for the US nuclear force. Strategy could be designed around a functional continuum rather than revolving solely around the conventional nuclear firebreak. Hence, it is possible that expanded options for strategic retaliation, beyond the accurate delivery of nuclear munitions against hard targets, could defuse the political tensions that potentially surround the division of labor within the alliance. By reducing the Soviet sanctuary position vis-à-vis the other states in Europe, the importance and nature of the hostage position of Western Europe vis-à-vis the Soviet Union would be altered as well.

We should caution here about the danger of oversell and of overreliance on indirect strategies of deterrence. A good many of the potential contingencies which may arise in Europe, and in relation to which force postures would be designed, involve spillover and escalation from regional or national conflicts into which outside powers are drawn by default or by a process of gradual engagement. Strategic deterrence would in such instances constitute an extension of local resistance capabilities, not a substitute for them. Secondly, strategies of deterrence and strategic punishment can imply a test of will and an exchange of threats which will involve a rather heavy load for democratic states, particularly small ones, to carry. Thirdly, there is the danger of viewing strategic bombing as a panacea, substituting for the economically and socially more costly policies of maintaining substantial standing forces in peacetime. Finally, a pattern of interstate politics based on threats of strategic penetration to valuable targets could become rather destructive to the maintenance of world order. A certain amount of small-power hubris, deriving from a perceived ability to hurt the great powers, could cause the former to abandon prudence in the mistaken belief of having achieved approximate equality.

Shallow retaliatory strikes at adjacent Warsaw Pact territory from a European country—or an extra-European country such as Iran or Japan —that was subjected to attack could be concentrated on targets of substantial industrial or military value. Their execution could be thought of as punitive deterrence, but also as an attempt to reduce the Soviet ability to project forces into the territory under attack. They could substitute for direct defense in cases where the local correlation of forces does not permit local defense, and could constitute a complement in other instances. There would presumably be a high premium on reducing the side damage to the population in the target area. In this connection, precision guidance and tailored weapon effects are particularly important. Furthermore, a strategy of this kind would presumably be pursued with the aim of exploiting geographical boundaries in order to establish limits to the war and facilitate its termination. The existence of such boundaries would make allied assistance less risky and hence more likely. The Soviet Union would, of course, have available the option of expanding the conflict by threatening nuclear retaliation against key population centers. But escalation to such level would transform the conflict and increase the chances of direct strategic confrontation with the United States. A strategic option of shallow retaliatory strikes would in no way obviate the need for the American nuclear umbrella. But it constitutes an intermediate step which may make the latter more credible and transfer more of the onus of escalation to the Soviet Union.

Beyond-line-of-sight weapons would pose increased requirements to intelligence and data processing. New dependence may develop between the United States on the one hand and countries interested in executing retaliatory missions on the other. Paradoxically, the dispersion of capabilities for beyond-border strikes may entail requirements for centralized decision-making and control and access to Amreican infrastructure, as, for example, in the case of GPS (Global Positioning System). In general, of course, wars should not be fought on the principle that the fighting should only take place on the territory of the attacked party. The objective must be to reestablish the status quo ante with the most appropriate means. Blurring the distinction between tactical and strategic missions, and particularly separating it from the nuclear/conventional distinction, will generate ambiguities which may be good for deterrence, but which may, on the other hand, generate preemptive pressures and "forward diplomacy" designed to break the will of the peripheral power by assertive references to the Soviet power of escalation. This problem is particularly acute in areas where it may be difficult to separate targets associated with central war systems from targets of direct relevance only to a local conflict. Major air bases, useful for both conventional and nuclear war, illustrate this difficulty.

In fact, a strong argument can be made that the security of small peripheral powers is better served by a posture for local defense, dependence on outside assistance, and integration into a system of political commitments to collective defense. In this connection, it should be pointed out that the ability of NATO to cope with escalation on the Central Front will continue to constitute a primary measure of the credibility of deterrence extended to the peripheral areas, that is, of the drawing rights of the latter on the general equilibrium. Technological developments are likely to introduce inherent options and ambiguities with respect to responses to attack. Such ambiguities will presumably contain incentives for restraint. They can be beefed up by transfers and redeployments in a war. The new weapons technologies however, promise to greatly improve options for direct defense against invasion. Thus, cannon-launched guided projectiles (CLGPs), as well as highly accurate surface-to-surface missiles and ATWs, may provide a country like Norway with a much better capability to resist invasion from the sea and over land. And the acquisition of such capabilities would not entail the political and strategic costs associated with acquisition of a capability for cross-border retaliation. Considerations of regional political equilibriums have to be taken into account as well. The major problem confronting the countries of the Western Alliance is to establish plausible options for defense, options that will appear credible and plausible to potential enemies and domestic audiences alike. Such options should not put excessive demands on will power, risk-taking, and the exercise of indirect pressure, which was always the major difficulty with a nuclear emphasis posture. There has been a Western propensity to focus on the *rules* of the game in war, while

Moscow has been concentrating on the *aims* of the game. The aim must be to win, and that implies a credible posture for denying the Soviet Union certain feared attack options.

The new technology does not provide a basis for a revolutionary transformation of the international system at the expense of the great powers. But it promises to introduce a greater degree of complexity into the pattern of interdependence obtaining among allies as well as adversaries. The options created, the distribution of roles and responsibilities, the claims in regard to what is attainable, the restructuring of forces and reconfiguration of postures—all will determine the systemic impact of the new technologies on the pattern of politics in Europe.

Generally speaking, it would seem that improved accuracy and efficiency of conventional munitions will tend to raise the nuclear threshold. There will undoubtedly be many cases in which modern conventional munitions could destroy targets with less or roughly the same resource costs as nuclear weapons. It may be easier to exploit the particular vulnerabilities of a given target system with tailored conventional munitions. High accuracy is not always required, but new area-effect weapons would improve the ability to destroy certain broad targets by exploiting a new line in the application of chemical energy so as to accomplish a uniform distribution of blast coverage, fuel air explosives (FAE) or the combination of kinetic and chemical energy produced by shaped charges and earth penetrators. Such target destruction would involve a significant reduction in collateral damage compared with the use of nuclear weapons. The political problems of initial and continued release would ceteris paribus be ameliorated, as would the structural problem of preemptive instability. In general, we should expect that a raising of the nuclear threshold and a weakened dependence on nuclear response to conventional attacks, without a reduction in the capacity for defense, would strengthen the internal cohesion of the alliance. But, as we have observed, much will depend on how decisions are processed.

New technologies will provide more flexible options for the employment of nuclear weapons through the exploitation of increased accuracy and discriminate use by the employment of increased radiation (IR) or suppressed radiation (SR) warheads. Nuclear weapons would, however, remain nuclear weapons; deliberate attempts to blur the distinctions between nuclear and conventional munitions through the introduction of so-called "mininukes" appear to have been halted. There is a need for prudent choice here. Technology should not be allowed to drive decision-making in undesirable directions. The interest in generating options should not be an indiscriminate one. It has to be precisely targeted on those options which are deemed desirable from the point of view of strategic stability. In this context, insertable weapons —insertable nuclear components (INCs)—which would blur the distinction between nuclear and nonnuclear warheads, do not constitute a desirable option.

INTRA-ALLIANCE RELATIONS AND THE COHERENCE OF THE POLITICAL ORDER IN EUROPE

Introduction of the new technologies into the NATO defense posture in a comprehensive and systematic manner will involve an important effort at intra-alliance consensus-building. There is always the residual fear aroused by arguments to the effect that PGMs may be a way of sweetening the pill of US manpower reductions in Europe. As such, they could be symbols of a weakened rather than a strengthened posture for deterrence. The timing of decisions and the manner of implementation, therefore, will remain critical.

From the point of view of intra-alliance relations, a critical issue is likely to be the question of whether the new technologies will create pressures for a centralization of decision-making power or will provide options for its decentralization. That issue, in turn, is connected with the issue of how the technology affects the relative range of European and American options for engagement and disengagement in a war. Decentralized decision-making power may provide for greater operational flexibility, enhanced deterrence, and more equal involvement. However, the very nature of the political environment in the years ahead could cause a decentralized decision structure to have serious divisive impact, to the extent that it is perceived as giving each of the member states an enhanced ability to commit the rest of the alliance to a given conflict in a manner that some will be unwilling or reluctant to accept. The confluence of operational flexibility and contextual fluidity at the level of potential military conflict would seem to exacerbate the problem of consensus-building within the alliance.

The centralization/decentralization issue is ambiguous. The nature of the weapons involved is such as to permit decentralized release; however, the nature of any war in which PGMs are used may create strong pressures for centralization. Such a war is likely to be one of

high intensity and velocity, a condition which will make war termination and intrawar deterrence more urgent. Such objectives are likely to
generate incentives for centralized release and control. But a centralized
release procedure could also be interpreted as a way of establishing
extensive US control. Decentralized release and control, on the other
hand, could become politically divisive in conflicts with strong differential impacts on the interests and stakes of the NATO allies. As
we have noted, increased requirements for intelligence and data processing may produce pressures for centralized control and more elaborate mission planning. This could entail increased uncertainties with
respect to actual combat performance as opposed to test-site performance. Increased dependence on data-handling technology may also open
up for increased enemy countermeasures.

The intensity of operations in a war where PGMs are employed is
likely to lead to a high rate of stockpile consumption. That could cause
an early pause in the fighting, and could enhance the influence of the
supplier country. Hence the issue of who is in control of the logistics
system will in effect concern who will have dominant leverage on the
conduct of war beyond the initial phase. In principle, selective targeting,
erosion of the Soviet homeland threshold, the availability of precision-
guided, tailored, nuclear weapons, as well as precision-guided conventional munitions, area-effect weapons, RPVs, battlefield sensors, etc.,
would seem to expand European options. Yet that very expansion might
be troublesome in the sense of highlighting intra-European tensions—
which Europeans should decide for which Europeans?—as well as trans-
Atlantic fears in regard to coupling and catalytic effects. Such conflicts
could become stark to the extent that several European countries become capable of substantial shallow retaliatory strikes, albeit with conventional munitions, against targets in the Soviet Union. The latter may
militate against the diplomatic objective of establishing a great-power
code of conduct based on reciprocal restraint.

Cost is an important parameter in this connection. If short-range
weapons should remain significantly cheaper than those of longer
range, and if the industrial base for making long-range "smart" weapons
remains largely unavailable to Europeans, the whole problem of mission responsibilities could become rather sensitive. On the level of
political symbolism, it would raise issues connected with the linkage of
the US guarantee to Europe, the "seamless web of deterrence," and the
disparities between US and European decisions and options. The problems will be compounded by the degree to which the new technologies

give significant comparative advantages, or even monopolies, to US arms-production industries in relation to NATO as well as extra-NATO markets. Thus the new technologies are intimately linked with the broader issue of alliance cooperation in research, development, procurement, and logistics programs. A minimum requirement in this area would seem to be alliance agreement on multiyear, multiproject goals for cooperative research, development, and procurement. The United States would have to share technologies with the Europeans, and would have to be willing to buy European-produced weapons. There has to be a two-way street, as indeed was envisaged in the Culver-Nunn amendment adopted by the Senate Armed Services Committee on May 19, 1975. In the absence of cooperative arrangements in this sphere, PGMs may come to symbolize a US attempt to prolong and expand an industrial hegemony.

Extended deterrence in NATO serves the structural purpose of providing coherence for the security arrangements of the alliance. The framework of the alliance also provides coherence by linking the peripheral flank areas to the Central European core area. The former are conceded drawing rights on the general balance of power between East and West. Local asymmetries and imbalances are integrated into a total balancing framework. However, to the extent that political and/or strategic developments should serve to sever the links between the Center and the periphery, or exhaust the drawing rights, the local imbalances could cause conflicts and adjustments to power realities on the flanks. We should remember here that the flank areas are not very similar in any relevant way; the South and the North are very different areas indeed. The Northern flank is sociopolitically rather stable. There are no national minority problems of significance, no disputed borders, and a rather homogeneous sociocultural community, crosscutting divergent foreign policy orientations. In the South, tensions between society and the state are growing very rapidly and drastic political realignments or volte-faces may be expected. The political cultures are rather volatile. Regional disputes over minorities and real estate constitute serious sources of conflict among allies as well as across the lines of alignment. The Southern flank is linked in a complex way with the instabilities and rivalries in the Middle East. It can become an effective transmission belt for tensions from the domestic to the international level. On both flanks, the security problems are compounded by Soviet naval buildups and expanded operations.

Tensions and even conflict may arise between Northern-flank countries like Norway and Iceland, on the one hand, and the European Community countries, on the other, over access to protein and hydrocarbon resources in the coastal areas. The United States and Canada are unlikely to be directly involved, but would have the same interests as Norway and Iceland in coastal state jurisdiction with respect to resources. The Soviet Union, being a large distant-water fishing country, would have shared interests with the EEC. The legal issues are unlikely to be finally resolved during the Third United Nations Conference on the Law of the Sea, and the world community may have to cope with a highly contested mosaic of regulatory regimes for ocean management. Low-cost precision-guided weapons may provide the coastal states with credible powers of enforcement, but the same technologies would also enable intruders to contest attempts at denying them access to fishing grounds and the like. The prospects of uncontrolled conflict would, however, provide the states concerned with strong incentives to negotiate compromise arrangements. The principle of flag-state enforcement would tend to strengthen the incentives. Uncertainties and ambiguities persist, however, with respect to an area of activity where local emotions and interests are easily mobilized.

While overt Soviet aggression across the dividing line in Central Europe no longer looms as an immediate danger, the conclusion is not warranted that the danger can be ignored. The absence of an immediate threat is hardly unrelated to the military and political constraints on Soviet behavior imposed by the NATO Alliance. A viable Central Front constitutes a sine qua non for preventing a decoupling of the peripheral areas from the Center. It is important also for purposes of preventing Soviet preferred couplings through demonstrations of NATO weaknesses. A weak Central Front could provide the Soviet Union with incentives to generalize subregional conflicts for purposes of securing specific gains.

Current attitudes toward the military relation of forces are based on general confidence in the moderation of Soviet objectives and behavior, as well as on the absence of an immediate threat of war. Some rapid reassessments and restructuring of priorities and outlooks might have to take place in a crisis under the impact of a spectacular Soviet demonstration of prowess. American behavior will then determine the inferences drawn concerning the relationship between American will and capabilities.

Finally, any alterations in NATO strategy and force posture should be assessed in the context of how they would affect the prospect for reconstruction across the East-West division in Europe. It would seem important to shun alternatives which would tend to freeze the confrontational aspects of East-West relations or strengthen the structural dependence of the East-European states on the Soviet Union. Expanded options for direct attacks on the Soviet Union and the deliberate avoidance of large-scale destruction to Eastern Europe might influence the evolution of the political order in Europe in the direction of greater pluralism. However, the availability to the states of Western Europe of means to leapfrog the protective buffer zone in Eastern Europe could cause Moscow to adopt a more aggressive definition of its security needs in Europe. In relation to such issues, instrumentalities like PGM are at the most of marginal significance. Soviet incentives and interests will continue to be structured by the broad shape of East-West political relations and the framework and texture of constraints embodied therein.

GLOSSARY

AAA; AA	Antiaircraft Artillery
AAFCE	Allied Air Forces Central Europe
AAH	Advanced Attack Helicopter
ABM	Anti-Ballistic Missile
ACCHAN	Allied Command Channel
ACE	Allied Command Europe
ACLANT	Allied Command Atlantic
ACR	Armored Cavalry Regiment
ACRA	Anti-Char Rapide Autopropulse
ACTICE	Authority for Coordination of Inland Transport in Central Europe
AD	Air Defense
ADM	Atomic Demolition Munition
AEW	Airborne Early Warning
AFAADS	Advanced Forward-Area Air Defense System
AFCENT	Headquarters Allied Forces Center Region
AFE	Allied Forces Europe
AFNORTH	Allied Forces Northern Europe
AFSOUTH	Allied Forces Southern Europe
AGM	Air-to-Ground Missile
AIRCENT	Headquarters Air Forces Center Region
ALCM	Air-Launched Cruise Missile

Compiled by James Digby, with many entries from an earlier list prepared by Robert W. Komer

291

AMF	ACE Mobile Force
AML	French Wheeled Armored Vehicle Series
AMSD	Antiship Missile Defense
AMST	Advanced Medium Short (Takeoff and Landing) Transport
AMX	French Tank Series
APC	Armored Personnel Carrier
ASH	Advanced Scout Helicopter
ARM	Anti-Radiation Missile
ASM	Air-to-Surface Missile
ASW	Antisubmarine Warfare
ATAF	Allied Tactical Air Force
ATGM	Antitank Guided Missile
ATW	Antitank Weapon
AWACS	Airborne Warning and Control System
AWX	All-Weather
BAOR	British Army of the Rhine
BCT	Battalion Combat Team
CAP	Combat Air Patrol
CAS	Close Air Support
CBR	Chemical/Biological/Radiological (warfare)
CBU	Cluster-Bomb Units
CCC; C³	Command/Control/Communications
CENTAG	Central Army Group
CEP	Circular Error Probable
CINCCENT	Commander-in-Chief, Center Region
CINCCHAN	Commander-in-Chief, Channel Command
CLGP	Cannon-Launched Guided Projectile
CNAD	Conference of National Armaments Directors
COMM Z	Communication Zone
CONUS	Continental United States
CPX	Command Post Exercise
CRAF	Civil Reserve Air Fleet
DAD	Decentralized Area Defense
DCPG	Defense Communications Planning Group
DISCOM	Division Support Command
DME	Distance Measuring Equipment
DOD	Department of Defense
DOT	Défense Opérationelle des Territoires (France)
DPC	Defense Planning Committee
DPPG	Defense Planning and Program Guidance

DPQ	Defense Planning Questionnaire
DRC	Defense Review Committee
DSA	Defense Supply Agency
DSRS	Division Support Rocket System
ECCM	Electronic Counter-Countermeasures
ECM	Electronic Countermeasures
EDC	European Defense Community
EDIP	European Defense Improvement Program
EDP	Emergency Defense Plan
EEC	European Economic Community
EMP	Electromagnetic Pulse
EOB	Electronic Order of Battle
EOGB	Electro-Optical Guided Bomb
EP	Earth Penetrators
EUCOM	European Command (US)
EW	Electronic Warfare; Early Warning
EWG	Executive Working Group (of DRC)
EWS	Electronic Warfare Support
FAC	Forward Air Controller
FAE	Fuel Air Explosive
FASCOM	Field Army Support Command
FBM	Fleet Ballistic Missile
FBS	Forward-Based Systems
FEBA	Forward Edge of the Battle Area
FLIR	Forward-Looking Infrared
FSTS	Forward Storage Sites
FTX	Field Training Exercise
FUFO	Full-Fusing Option
GAF	German Air Force
GCI	Ground Controlled Intercept
GDP	General Defense Plan
GEEIA	Ground Electronics Engineering Installation Agency
GIUK	Greenland, Iceland, United Kingdom
GNP	Gross National Product
GOPL	General Outpost Line
GPF	General-Purpose Forces
GPS	Global Positioning System (NAVSTAR)
GSFG	Group of Soviet Forces Germany
GSRS	General Support Rocket System
GTA	German Territorial Army
HARM	High-Speed Anti-Radiation Missile

HE	High Explosive
HOT	German-French Antitank Missile
ICBM	Intercontinental Ballistic Missile
IFF	Identification Friend or Foe
INC	Insertable Nuclear Components
IOC	Initial Operational Capability
IR	Infrared; Increased Radiation (warhead)
IRBM	Intermediate-Range Ballistic Missile
IS	International Staff
ISI	Initial Support Increment
JCS	Joint Chiefs of Staff (US)
JSCP	Joint Strategic Capabilities Plan
JSOP	Joint Strategic Operations Plan
JSTPS	Joint Strategic Target Planning Staff
KE	Kinetic Energy
LARS	Light Artillery Rocket System
LAW	Light Antitank Weapon
LGB	Laser-Guided Bomb
LNNO	Limited Nonnuclear Option
LNO	Limited Nuclear Option
LOC	Line of Communication
LOCPORT	Line of Communications/Port Package
LOGSTARS	Logistic Status Reporting System
LOH	Light Observation Helicopter
LRRP	Long-Range Reconnaissance Patrol
LSI	Large-Scale Integration
LWIR	Long-Wave Infrared
MAAG	Military Assistance Advisory Group
MAB	Mobile Assault Bridge
MAC	Military Airlift Command (US)
MAE	Mean Area of Effectiveness
MAF	Military Amphibious Force (US)
MAP	Military Assistance Program
MARS	Medium Artillery Rocket System
MARV	Maneuverable Reentry Vehicle
MBFR	Mutual Balanced Force Reductions
MBT	Main Battle Tank
MFR	Mutual Force Reduction

MGGB	Modular Guided Glide Bomb
MICV	Mechanized Infantry Combat Vehicle
MIRV	Multiple Independently Targetable Reentry Vehicle
MIT	Military Implications Team (NATO)
MLF	Multilateral Force
MNC	Major NATO Commander
MOB	Main Operating Base
MOD	Ministry of Defense
MRBM	Medium-Range Ballistic Missile
MRCA	Multi-Role Combat Aircraft
MRR	Minimum Residual Radioactivity
MSC	Major Subordinate Commander; Military Sealift Command
MTOE	Modified Table of Organization and Equipment
NAC	North Atlantic Council
NADGE	NATO Air Defense Ground Environment
NAMSA	NATO Maintenance and Supply Agency
NATO	North Atlantic Treaty Organization
NAVSTAR	US Satellite Navigation System
NCA	National Command Authority
NGA	NATO Guidelines Area
NIAG	NATO Industrial Advisory Group
NICS	NATO Integrated Communications System
NORTHAG	Northern Army Group
NPG	Nuclear Planning Group (NATO)
NSC	National Security Council (US)
NSDM	National Security Decision Memorandum
NSTAP	National Strategic Targeting Attack Policy
NSTL	National Strategic Target List
NWCS	NATO-wide Communications System
NWT	New Weapons Technologies
O&M	Operations and Maintenance
O&S	Operations and Support
PAL	Permissive Action Link (lock on nuclear weapon)
PBEIST	Planning Board for European Inland Surface Transport
PBOS	NATO Planning Board for Ocean Shipping
PEMA	Procurement Equipment and Munitions/Army
PGM	Precision-Guided Munition
PHM	Patrol Hydrofoil (Missile)
PIT	Political Implications Team (NATO)

PLSS	Precision Location and Strike System
POL	Petroleum/Oil/Lubricants
POMCUS	Prepositioned Materiel Configured to Unit Stocks
PPBS	Planning, Programming, and Budgeting Systems
PPGM	Planning and Programming Guidance Memorandum
PRF	Pulse Recurrence Frequency
QRA	Quick Reaction Alert
RAF	Royal Air Force (UK)
RAM	Remote Area Mine
RAP	Rocket Assisted Projectiles
R&D	Research and Development
RD&P	Research, Development, and Procurement
RDT&E	Research, Development, Testing, and Evaluation
REMBASS	Remote Battle Area Sensor System
RNA	Royal Netherlands Army
RPV	Remotely Piloted Vehicle
R/S	Rationalization and Specialization
RV	Reentry Vehicle
SACEUR	Supreme Allied Commander Europe
SACLANT	Supreme Allied Commander Atlantic
SALT	Strategic Arms Limitation Talks
SAM	Surface-to-Air Missile
SAP	Semi-Armor-Piercing (munitions)
SCEPC	Senior Civil Emergency Planning Committee
SCS	Sea Control Ship
SETAF	Southern European Task Force
SF	Special Forces
SHAPE	Supreme Headquarters Allied Powers Europe
SHORADS	Short-Range Air Defense System
SIOP	Single Integrated Operations Plan
SLAR	Side-Looking Radar
SLBM	Submarine-Launched Ballistic Missile
SLCM	Sea-Launched Cruise Missile
SLOC	Sea Lines of Communication
SP	Self-Propelled
SR	Suppressed Radiation (warhead)
SSBN	Ballistic Missile Submarine (nuclear)
SSM	Surface-to-Surface Missile
STAMP	Standard Air Munitions Package
STANAG	Standardization Agreement

STC	SHAPE Technical Center
STOL	Short Takeoff and Landing (aircraft)
STRATCOM	Strategic Communications Command
STRICOM	Strike Command
SYG	Secretary General
TA	Territorial Army
TAC	Tactical Air Command
TAC NUC	Tactical Nuclear
TACS	Tactical Air Control System
TAC SAT	Tactical Communications Satellite System
TC	Tank Corps
TD	Tank Destroyer; Table of Distribution
TNF	Theater Nuclear Forces
TNW	Tactical Nuclear Weapon
T/O	Table of Organization
TOA/DME	Time of Arrival/Distance Measuring Equipment
TO&E	Table of Organization and Equipment
TOT	Time on Target
TOW	Tube-Launched, Optically Tracked, Wire-Guided (missile)
TRAM	Target Recognition and Attack Multisensor
TRAP	Tanks, Racks, and Pylons
TRICAP	Triple Capability
UCMS	Unit Capability Measurement System
UE	Unit Equipment
USAFE	United States Air Forces Europe
USAREUR	United States Army Europe
USASTRAT-COMEUR	United States Army Strategic Communications Command/Europe
USEUCOM	United States European Command
USMC	United States Marine Corps
USNATO	United States Mission to NATO
UTTAS	Utility Transport Tactical Aircraft System
VLSI	Very Large Scale Integration
VPWG	Verification Panel Working Group
VSTOL	Vertical/Short Take-Off and Landing (aircraft)
WEI	Weapons Effectiveness Indicator
WIG	Wing-in-Ground (Aircraft)
WP	Warsaw Pact
WRM	War Reserve Materiel

BIBLIOGRAPHY

Documents

Policy, Troops, and the NATO Alliance. Report of Senator Sam Nunn to the Committee on Armed Services, United States Senate, April 2, 1974, 93d Congress, 2nd Session. Washington, D.C.: U.S. Government Printing Office, 1974.

Report of the Secretary of Defense James R. Schlesinger to the Congress on the FY 1975 Defense Budget and FY 1975-1979 Defense Program, March 4, 1974. Washington, D.C.: U.S. Government Printing Office, 1974.

Report of the Secretary of Defense James R. Schlesinger to the Congress on the FY 1976 and Transition Budgets, FY 1977 Authorization Request and FY 1976-1980 Defense Programs, February 5, 1975. Washington, D.C.: U.S. Government Printing Office, 1975.

Schlesinger, James R., *The Theater Nuclear Force Posture in Europe. A Report to the United States Congress in Compliance with Public Law 93-365.* Washington, D.C.: U.S. Government Printing Office, 1975.

Report of Secretary of Defense Donald H. Rumsfeld to the Congress on the FY 1977 Budget and Its Applications for the FY 1978 Authorization Request and the FY 1977-1981 Defense Programs, January 27, 1976. Washington, D.C.: U.S. Government Printing Office, 1976.

The Department of Defense Program of Research, Development, Test and Evaluation, FY 1977, Statement by Dr. Malcolm R. Currie, Director of Defense Research and Engineering, to the Congress of the United States, 94th

Congress, 2nd Session, February 3, 1976. Washington, D.C.: U.S. Government Printing Office, 1976.

Books/Publications

Aron, Raymond. *The Great Debate: Theories of Nuclear Strategy*. New York: Doubleday & Company, 1965.

————. *On War*. New York: W. W. Norton & Company, 1968.

Biryukov, G., and Melnikov, G. *Antitank Warfare*. Moscow: Progress Publishers, 1972.

Burt, Richard. "New Weapons' Technologies and European Security." *ORBIS*, vol. XIX, no. 2 (Summer 1975), pp. 514-32.

Canby, Steven. *The Alliance and Europe: Part IV: Military Doctrine and Technology*. Adelphi Paper No. 109. London: The International Institute for Strategic Studies, Winter 1974/75.

Cliffe, Trevor. *Military Technology and the European Balance*. Adelphi Paper No. 89. London: The International Institute for Strategic Studies, 1972.

Cohen, Samuel T. *On the Stringency of Dosage Criteria for Battlefield Nuclear Operations*. The RAND Corporation, P-5332, January 1975.

————, and Lyons, W. C. "A Comparison of U.S.-Allied and Soviet Tactical Nuclear Force Capabilities and Policies." *ORBIS*, vol. XIX, no. 1 (Spring 1975), pp. 72-92.

Davidson, Charles N. "Tactical Nuclear Defense—the West German View." *Parameters*, vol. IV, no. 1 (1974), pp. 47-57.

Davis, Lynn Etheridge. *Limited Nuclear Options: Deterrence and the New American Doctrine*. Adelphi Paper No. 121. London: The International Institute for Strategic Studies, Winter 1975/76.

Digby, James. *Precision-Guided Weapons*. Adelphi Paper No. 118. London: The International Institute for Strategic Studies, Summer 1975.

Hammond, Thomas T., ed. *The Anatomy of Communist Takeover*. New Haven: Yale University Press, 1975.

Hassner, Pierre. *Europe in the Age of Negotiation, The Washington Papers: 8*. Beverly Hills/London: Sage Publications, 1973.

Hunt, Kenneth. *The Alliance and Europe: Part II, Defense with Fewer Men*. Adelphi Paper No. 98. London: The International Institute for Strategic Studies, Summer 1973.

Kemp, Geoffrey, Pfaltzgraff, Robert L., and Ra'anan, Uri. *The Other Arms Race: New Technologies and Nonnuclear Conflict.* Lexington, Mass.: Lexington Books, 1975.

Lomov, N. A., ed. *Scientific-Technical Progress and the Revolution in Military Affairs.* (Moscow: Voenizdat, 1973.) Washington, D.C.: U.S. Government Printing Office, 1974.

Martin, Laurence. *Arms and Strategy.* London: Macmillan, 1975.

————. "Theatre Nuclear Weapons and Europe," in *Survival*, November/December 1974. London: The International Institute for Strategic Studies, pp. 268-76.

Mayne, Richard, ed. *The New Atlantic Challenge.* London: Charles Knight, 1975.

Nerlich, Uwe. *The Alliance and Europe: Part V: Nuclear Weapons and East-West Negotiation.* Adelphi Paper No. 120. London: The International Institute for Strategic Studies, Winter 1975/76.

Record, Jeffrey. *Sizing Up the Soviet Army.* Washington, D.C.: The Brookings Institution, 1975.

Schmidt, Helmut. *The Balance of Power.* London: Kimber, 1971.

Sidorenko, A. A. *The Offensive.* (Moscow: Voenizdat, 1970.) Washington, D.C.: U.S. Government Printing Office, 1974.

Urban, G. R., ed. *Detente.* London: Temple Smith, 1975.

Wohlstetter, Albert. "Threats and Promises of Peace: Europe and America in the New Era." *ORBIS*, Winter 1974, pp. 1122 ff.

CONTRIBUTORS

Graham T. Allison is Professor of Politics and Associate Dean of the John F. Kennedy School of Government at Harvard University. He is the author of *Essence of Decision: Explaining the Cuban Missile Crisis* (1971) and co-author with Peter Szanton of *Remaking Foreign Policy: The Organizational Connection*, to be published by Basic Books later this year.

Richard Burt is Assistant Director, International Institute for Strategic Studies (since 1976). He is formerly Research Associate of IISS and an Advanced Research Fellow of the U.S. Naval War College. Among his most recent publications is *The Debate over New Weapons Technologies*, Adelphi Paper No. 126, IISS, London.

James Digby is a member of the senior staff of the Rand Corporation. He was an early contributor to Rand thought on the use of counterforce attacks and the design of forces for controlled response. In the 1950s he headed Rand's Operations Department, and later was its program manager for international studies. He headed a group with the NATO Force Planning Exercise, and recently he has worked on the implications of new technology for military postures and arms control. In addition to his Rand work, Mr. Digby is Executive Director of the California Seminar on Arms Control and Foreign Policy. His published work includes

Precision-Guided Weapons, Adelphi Paper No. 118 (International Institute for Strategic Studies, Summer 1975) and contributions to *Neuerungsorientierte Unternehmungsfuhrung* (Haupt, Bern, 1972) and *The Other Arms Race* (Heath, Lexington, 1975).

David Greenwood is Director of the Centre for Defense Studies at Aberdeen and Reader in Higher Defence Studies at the University of Aberdeen, Scotland. In the mid-1960s he worked as an Economic Advisor in the Ministry of Defence, London, in the Secretary of State's Programme Evaluation Group. Since 1974 he has been a member of the Foreign and Commonwealth Office's Advisory Panel on Arms Control and Disarmament. Among his publications is *Budgeting for Defense* and several articles on defense issues.

Peter H. Haas is the Deputy Director (Science and Technology) of the Defense Nuclear Agency. He was born in Frankfurt, Germany and came to the U.S. in 1937. He was employed by the National Bureau of Standards from 1949 to 1954, by the Army's Harry Diamond Laboratories from 1954 to 1965, and joined the Defense Nuclear Agency in 1965. Mr. Haas is a physicist who has specialized in solid state physics and electromagnetism. He has been associated with nuclear weapon effects programs for over twenty years.

Pierre Hassner is Senior Research Associate (Maitre de Recherche), Centre d'Etude des Relations Internationales, Fondation Nationale des Science Politiques, Paris, and Professor of Politics, Johns Hopkins University, European Center, Bologna. Among his numerous publications are *Les alliances sont-elles dépassés?*, *Change and Security in Europe,* and *Europe in the Age of Negotiation.*

René Herrmann has been (1967-69) an assistant to a member of the Bundestag. Since 1973 he has been Research Associate of the Research Institute of the SWP, Ebenhausen.

Johan Jørgen Holst is now Undersecretary of State for Defence in Oslo (since 1976). Formerly Research Associate at the Norwegian Defence Research Establishment, the Center for International Affairs of Harvard University and at Hudson Institute. 1969-75 Director of Research at the

Norwegian Institute of International Affairs, Oslo. He is a member of the Council of the IISS. He has published and lectured widely on subjects relating to international relations, strategy, and arms control.

Cecil I. Hudson is Vice President and Deputy General Manager of the Systems Group, Science Applications, Inc. From 1961 to 1972 he was on the staff of the University of California's Lawrence Radiation Laboratory (later Lawrence Livermore Laboratory) where he became a noted expert in the design of nuclear explosives and their potential industrial or military applications. Dr. Hudson's main interests are in large scale systems and their interaction with each other, and in the processes by which choices are made concerning the development of new technologies.

Erik Klippenberg since 1959 has been Chief Scientist/Operational Research at the Norwegian Defence Research Establishment. From 1951 to 1956 he was Project Leader for hardware development, Norwegian Defence Research Establishment. From 1956 to 1959 he was Chief of the Operational Research Division, SHAPE Technical Centre. Since 1974 he has been a member of the Norwegian Review Commission.

Benjamin S. Lambeth is a senior staff member of the Social Sciences Department of the Rand Corporation, specializing in Soviet military affairs and U.S. strategic policy. He has previously worked with the Georgetown Center for Strategic and International Studies, the Institute for Defense Analysis, the Center for International Affairs at Harvard University, and the Office of National Estimates and Office of Political Research, Central Intelligence Agency. He is co-author of *The Soviet Union and Arms Control: A Superpower Dilemma* (1970) and has published numerous journal articles on U.S. and Soviet military matters.

Laurence W. Martin is Professor and Head of Department of War Studies, University of London King's College. Former academic assignments at Yale University (1955-56), MIT (1956-61), School of Advanced International Studies of Johns Hopkins University (1961-64) and University of Wales (1964-68). He is a member of the Council of IISS, Academic Advisor to the NATO Defense College, Rome, and consultant to various research organizations (Sandia Laboratories, Los Alamos Scientific Laboratories, SAI, Hudson, etc.). Among his numerous publications are *The Anglo-American Tradition in Foreign Affairs* (with Arnold Wolfers), *Neutralism and Non-Alignment, The Sea in Modern Strategy, America and the World* (co-author), and *Retreat from Empire? The First Nixon Administration* (co-author).

Uwe Nerlich is currently Director of Research, Research Institute of the SWP, Ebenhausen (since 1966). Formerly he was Head of the Security Studies Department of the Research Institute of the German Society for Foreign Affairs (1962-65). In 1974-75 Fellow at the Center for Advanced Study in the Behavioral Sciences at Stanford. Consultant to various research organizations in the United States and Western Europe. He has published and lectured widely on subjects relating to international relations, strategy, and arms control.

Frederic A. Morris is a student at the Harvard Law School and in the Public Policy Program of the Kennedy School of Government, Harvard University.

Henry S. Rowen is Professor of Public Management and Director of the Public Management Program at the Graduate School of Business, Stanford University. From 1967 to 1972 he served as President of the Rand Corporation. He was Assistant Director of the Bureau of the Budget in 1965-66 and Deputy Assistant Secretary of Defense for International Security Affairs from 1961 to 1964. Mr. Rowen is a member of the Executive Panel of the Office of the Chief of Naval Operations and serves on the Executive Committee of the California Seminar on Arms Control and Foreign Policy. He serves as consultant and as a member of various advisory groups in the areas of foreign policy, arms control and disarmament, and public policy. He is the author of numerous articles on these topics.

James R. Schlesinger, former Secretary of Defense, is now visiting scholar at Johns Hopkins University.

Karl Peter Stratmann is a Research Associate at the Research Institute of SWP, Ebenhausen, West Germany. He has published several articles on strategy and decision-making.

Albert Wohlstetter is University Professor at the University of Chicago, a Fellow of the Center for Policy Studies, the University of Chicago, and a Fellow of All Souls College, Oxford University. In 1965 he was awarded the Department of Defense Medal for Distinguished Public Service. For the last 25 years he has done research on problems of defense and political-military affairs, specifically on protecting strategic forces and stabilizing deterrence. His most recent publications, "Is There a Strategic Arms Race?," "Rivals, But No Race," and "Optimal Ways to Confuse Ourselves" appeared in volumes 15, 16, and 20 of *Foreign Policy*, 1974 and 1975.

INDEX

Adenauer, Konrad, 28
AFSATCOM (US), 200
Aillert, Gen., 68
All-out war, search for alternatives
    to, 64
Amalrik, Andrei, 56
Angola, 18, 31, 35; Cuban and
    Soviet presence in, 57
Antitank guided missiles (ATGMs),
    244
Antitank vehicles, high-mobility,
    124-25
Area munitions, 128-33
Armored personnel carriers (APCs)
    243
Aron, Raymond, 51, 65-66 *passim,*
    68, 71, 174 n. 1
Atomic demolition munitions
    (ADMs), 135-37, 250-51
Attlee, Clement, 65
Austria, 32
AWACS (Airborne Warning and
    Control System), 126, 200, 277

Backfire bomber (Soviet), 98, 186
Beaufre, André, 66, 72
Bell, Daniel, 197
Blackett, Patrick, 65, 68

Brandt, Willy, 45, 47
Brezhnev, Leonid, 32
Brezhnev-Kosygin regime, 85, 88
British defense budget, 196, 199,
    201, 202-03; defense posture,
    268; nuclear program, 64, 72,
    188
Brown, General George, 214
Brown, Harold, 214
Buzzard, Sir Anthony, 66, 67, 69, 70

Cannon-launched guided projectile
    (CLGP), 159, 220
Cape of Good Hope, 31
Carrillo, Santiago, 46
Catton, Bruce, 209
Central nuclear war, 86-87, 93; large-
    scale, 164-68; limited, 162-64
Chile, 32
Chinese-American relations, 43
Churchill, Winston, 210, 212
CIA influence, 54-55
Circuits, integrated, 147 n. 3
Circular error probable (CEP), 116-
    118, 119, 121, 131, 135
City-avoidance strategy (US), 83-84,
    85
Clay, Gen. Lucius, Jr., 214, 215

Cold War, 43-44, 48, 51

Collateral damage, effects of, 139-40

Command/control/communications (CCC), 249, 251, 280

Condor AGM-53A (US), 160

Conservative alliance framework, 20-21, 39 n. 5

Continental United States (CONUS), 80, 94, 98, 99, 123

Conventional capabilities (NATO), 10-11, 242-48; *See also* Defense, Conventional (NATO)

Conventional defense strategy. *See* Defense, Conventional (NATO)

Conventional technology, new, 9-10, 126-35, 143-147

Correlation guidance, 111

Crossman, Richard, 66, 70

Cruise missiles, 248

Cuban Missile Crisis, 232

Cuius regio, eius, religio, principle of, 45, 56

Culver-Nunn amendment, 287

Currie, Malcolm R., 207

Cyprus, 32, 50

Davis, Col. Joseph, 213

Defense budgets, 193-205; British, 196, 199, 201, 202-03; constraints, 115, 198-200; French, 196, 198; funds, committed, 200-02; German, 202-03; Italian, 196, 202-03; NATO, 15, 153-54, 194-205, 217-18, 277; priorities, 196-98, 202-05; postural change, need for, 194-96; United States, 199, 201, 237

Defense, conventional (NATO), 9-11, 126-35, 143-47, 217, 242-48; forward, 243-46; interdiction, 246-47; long-range, 247-48; recourse to, 262-63; reduction of, 257-58

Defense, nuclear (NATO), battlefield, 250-52; coercive bargaining, 252-53; interdiction, 252; substitute for conventional, 268;

survivability, 249-50; tactical, 255-65

de Gaulle, Charles, 13, 47, 72, 73

Delivery accuracy (PGMS), collateral damage, reduced, 120-22, 145-46; logistics requirements, reduced, 119, 146-47; military effectiveness, improved, 119-20

Detente, 28, 33, 35-36, 42-59; debate on, 41; Kissinger's policy, 44, 45, 56; skepticism about, 41, 196; unconditional, 56

Discriminate attacks, focus on, 232-36, 253

Doctrine of generalized threats, 24-29

Domino effect, limits of, 53

Earth penetrators (EP), 135-37

Economic interdependence, constraints of, 42, 54, 55

Economic pressures (NATO), 55

Economist, on deterrence, 69

Egypt, 31

Eisenhower, Dwight D., 64, 211, 220

Electronic circuits, lage-scale integration of (LSI), 150-52

Electro-optical technology, 113

European Defense Community (EDC), 19-20; economic role, 55, 58; as mediator, 58; military role, 58-59

Exocit (French), 182

Explosives, fuel air (FAE), 128-30

FEBA, 165, 167

Finlandization, 47

Flax, Alexander, 213-14

France, European military balance, effect on, 57; and Germany, 53

French communist party, 36, 37; defense budget, 196, 198; defense posture, 14, 268; nuclear program, 72-73, 188

Fuel air explosives (FAE), 128-29, 284

Gallois, General, 72, 73
GAMO, 200
GBU-15, 159-60
German defense budget, 202-03
Germany, 21, 22, 24, 33, 45, 53
Global positioning system (GPS), 283
Gorshkov, Admiral, 98
Grail and SA-7 (Soviet), 159
Grechko, Marshal Andrie, 99
Greece, 24, 32, 35, 50, 51; and American bases, 57; and U.S. bilateral relationship, 58
Guderian, Col. Hans von, 211-12
"Gun Ship" (US), 109

Harpoon (US), 182
Hart, Liddell, 65, 66, 67, 210, 212
Healey, Denis, 65, 66, 73
Helsinki, 32
High-Speed Anti-Radiation Missile AGM-88A (HARM), 160
Hoffman, Stanley, 27
Holst, Johan J., 199
Home-on-beacon, 113
Hungary, 45

ICBM force (Soviet), 85, 180, 227
ICBM force (US), 79, 180 n.
Iceland, 36
Il Manifesto, 46
Iklé, Dr. Fred C., 176 n. 22
Indochina, 65
Infrared seeker, 113
Insertable nuclear components (INCs), 285
Iran, 32
IRBM force (Soviet), 85, 227
Italian communist party, success of, 53-54; U.S. attitude toward, 56
Italian defense budget, 196, 202-03
Italy, 21-22, 32, 49, 50; and American bases, 57; communist party, 36, 53-54; economic interdependence, constraints of, 54

Johnson, Lyndon B., 14, 213

Kadar, Janos, 45
Karamanlis, 32
Kennedy, John F., 232
Khrushchev, Nikita, 85, 88
Kissinger, Henry, 21, 36, 37, 47
    African tour, 35
    attitudes toward European Third World, 52-53
    detente, policy of, 44, 45, 56
    SALT, comments on, 185
Kola Peninsula, 235, 283
Korea, 65
Kulikov (Sov. gen. staff chief), 99

Laser-guided weapons, 113, 151-52, 156
Lavelle, Gen. John, 213, 215
Limited nuclear options (LNOs). *See* Central war, limited
Limited nonnuclear options (LNNOs), *See* Central war, limited
Lomov, Col. Gen. N., 94-95
Lowenthal, Richard, 68

Main battle tank (MBT), 203
Martin, Laurence, 38 n. 1, 169, 172
Massive retaliation strategy, 69-70
    SIOP, 79
Matador (US), 181
Maverick AGM-65A (US), 159, 219
Map matching, 113
MC 14/, 3, 14
McNamara, Robert, 83-85, 213
Mean area of effectiveness (MAE), 116
Middleton, Drew, 220
Military implications team (MIT), 270
Mines, 133-35
Minimum residual radioactivity (MRR), 140-41, 143
Mininukes, 166, 171, 258, 261, 263, 284
Minuteman (US), 85, 181
MIRVed ICBM force (Soviet), 79, 80, 98, 180
Missile gap, 64

Missiles, cruise, 179-191 *passim*

Mitterrand, François, 37

Morgenthau, Hans, 51

Morison, Elting, 208

Mozambique, 18

Multi-Role Combat Aircraft (MRCA), 202-03

Munitions, improved area, 128-33
  cluster, 130
  weapon-tailoring techniques, 130

Munitions, precision-guided (PGMs), 11, 108-111, 119, 121, 123, 157, 158-162, 164-174, 212-215, 247, 271, 280, 281, 285-286, 287
  cost effectiveness, 147
  damage, target, 114-19, 143-45
  definition, 158
  nonnuclear, 172-73
  size, importance of, 113-14
  targets, types of, 114

Munitions and targets, matching of, 133-35

Mutual and balanced force reduction (MFBR), 17-19, 188, 189-90

National Command Authority (NCA), 80, 81

Netto (Angola), 35

New Left attitude toward alliance, 27-28

Nixon administration, 80

Nixon, Richard M., 43, 79, 80

North Atlantic Treaty Organization (NATO)
  air threat, 125
  bureaucratic inertia, 13, 15
  conflict situations, 123
  defense budget, 15, 153-54, 194-205, 217-18, 277
  defense options, 10-12, 35, 240-54, 273-77, 279
  defense posture, 18, 22, 33-36, 153, 216-20, 242-54, 255-65, 269
  as deterrent, 27, 29, 59, 256, 277-85
  doctrine, changes in, 12-29, 228-229
  inadequacies, 216
  instability, risks of, 16-17
  member nations, 217
  priorities, shifting, 15-16, 20
  SALT, consequences of, 187
  strategy, 11-29, 33, 267
  uniqueness of, 66
  vulnerability, 167

Norway
  defense budget, 197
  and NATO, 39 n. 8
  Soviet pressures against, 57

NSDM 242, 79

Nuclear employment, flexible, 80

Nuclear munition technology, new, 135-47, *See also* Weaponry, nuclear, new

Nuclear parity, 64

Nuclear Planning Group (NPG), 270

Nuclear strategy, limited, 66-67
  enemies of, 68
  relation toward national nuclear power, 74

Nuclear weapons, tactical, 67-68, 165
  for local defense, 67
  as deterrent, 67
  as supplement to strategic strikes, 67

Nunn amendment, 169-70

Observer, The, on Western public opinion, 69

October War, 17, 110, 156, 166, 173

Offensive, The (Sidorenko), 91-93

Offset aiming from beacon, 113

Operation Linebacker, 215

Patton, Gen. George, 211

Pershing (US), 160, 181

Ping-Pong diplomacy, 43

Point munitions, 127-128

Poland, British guarantee in WW II, 65-66

Polaris (US), 85, 181
Polarka Plan, 32
Political implications team (PIT), 270
Portugal, 28, 31, 36, 37, 49, 50
    and American bases, 57
    economic interdependence, constraints of, 54
    moderation, move toward, 53
    Soviet influence on, 228
Poseidon (US), 189
Position-fixing systems, 112-13
    DME (distance measuring equipment), 112
    GPS (global positioning system), 112
    higher frequency (GHz) of operation, 112
    LORAN, 112
    OMEGA, 112
Precision guidance technology. *See also* Munitions, precision-guided (PGMs)
    electro-optical, 113
    laser-designated, 113
    infrared seeker, 113
    radar area correlation, 113
    time of arrival/distance-measuring equipment (TOA/DME), 113
    home-on-beacon, 113
    Map matching with aircraft, 113
    offset aiming from beacon, 113
Precision-guided munitions (PGMs). *See* Munitions, precision-guided (PGMs)

Quick Reaction Alert (QRA) aircraft, 183

Radar area correlation, 113
Radiation warheads. *See* Warheads, radiation
Remotely piloted vehicle (RPV), 123, 243
Rocket systems, multipurpose, 124

SACEUR, 272

SACLANT, 272
SALT. *See* Strategic Arms Limitation Talks
Surface-to-air missiles (SAMs), 125
Sandys, Duncan, 69
SA-6 (Gainful) (Soviet), 159
Saudi Arabia, 32
Schlesinger, James R., 79, 96-97, 98, 157, 196
Schmidt, Helmut, 65, 68, 69, 71, 72
Sea Launched Cruise Missile (SLCM), 160-61, 182
Seamans, Robert, 207, 214
Semi-armor-piercing munitions, (SAP), 127
Sensor technology, 150-52
Shaddock SS-N-3 (Soviet), 160, 182
Sidewinder AIM-9 (US), 159
Single Integrated Operational Plan (SIOP) 79, 80
SLBM force (Soviet), 85, 98, 180 n, 227
Slessor, Sir John, 64, 69
SLOP, 80, 83, 98
"Smart bombs." *See* Munitions, precision-guided (PGMs)
Soares, Mario, 32, 37
Sonnenfeld Doctrine, 33
South Africa, 32
Soviet
    conventional forces, 84-85
    military posture, 24-36, 82, 86-101, 187, 226-27, 243
    strategic rocket forces, 85
Spain, 49, 50
    and American bases, 57
Spanish communist party, 46
Spasm-war threshold, 79
Spitzbergen, 31
SS-9 force (Soviet), 85
SS-N-6 (Soviet), 85
SS-NX-13 (Soviet), 98
Strachey, John, 65, 66, 68, 71
Strategic Arms Limitation Talks (SALT)
    missiles, cruise, 179-180, 184-88

mutual and balanced force reduction (MBFR), 17-19, 188, 189-90
SALT I, 79, 186
SALT II, 186
skepticism about, 196
Vladivostok guidelines, 179-80, 185
Strategic policy (NATO)
negotiating requirements, fallacy of, 17-19
West European Institutionalism, fallacy of, 19-20
Suez, 13
Surveillance, advances in, 231
Suvorov, Gen., 92
Swinton, Lt. Col. Ernest, 210

Tactical nuclear weapons (TNW), 255-265, 270, 278-80
instant action, 259-61
political aspects, 259-60
Targets, determining accurately, 122-23
Terminal guidance schemes, 111-12
Terminally Guided ICBM (US), 161
Thanh Hoa Bridge, 109-207
Theater warfare, 10, 86-87, 89, 91, 98, 168-72
Third World in Europe, 48, 51
Britain, 52
France, 52
internal politics, primacy of, 52
Kissinger, Henry, attitudes toward, 52-53
Time of arrival/distance measuring equipment (TOA/DME), 113
Times (London), on tactical nuclear strategy, 68
Tito, Marshal, 32, 50
Tomahawk (US), 182-83
TOW BGM-71A (US), 159
Treaty of Washington, 38
Truman, Harry S, 24
Turkey, 24, 50, 51
and American bases, 57, 58
European military balance, effect on, 57

United States
defense budget, 199, 201, 237
economic pressures, use of, 55
nuclear policy, 79, 80-81, 83, 85, 87, 98
reluctance to use nuclear weapons, 65
support of NATO, 23

Vietnam War, 14, 28, 85-86, 109-10, 156, 213-215
Vladivostok guidelines, 179-80, 185
Vogt (AAFCE Comm. in Chief), John, 219

Warheads, radiation
increased (IR), 137-40, 284
low-yield, 141-142
suppressed (SR), 284
Warsaw Pact
countermeasures against PGMs, 110
influence of sophisticated NATO weaponry, 152-53
Weaponry, nuclear, new, 135-47
antitank vehicles, 124-25
area munitions, 128-33
atomic demolition munitions (ADMs), 135-37
correlation guidance, 111
earth penetrators (EP), 135-37
mines, 133-35
point munitions, 127-28
position-fixing systems, 112-13
precision-guided munitions. *See* Munitions, precision guided (PGMs)
radiation warheads, 137-40
SAMS (surface-to-air missiles), 125
terminal guidance schemes, 111-12
Weapons systems, new, 9-10
Western alliance
debates in mid-seventies, 63-64
defense posture, 225

Yugoslavia, 32, 37, 50

ZI (Soviet), 101
Zuckerman, Sir Solly, 69